Beyond Analytic Philosophy

Beyond Analytic Philosophy

Doing Justice to What We Know

Hao Wang

A Bradford Book
The MIT Press
Cambridge, Massachusetts
London, England

© 1986 by The Massachusetts Institute of Technology

All rights reserved. No part of this book may be reproduced in any form by any electronic or mechanical means (including photocopying, recording, or information storage and retrieval) without permission in writing from the publisher.

This book was set in Palatino by The MIT Press Computergraphics Department and printed and bound by Halliday Lithograph in the United States of America.

Library of Congress Cataloging in Publication Data

Wang, Hao, 1921–
  Beyond analytic philosophy.

  "A Bradford book."
  Bibliography: p.
  Includes index.
  1. Analysis (Philosophy). 2. Logic. 3. Knowledge, Theory of. 4. Philosophy, Modern—20th century.
  I. Title.
  B808.5.W36   1986   146'.4   85–70
  ISBN 0–262–23124–7

Contents

Preface

From one perspective, all intellectual and artistic pursuits are efforts to understand the world, including ourselves and our relation to the rest of the world. If successful, they would not 'leave everything as it is' but bring about some, however slight, desired change of the world in the form of modifications of our surroundings or our consciousness. Indeed, it is in striving for changes in the sense of finding something new (novel), be it new purposes, new ways of attaining them, new inventions, new discoveries, or new outlooks, that the mind finds a focus to help it function more effectively. This fact of life is, I think, the central factor that makes it harder to study philosophy as a quest for some comprehensive understanding of the world as a whole, especially in the contemporary context of greatly increased and diversified human experience.

The preliminary task of finding an appropriate focus becomes, to a considerably greater degree than in other pursuits, a major difficulty in itself. Indeed, it is by no means clear that the attempt is not futile and aiming at something impossible. Hence, even though the goal appears 'higher,' it need not be a 'better' one in the sense of being capable of yielding in practice a greater improvement of our understanding. It is familiar that more decisive advances are generally made in more restricted directions, which, even for the specified purpose of philosophy, often accomplish more than work consciously and directly aimed at it.

If, for one reason or another, anybody, despite the obvious odds against its being rewarding, still chooses to concentrate on philosophy in the tradition of being comprehensive, then it is necessary to search for some suitable way of selection from the vast amount of data and the many competing leading questions. The 'problem of beginnings' is exceptionally acute in this case. It is necessary to find out what are 'fundamental,' a problem to which a diversity of familiar answers have been proposed. Kant formulates the central question as: What is man? He breaks it up into three more limited questions (1781/1787, A805-

B833; 1800, p. 29): What can I know? What must I do? What may I hope? Two hundred crowded years later, most of us would now be more modest in choosing the questions. Instead of beginning (or ending) with philosophical questions in Kant's manner, I would like to begin and end with a classification of what philosophy has to attend to. The guiding principle is, I believe, to do justice to what we know, what we believe, and how we feel.

Philosophy guided by this principle is a sort of 'phenomenology' in the sense as employed, for example, by physicists. Since, however, the term has acquired different associations through the work of Hegel and Husserl, I propose to use instead the perfectly reasonable combination 'phenomenography,' and this book and its planned sequels can be viewed as steps toward explicating this ill-defined idea by an actual development of its implications. One implication is the emphasis on appropriate selections and arrangements rather than on new discoveries (as in the sciences) and new creations (as in the arts). Of the three components I propose to begin, suitably for my preparations, with what we know. This procedure appears to agree also with the main tradition of philosophy, as well as to conform with the natural desire to consolidate first what is relatively certain. More objectively, the other two components have to pass through the sieve of this one before they can enter philosophy (at least as is done in the familiar prosaic manner), because we use here only what we know about what we believe and how we feel. Indeed, for instance, Dewey, who is well known for his central concern with practice, seems to share this attitude toward what we know (1929, p. 297):

> The colder and less intimate transactions of knowing involve temporary disregard of the qualities and values to which our affections and enjoyments are attached. But knowledge is an indispensable medium of our hopes and fears, of loves and hates, if desires and preferences are to be steady, ordered, charged with meaning, secure.

Clearly, in aiming at originality and erudition, a dilemma of the 'narrow gate,' that of striving to avoid the Scylla of pedantry and the Charybdis of dilettantism (a dilemma discussed extensively by Unamuno), is particularly acute for this style of philosophizing. It is, therefore, necessary to divide up the difficulty also within the realm of what we know. As a more manageable and more effective way of developing and communicating what I take to be a moderately satisfactory account of this domain, I shall consider in this book the treatment by what is known as 'analytic philosophy,' which takes it as the central area and the home ground. I shall point out its inadequacies to what we know and at the same time contrast it with my own alternative perspective which at present remains more definite in its applications than in its articulate formulation. More specifically, I feel a pretty conclusive refutation of the position, represented in different forms by Carnap and Quine, can be offered, along a line explained all too briefly by Gödel (which, by the way, may be viewed as a critical development of Russell's early position).

The term 'analytic philosophy,' unfortunately, means quite different things as a proper name and as a description. In the broad (and natural, I think) sense it includes not only the work of Gödel (in philosophy) and Russell (in its varied aspects), but also, I believe, for example, the work of Aristotle and Kant. In the narrow (and historically accidental) sense, the most distinguished and least ambiguous representatives would seem to be Carnap and Quine. At any rate, it will be more convenient for me, particularly with the deliberate emphasis on mathematics and physics in this book, to concentrate on their work as representative of analytic philosophy in the narrow sense (which is, of course, rather indefinite in itself); I shall call this more sharply defined type of work 'analytic empiricism.' (Inevitably these short labels have to pay the price of inaccuracy. The name 'empiricism' can be understood as being more hospitable, as covering more possibilities.) By centering on a critique of analytic empiricism, I believe that the observations also point to inadequacies of the whole spirit of 'analytic philosophy' in its accidental sense. Hence, the title of the book appears justified.

In a famous passage Aristotle contrasts history with poetry. 'The distinction between historian and poet,' he says, 'consists really in this, that the one describes the thing that has been, and the other a kind of thing that might be. Hence poetry is something more philosophic and of graver import than history, since its statements are of the nature rather of universals, whereas those of history are singular' (*Poetics*, 1451). I am certainly not concerned with offering a history of the analytic movement in its varied manifestations. Rather I am interested in another kind of interplay between the universal and the particular. Instead of approaching philosophy by moving from history to poetry, history is brought in to deregimentize, and thereby to clarify intuitively, rigidified philosophical positions. By looking at the conceptual changes and equivocations at a few turning points, we arrive at a decomposition which reveals alternative recombinations. In another aspect, the concentration on a small number of central philosophers and topics has the 'poetic' advantage of being better able to capture the important and universal points at issue between current practice and the envisaged alternative.

I shall begin with a few aspects of Russell's wide-ranging work, paying special attention both to his influence on Carnap and Quine, and to several alternative approaches to philosophy, all suggested by his varied experiments with the theory and the practice of philosophy. Russell is followed by a digression on the *Tractatus*, partly for its relation to Russell's work before 1914, but especially for its puzzling influence on later Russell and on the logical positivists. The rest of the book is devoted to a preliminary formulation of my own position, largely by means of a critical exposition of some aspects of Carnap's work and nearly all aspects of Quine's. An extended development of my own views, which, at least with respect to the philosophy of mathematics, to a large extent overlap with Gödel's and owe much to discussions with him, will be given in a book under preparation, tentatively entitled *Reflections on Kurt Gödel*.

A major theme of the present book is that analytic empiricism does not and cannot give an adequate account of mathematics. The meandering arguments for this are pulled together in section 2 (of the Introduction), which questions the 'Two commandments' shared by Carnap and Quine. The comprehensive treatment of Quine's work (under the label 'logical negativism') both in philosophy and in logic, in Chapter 4 (and sections 13 and 14), is meant to provide a model representation of the current ramifications of analytic empiricism; it should reduce the danger of my being accused of dilettantism. A more detailed map of the book is included in the Introduction.

In revising the preceding version of this book, I have benefited from wise comments by Jay D. Atlas, Charles Chihara, Martin Davis, Charles Parsons, Hilary Putnam, Peter Strawson, and G. H. von Wright. Previously, around the end of 1981, a first draft of about a third of this book had been sent around to solicit comments; Richard Rorty graciously wrote me several pregnant pages that enabled me to make several corrections and deletions.

For well over fifteen years I have enjoyed the most valuable assistance of Mrs. Marie Grossi, who has, among other things, uniformly turned ugly manuscripts and revisions into elegant manuscripts, quickly and accurately. I am grateful to her indeed for relieving me of all the tedious parts of preparing a paper or a book (in particular, this one) for publication.

I have found it convenient to use a number of abbreviations, which are all explained in the list of references. In addition, I have always found the Chinese custom of compiling chronologies attractive and decided to include a chronological table at the end of the book.

April, 1985

Introduction

Over the years I have often wondered why philosophy does not occupy
a more central place in contemporary life. Repeated encounters with
polite indifference have transformed the puzzle to an opposite one:
Why should anybody capable of securing more acclaim in other pursuits
be obsessed with philosophy? Perhaps there is a 'metaphysical' instinct,
a potential instinct to strive to see the world as a whole, which, given
free rein, would generate a strong wish to strive consciously for an
articulate worldview. This wish as a matter of fact is extinguished in
the vast majority of cases, but only by the cumulative force of the
circumstances.

In my own case I see also a more specific puzzle and challenge. I
feel I notice a large number of what I take to be fundamental issues
and principles which, as far as I can determine, are not studied in the
existing disciplines (including current philosophy). Taken together these
issues and principles would seem to be sufficient to make up a 'backbone'
(or an approximation to it) of human understanding, which might give
a less formless structure and guide to the diversified human pursuits.
But try as I may, I see no feasible approach toward pulling them together.
Hence, I would like to meet the challenge or, failing that, to resolve
the puzzle by determining why the desired synthesis is unattainable.
Moreover, just because philosophy in this sense calls for a broad range
of attention and an open-ended search for unity, it leaves larger room
or more freedom for the directed continuation of curiosity and its
satisfaction.

The lessons from the history of philosophy suggest to me that the
quest for absolute certainty (for some clean foundation once and for
all), while seductive, is unlikely to succeed. Familiar forms of relativism,
on the other hand, all appear to me to give up the quest for a backbone
too soon. A more attractive (to me) form of relativism is to consciously
restrict oneself to a limited large area and reflect on some fundamental
concept, be it that of time or life or mind or intuition or set or justice
(even just in a given type of society), in its full richness. This type of

work is of philosophical significance and might be more fruitful than the attempt to find a comprehensive and not too formless framework. Yet I feel there remains a middle course between absolutism and relativism (in the specified senses).

What I have in mind is a sort of skeleton system that gives each part its due and reflects the current state of human understanding in a fairly faithful and structured manner. I envisage few, if any, arguments at the center of the system. The main concern will be to select and arrange what are taken to be fundamental, and paint (only) what we see clearly (and also, with adequate qualifications, what we see not so clearly) about them. In this way, the contact with our educated intuitions will be spread out while interconnected. Such a system will confront (as a body) the judgment of adequacy more flexibly and permit more localized repairs and revisions. The difficulty with this suggested project is obviously the reasonable doubt about how far anyone could execute it and how far it could be made sufficiently definite to allow and attract cooperative efforts toward its development.

There remains a huge gap between this project and the minimal requirement that we do justice to what we know, what we believe, and how we feel. It is with the intention of filling in a small part of this gap that this book and its sequels were planned. It is to be expected that in the process of working on these books the project itself will acquire a more definite shape; indeed, such a prospect is in no small measure the driving force behind the work. It is clear that anyone trying to develop such a project must inevitably be bound by his necessarily extremely limited range of vision and his irradicable stubborn prejudices, however diligently he may try to transcend and shake them off. But at any rate a concrete example, with all its shortcomings, will in its elaboration communicate much more (and more effectively) what is envisaged, than repeated attempts at an abstract specification.

1. A map of this book

In philosophy I tend to meander and ramify and be noncommittal. This is partly a reaction to oversimplifications, partly the effect of my failure to find satisfactory evidence for my beliefs, and partly the influence of later Wittgenstein. [This influence is most obvious in my 1961.] As a result, there is usually a real or apparent lack of focus. When I try to correct this defect, I often make strong assertions which seem insufficiently warranted by the detailed evidence I present. To partially remedy this confusing style, I propose to outline a few of the major themes of this book here.

I begin with Russell's work at the beginning of the century. He was in quest of a conception of logic that would include set theory and serve philosophy as mathematics serves physics. Unfortunately he got entangled with the paradoxes of set theory and was conditioned, in different degrees at different stages, by the empiricist tradition. Over the years he experimented with different possibilities. With regard to philosophy as a whole he wavered between technical and popular philosophy and between emphasizing what we know and how I know. With regard to logic he moved gradually from realism to nominalism.

The years from 1910 to 1914 were a crucial transition period for Russell. He had done the most interesting and solid part of his work in logic and was looking for another major philosophical project. He thought of doing for physics what he had done for (the 'foundations' of) mathematics. What he actually did during the period was to begin but not to complete a large book on the 'theory of knowledge' [1984 (1913)]. The book was to encompass human knowledge, with knowledge of logic followed by sense knowledge and science. It aimed at an account of logic and, with its help, an account of scientific knowledge. Criticisms by Wittgenstein caused him to discontinue the work.

Wittgenstein transformed the program by dropping the theory of knowledge and concentrating on a theory of the world. Two strong oversimplifying (and mistaken) assumptions were made concerning infinity and atomicity. The result was the awe-inspiring brief and elegant *Tractatus*. This seminal work appeared to give a surprisingly simple and compelling theory of logic and its sharp separation from science. An astonishing episode in intellectual history is how this powerful book misled Russell and the logical positivists, who were largely familiar with and greatly interested in mathematics, to adopt an obviously unreasonable and trivializing conventionalist conception of mathematics. This misconception produced in Russell a disenchantment with mathematics and was particularly attractive to those who were predisposed to empiricism. It promised to supply or strengthen the missing or fragile link in the neat and alluring picture of knowledge and the world, which the logical positivists were striving to complete.

1.1. The concept of logic

Russell completed his first version of *Principles* 'on the last day of the century' (December 31, 1900). In May or June 1901 he discovered his famous paradoxes. The efforts to resolve these paradoxes lasted for nearly a decade. Three things were at the center: mathematics, logic, set theory. Of the three, mathematics was and is the most fully developed, the most certain, and intuitively the least open to alternative interpretations. In the last respect, we have by now, I believe, reached also a pretty definite consensus on set theory, at least as a framework in which new axioms can be studied in a controlled manner. Logic remains for most of us an ambiguously defined domain. I shall, however, adopt a conception of logic sketched by Gödel, which seems to put things in a satisfactory perspective. Roughly speaking, logic is the theory of (pure) concepts and includes set theory as a (proper) part: every set is the extension of some concept but the range of a concept need not be a set. More about this will be said in the book under preparation (mentioned in the Preface), and I mention this here only to make explicit the perspective from which the development since Russell is viewed.

The paradoxes have both helped us in deepening our understanding of logic and distracted Russell (and others) from developing what now appears to be a more promising initial conception of logic. I have not seen the original draft of *Principles*, but it is clear that the complications about types (or restricted ranges) were introduced in the published version after the discovery of the paradoxes. If we take away this and related features and simplify matters in the light of later work, we seem to arrive at the following basic features of Russell's concept of logic.

(1) A term is anything; it may be an object (a 'thing') or a concept (pp. 43–44). (2) The range of variables is completely universal (p. 91). (3) A set is an object, but a class ('range') is not (p. 523; I am changing Russell's terminology to suit current usage). (4) Propositions and their constituents are logically indefinable (p. 356, p. 510, p. 84, p. 107). (5) The analysis of a proposition to find its constituents does not restore its unity (pp. 466–467, pp. 50–51). (6) The logical constants are the indefinables of logic (first page of the Preface). (7) The logical truths are those true in virtue of their form (as determined by the occurring logical constants). Of course this outline leaves open explanations of the crucial concepts of logical constant, analysis, constituent, etc., and it omits the many complex ramifications in Russell's book.

The above selection appears to me to give a first approximation (which, I hope, will be perfected by the specialists) to a formulation of the leading task which guided Wittgenstein's research from 1908 (or 1909) to 1918. He managed to bypass the involvement with set theory (and with the theory of knowledge) and came up with an attractive concept of logic by taking four radical steps: (a) the merging of concepts with things into 'objects'; (b) the principle of finitude; (c) the principle of atomicity; (d) the principle of extensionality. By (b), set theory can be eliminated because we need only to consider finite sets and they can all be eliminated (in principle) contextually. By (a), the thorny issue of the relation between universals and particulars is bypassed. Atomicity and (a) yield the idealized possibility of analyzing all propositions into their ultimate constituents and their logical form.

Extensionality and (a) serve to exclude the theory of knowledge. As a result, the only logical constants are the truth-functional connectives, and the only logical truths are the tautologies in the exact sense of the propositional calculus. In this way we arrive at the concept of logic of ultimate simplicity, powerfully depicted in the *Tractatus*.

The strange influence of this concept on the logical positivists will be considered in the next section. Its influence on Russell, apart from the disenchantment with mathematics, includes also his introduction to the second edition of *PM*, which applies (d) to set out the ramified type theory as a separate system. Ramsey took a different course and attempted to restore the simple theory of types also on the basis of an interpretation of the *Tractatus*. Russell's system can be improved by extending it to my systems Σ_ω and a form of its completion by using all and only recursive ordinals as indices (see section 14.3). A natural rectification and completion of Ramsey's ideas would seem to be the current conception of set theory.

Another way of looking at the *Tractatus* concept of logic is to see how we can retain as much as possible its attractive features and recover the distinctions it unjustly omitted in (a) and (b). Let me follow Gödel and restore the distinction between objects and concepts, and include sets (many infinite ones) among the objects. The extensional (set-theoretic) paradoxes are taken care of by the iterative concept of set. The linguistic (semantic) paradoxes are resolved in the manner familiar today, and widely accepted at least up to the 1960s. What remain are the intensional (or logical) paradoxes and their resolution, according to Gödel, is an important problem which is a symptom and consequence of the fact that we do not yet have any moderately satisfactory theory of concepts. (By the way, Russell does make a similar separation but says that 'the logical and mathematical contradictions are not really distinguishable'; see *Principles*, p. xiii.) It could be argued that this broad concept of logic corresponds more closely to Russell's early ideas than to those of the *Tractatus*. We may still say that logical truths are analytic or even tautological, provided we do not understand it in a nominalistic or linguistic sense. Moreover, as I shall consider briefly in the next section, we may also restore Russell's concern with the theory of knowledge in the different form of an attention to mathematical and conceptual intuitions, as well as their connections with our physical experience.

1.2. Set theory and mathematics

Russell published a very interesting discussion of set theory in 1906, which includes a characterization of the three basic approaches: the zigzag theory or the intensional approach, the theory of limitation of size or the extensional view, and the no-class theory or the 'method' of elimination by equivocation. Across this classification, there is also a distinction between what may be called the intrinsic and the extrinsic views. The former allows set theory a more autonomous intuitive development, while the latter is preoccupied with the instrumental value of containing 'enough ordinary mathematics.' Russell's own subsequent work was largely along the line of no-class theory. (For an instructive study of this, see Gödel 1944.) This approach tends to be forced to an extrinsic view, and it leads to systems like Σ_ω (just mentioned) and to considerations about how much mathematics can be carried out in each system. (There has recently been a reversal of direction by considering for each given piece of mathematics the alternative systems in which it can be carried out. This is of interest to mathematical practice but need not concern us here.)

The intensional approach usually takes it as an axiom that every property or concept determines a set which is its extension. This, for instance, appears to be the axiom which led to the inconsistency of Frege's system. (Russell did suggest, on p. 104 of his *Principles*, that 'this axiom need not be universally admitted, and appears to have been the source of the contradiction.') It is associated with the idea that the properties, 'simple' in some sense, should all determine sets. For example, the complement of a set should be a set; when applied to the empty set, this 'obvious' principle yields the questionable consequence of there being the universal set. It is, therefore, not surprising that theories of the type 'all have a certain zigzag quality.' Quine's systems considered in the section on his logical ideas (section 17) are clearly of this type. Russell says of this type of theory that 'I have found no guiding principle except the avoidance of contradictions; and this, by itself, is a very insufficient principle' (Lackey, p. 147). It now appears that this approach is no longer of interest for set theory but may still be a loose guide to the search for a theory of concepts.

The extensional approach is what is commonly accepted today, and it is of interest to see why Russell did not follow it. 'This theory has, at first sight, a great plausibility and simplicity, and I am not prepared to deny that it is the true solution.' 'A great difficulty of this theory is that it does not tell us how far up the series of ordinals it is legitimate to go' (p. 153). He then seems to go back to the intensional approach by asking under what circumstances a defining property is legitimate. He does recognize the intention 'that all ordinals should be admitted which can be defined, so to speak, from below' (p. 154). His main discomfort over the approach is, I believe, its open-endedness which, from another viewpoint, is seen to be both natural and attractive in conforming to the basic pattern of human knowledge.

The idea of 'foundations' of mathematics appears to be more a favorite one in Germany, from Frege's *Foundations of Arithmetic* (1884) to the Hilbert school's *Foundations of Mathematics* (1934 and 1939), than with Russell. More specifically, at least in his early work, Russell does not, correctly in my opinion, suggest that logic can make mathematics more indubitable. In 1907 he wrote about the 'inductive' evidence for axioms in two papers. For example, in one of them: 'If the axiom itself is nearly indubitable, that merely adds to the inductive evidence derived from the fact that its consequences are nearly indubitable.' 'Infallibility is never attainable, and therefore some element of doubt should always attach to every axiom and to all of its consequences. In formal logic, the element of doubt is less than in most sciences, but it is not absent' (Lackey, p. 251). The other paper is wholly devoted to this matter by talking about 'the regressive method of discovering the premises.' It was 'to explain in what sense a comparatively obscure and difficult proposition may be said to be a premise for a comparatively obvious proposition, to consider how premises in this sense may be discovered, and to emphasize the close analogy between the methods of pure mathematics and the methods of the sciences of observation' (p. 272). He went on to elaborate the analogy between science and mathematics and would probably not object to drawing a parallel between set theory and fundamental physics.

However, Russell's healthy denial of infallibility was tainted by an empiricism which I believe is demonstrably false in the particular application which he made of it. He spoke of the Peano axioms as though they could only have been gotten by empirical induction. 'It is to be observed that they go beyond the empirical premises out of which they are distilled' (p. 276). Indeed, Dedekind first arrived at the axioms by conceptual reflection (I shall return to this in a larger context in the next section). This appears to me an example of what Santayana took to be Russell's basic limitation in philosophy: 'He couldn't entertain the hypothesis that Berkeley, Hume, and Mill might have been fundamentally wrong' (compare a longer discussion of this in the first chapter below).

While most physicists accept the central place of fundamental physics within physics, few mathematicians would concede a similar place to logic within mathematics. This is rather disappointing to logicians, and the reason undoubtedly is the fact that, at least up to now, logic has had a surprisingly small impact on general mathematical practice. In this regard it may be of interest to mention a report on Einstein's somewhat different opinion. 'Einstein often mentioned that he felt that he should not become a mathematician because the wealth of interesting and attractive problems was so great that you could get lost in it without ever coming up with anything of genuine importance. . . . But he told me once, "Now that I've met Gödel, I know the same thing does exist in mathematics" ' (Woolf 1980, p. 485). Presumably Einstein had in mind both Gödel's incompleteness theorems and his work in set theory.

1.3. Carnap and Quine

Much of this book is concerned with a critique of the work of Carnap and especially that of Quine. I consider Carnap the representative of logical positivism and Quine the creator of what I call a 'logical negativism.' I disagree with both of them, and my disagreement goes to what I take to be their shared outlook which I call 'analytic empiricism.' A central theme of mine is that their philosophies fail to give an adequate account of logic (or of mathematics). This, in my opinion, discredits their views in a basic way in the light of the fact that logic is so central for both of them. An outline of the more definite points (on the theme) in the observations dispersed throughout this book is given in the next section in a sharper form than I am accustomed to. (In connection with the related issue of analyticity and necessity, I would like to mention also my more extended and more leisurely discussions in the 1955 paper and in Chapter 8 of MP.)

Another issue of relatively broad interest is the debate on 'ontology' between Carnap and Quine. While Carnap seems to evade the issue altogether, I find Quine's famous doctrine, while suggestive, rather arbitrary and elusive. For example, the system Σ_ω mentioned before is conceptually quite transparent. Quine at first could not appreciate this or relate this transparency to his criterion of 'ontic commitment.' Only after the term 'substitutional quantification' had been introduced, Quine began to notice an 'ontological' difference between systems like Σ_ω and the familiar simple theory of types. It appears to me that Σ_ω satisfies all the requirements Quine puts on a desired system of logic. Yet at the same time it fails to conform to other standards which seem perfectly reasonable. It is not a natural 'stopping place,' and there is no good reason to give up the intuitively attractive and much richer iterative concept of set even though we have no proof of its consistency (as we have of Σ_ω and its extensions). Hence, we seem to have another indication that Quine's concept of logic is defective. Moreover, this case also illustrates the fact that we have better intuitive guides than Quine's criterion in determining the transparency of a theory.

Over the years the most widely influential and widely discussed work of Quine would seem to be his two articles on ontology (1948) and analyticity (1951). Each elaborates what appears to be a simple observation about a central issue in philosophy. In the case of the latter paper, as will be considered in the next section, there is no question of its being about a central issue, but the response given in it seems to me to rest on a prejudiced preconception. In the case of the former it is not clear that a central issue is captured. I remember reading the paper in manuscript early in 1948 and being impressed by its sweep and clever novelty. For several years afterwards I tried to do something with it but was thoroughly frustrated. A brief review of the history of its fate over almost forty years may illustrate the sort of reason underlying my negative sentiment toward this type of philosophical work.

A flood of papers followed in the next ten years or so. In the authoritative collection of selected readings in the philosophy of mathematics (BP, 1964), both the paper and two other papers closely related to it were included, which have all been deleted in the second edition (1983). Quine speaks of the 'ontological commitments' of 'theories.' Many, including myself, fail to understand the relation between theories and languages in Quine's mind. Moreover, his apparent restriction to first order theories, accompanied by indeterminate interpretations, seems to exclude most of the more interesting theories, and yet not to profit from the precision (at least in form) of first order theories. In 1964 he began to extend or develop his ideas to a criterion of 'ontological reduction,' which, in my opinion, has been demonstrated in the literature to be entirely arbitrary and artificial.

Quine had initially no distinction between what are known as referential and substitutional quantification. When the distinction became popular, Quine modified his original criterion by excluding substitutional quantification from it. And in 1977 we find him saying that the connection between 'ontology' and referential quantification 'is trivially assured by the very explanation of referential quantification' (TT, p. 174). An obvious question is then: Does his concept of ontology capture the more interesting aspects of the different meanings of the term 'ontology,' familiar mainly from the history of philosophy?

He also speaks of the tendency of the 'anti-formalists' to attribute the views of the Vienna Circle and of himself to the symbolic or formal logicians (TT, p. 175). This reminds me of Gödel's eagerness to dissociate himself from the Vienna Circle and his observation on several occasions that Carnap's misuse of logic gives logic a bad name among the philosophers. In my opinion, both Carnap and Quine have inadequate conceptions of logic and apply logic in philosophy in misleading manners, which do not do justice to logic in its more developed state and, through the conspicuity of their work, give to philosophers wrong ideas about logic. Unfortunately, as logic acquires more content, fewer good logicians remain interested in philosophy. As a result, philosophers tend to be accustomed to the more superficial aspects of logic and find more serious philosophical reflections related to logic, such as Gödel's, obscure, 'old-fashioned,' or ununderstandable because of presupposing implicitly a familiarity with traditional philosophical as well as not so recent logical material.

In view of Quine's central position in current philosophy and of the fact that I feel I disagree with him on several levels, extensive comments on his ideas are scattered all through this book. In addition, the whole of Chapter 4 is devoted to a critical and fairly comprehensive exposition of his life and work (both in logic and in philosophy). In my opinion, this effort is justified both because the result, through the central figure of Quine, reflects a major aspect of the general state of American philosophy in this century, and because my wide-ranging disagreement is not only with Quine but with a large group of philosophers represented by him.

There is also a chapter (5) of metaphilosophical observations which may be construed as fragments reporting on my gropings toward a 'phenomenography.' As such, it is not easy to summarize. Since these observations need not be read consecutively and do not make up an organized whole, I shall say no more about it here. It may, however, be noted that 'metaphilosophy,' in the sense of 'discourse about (the nature of) philosophy,' would seem to be naturally a part of philosophy. It is said (in the *Shorter O.E.D.*) that, e.g., 'metachemistry' and 'metaphysiology' are formed in supposed analogy to metaphysics. If, however, they are construed as discourses about chemistry and physiology, then the subjects with such names, when developed, would seem to belong also to philosophy. Metamathematics has evolved into a branch of mathematics itself. But it had formerly different connotations. For example, Cantor mentioned metamathematics in 1883 and 1889 (Cantor, p. 213 and p. 391). He seems to relate it to work attacking the validity of mathematical proofs and to protest against Wilhelm Wundt who apparently associated his work with 'the newer so-called "metamathematical" speculations.' Generally, I would like to suggest that a distinguishing characteristic of philosophy is that it properly includes metaphilosophy (indeed, as a major component), while, for instance, chemistry does not include metachemistry. Even metamathematics, according to this interpretation of 'meta-,' only belongs in part to mathematics and contains, in addition, also the philosophy of mathematics.

2. A refutation of analytic empiricism*

More than a third of a century has elapsed since Quine first published his epoch-making manifesto,[1] (to demolish the) 'Two dogmas' of the

*The notes to this section will be found immediately following it (pp.22–26).

analyticity of logic (and mathematics) and the reductionism of meaning (in our physical knowledge). All along I have been very unhappy about this article and have tried unsuccessfully from time to time to pinpoint the reasons for my dissatisfaction with it. The difficulty, I now realize, lies in the fact that we disagree on several levels, some of which, such as what we take to be the purposes of philosophy, are hard to state in an articulate form. Elsewhere in this book a contrast between Quine's perspective and my outlook is discussed along a variety of directions. Such a moderately full account has, however, the disadvantage that the reader needs to evaluate the plausibility of various aspects and reach a judgment on each. This would seem to demand more sympathetic patience than is available to those who are accustomed to the habit of concentrated local argumentations in current philosophy.

I believe, however, I can single out a central aspect which has a fairly definite formulation and may be of assistance in giving the larger issue an initial focus. The formulation, in my opinion, gets not only to the difference between Carnap and Quine, but also, more significantly, to the basic implicit presuppositions shared by them.[2] While the formulation is hardly conclusive in itself, it may motivate the reader to look for its supporting evidence and implications. It may also narrow down the area of disagreement, so that one may better concentrate on tracing the sources of disagreement.

One common feature of Carnap's and Quine's philosophical practice is their preoccupation with local (and mostly formal) precision accompanied by a surprising willingness to tolerate or even celebrate global indefiniteness. They differ in that Carnap tries (unsuccessfully) to map out larger localities. The appeal of their practice is undoubtedly connected with the predominance and relative success of specialization in the sciences. But I am sufficiently old-fashioned to believe that a major concern of philosophy remains the task of achieving some measure of global definiteness. Behind their practice is a shared wish to adhere to the physical and other more concrete or tangible objects and experiences (such as linguistic expressions and observation sentences).

What is fundamental is, I think, not the two dogmas of analyticity and reductionism which separate them but rather the denial of any autonomy to conceptual knowledge which unites them. Despite large differences between their conceptions of empiricism and logic, they share enough common preconceptions to warrant, I think, calling both of them 'analytic empiricists' (or, alternatively, 'logical empiricists'). After all, both are avowed empiricists and both center their philosophies on logic and 'logical analysis.' To parrot Quine's colorful manner of expression and to sacrifice some accuracy, I propose to label the intersection of their views on analysis (or logic) and empiricism the 'two commandments of analytic empiricism.' It is, unfortunately, in view of all the conspicuous differences between their positions, a little difficult to state the matter adequately in two elegant propositions. A tentative formulation might be:

(a) Empiricism is the whole of philosophy and there can be nothing (fundamental) which could be properly called conceptual experience or conceptual intuition.

(b) Logic is all important for philosophy, but analyticity (even necessity) can only mean truth by convention.

The separation into (a) and (b) is somewhat arbitrary, since the main point is their empiricism that denies conceptual knowledge any kind of independence. Of course the name 'empiricism' covers more possibilities than those which I associate with Carnap and Quine.

It is familiar that Quine developed his philosophy largely as a response to Carnap's position. In view of their sharing (a) and (b), I consider this an internal revolt. The work of later Wittgenstein (which I shall not consider here) and the philosophy of Gödel, while not developed (primarily) as responses to Carnap, both include important components which could be viewed as serious criticisms of the logical positivists. Indeed, I believe that my position in this respect is quite close to Gödel's and owes a great deal to my discussions with him. However, he considers the empiricist account of mathematics 'absurd.' Therefore, he is concerned more with establishing positively stronger assertions of his position of objectivism than with defending the weaker negative thesis of this section: that mathematics remains unaccountable by empiricism.

The unresolved and unresolvable difficulty for analytic empiricists (in my sense) is, I believe, the one which faced J. S. Mill (whose work is, by the way, more appealing to me than that of Carnap and Quine) in the last century:

(DE) How is empiricism to give an adequate account of the certainty, clarity, range, and applicability of mathematics?[3]

In my opinion many central issues in analytic philosophy can be viewed as ramifications involved in attempts to resolve this difficulty. In particular, logic and logicism come in (though not for Frege or early Russell) because it was thought that they help to make the task easier. It is not at all clear that the transformation helps in a basic way to clarify the matter. Indeed, I am inclined to believe that, without bringing in logic at all, were it not for the dominance of the 'two commandments,' we could see:

(A) Empiricism in the sense of Carnap or Quine cannot give an adequate account of mathematics.

This is the theme and thesis of this section. It is not surprising that a more definite refutation can be given of this more specific form of empiricism.

In order to persuade empiricists of this conclusion, it will be helpful, though not sufficient, to establish first the inadequacy of their attempts to refute it. The most direct approach to refute (A) is the one represented by Carnap, which may be broken up into the following steps:

(C1) Logicism: mathematics is reducible to logic.
(C2) Analyticity: logical truths are analytical.
(C3) Conventionalism: analytical propositions are true by convention and, therefore, void of content.

(DE) would be resolved by accepting these three propositions because it follows that 'mathematical knowledge,' as Russell once said,[4] 'is all of the same nature as the "great truth" that there are three feet in a yard.' Hence, there would be no more 'mystery' about mathematics.

But these assertions raise the familiar questions about the nature of logic, analyticity, and conventionalism. Numerous alternative accounts of logic can for the present purpose be divided into classes according to the range of logic they determine, of which only two classes need to be considered:

(1a) Logic is just first order logic (elementary logic).
(1b) Logic includes set theory (or at least enough of set theory to derive 'ordinary mathematics').

Since (1a) conflicts with (C1), its adoption essentially eliminates the relevance of logic to (DE). (It is only relevant to the 'if-then' interpretation of mathematics, treating mathematics as uninterpreted or hypothetically true only, which, however, is so clearly inadequate that it need not be considered here.) Indeed, (C1) commits Carnap to (1b). I shall, therefore, limit myself to the alternative (1b), which, incidentally, is also the position I now favor. The irresolvability of (DE) need not depend on this choice, which becomes irrelevant if we eliminate, as we can, logic as the intermediary between empiricism and mathematics.

Of the various senses of the term *analytic*, Gödel singles out two significant ones:[5]

(2a) Tautological. This term has been used equivocally. If it is to have a sufficiently definite and broad sense it has to involve in some manner definitions plus axioms and deductions. When applied to set theory or number theory, etc., it has 'the purely formal sense that terms occurring can be defined (either explicitly or by rules for eliminating them from sentences containing them) in such a way that the axioms and theorems become special cases of the law of identity and disprovable propositions become negations of this law. In this sense [i.e., if analytic is taken to mean tautological in this sense], even the theory of integers is demonstrably non-analytic, provided that one requires of the rules of elimination that they allow one actually to carry out the elimination in a finite number of steps in each case.' (To remove the restriction on being finite would beg the question of giving an account of mathematics and be circular in proving, e.g., the axiom of choice or the axiom of infinity tautological. Note that even first order logic is not tautological in the specified sense.)

(2b) Analytic. A 'proposition is called analytic if it holds, "owing to the meaning of the concepts occurring in it," where this meaning may perhaps be undefinable (i.e., irreducible to anything more fundamental).' In this sense the axioms and theorems of mathematics, set theory, and logic all are analytic, but need not, as a result, be 'void of content.' This is also the sense of analytic which I now favor.[6] But the irresolvability of (DE) need not depend on the acceptance of this choice, since, as remarked before, we could confront mathematics (independently of whether it is said to be analytic) directly with empiricism.

The crucial question in Carnap's argument is (C3), at least for those who choose (1b) and (2b), which are plausible for those who do not favor conventionalism (in its general sense) and nominalism (in its traditional sense).[7] I have just noted that (C1) commits Carnap to (1b). Now (C2), combined with (C1), appears to commit Carnap also to something like (2b). But once (1b) and (2b) are accepted, the acceptance imposes restrictions on the possible interpretations of (C3), or to the question whether being true by convention means being tautological or being analytic or something else. If it means tautological in the sense of (2a), then it is demonstrable that mathematics (and logic) cannot all be true by convention. If it means analytic in the sense of (2b), then being 'true by convention' need not be void of content; indeed, once the above distinction of (2a) and (2b) is made, it is hard not to see a problem in the conflict between (C3) and (2b). In this regard it is fortunate that Carnap, in his forthright manner, leaves a record of the crucial equivocation which he and other positivists rather naturally made at a time when (DE) was a dominant concern for their position.

The equivocation came in part from Wittgenstein's inclusion of logic under the tautological, based on a mistaken and puzzling obliteration of the finite and the infinite (as well as an idealized requirement that elementary or atomic propositions be mutually independent) in his *Tractatus*, as he himself acknowledged in 1932.[8] In addition, as Carnap concedes, the adaptation of the *Tractatus* view on tautologies by the Vienna Circle involved both modifications and conjectures.[9] 'But to the members of the Circle there did not seem to be a fundamental difference between elementary logic and higher logic, including mathematics. Thus we arrived at the conception that all valid statements of mathematics are analytic in the specific sense that they hold in all possible cases and therefore do not have any factual content.' It is indeed puzzling that, e.g., Hahn, Gödel's respected teacher in mathematics, could (and did) go along with this dubious equivocation.

Carnap goes on to recount his proof, as given in his *Logical Syntax*,[10] that the axioms of set theory (or rather the more restricted type theory) are analytic. Indeed, from all evidence (including this instance) available, it is clear that conventionalism in Carnap's work is primarily the syntactical viewpoint of logic and mathematics, or, in other words, the view that what is asserted in mathematics can be interpreted to be syntactical conventions and their consequences. (By the way, the 'semantic rules' for the conditions of truth are syntactical in that they govern sentences as syntactical objects.)

In this context, we have a sharper form of the equivocation between the tautological and the analytic. If syntax is understood in the standard (and proper) sense along the tradition of the Hilbert school, it has to be finitary and cannot, as a consequence of Gödel's incompleteness results, yield, unaided, enough of mathematics to resolve (DE) and refute proposition (A). If, on the other hand, syntax is stretched to include also nonfinitary components, then we are back to the original problem of giving an empiricist account of mathematics, since the only means available to us so far is to arrive at nonfinitary concepts and reasoning by an appeal to our mathematical intuition. In fact, Carnap seems not only to bring aids to syntax but actually to turn syntax itself into an aid to richer stuff, contrary to his claim to have reduced mathematics to the syntax of language. For example, in proving that the axiom of choice is analytic, Carnap used it in the metalanguage:[11] 'There is used a theorem of the syntax-language which corresponds with the theorem of the object-language whose analytic character is to be proved.' Hence, the reasoning is blatantly circular. We have to take logic to be true before we can add syntactical conventions to derive the conclusion that the theorems of logic are analytic (i.e., true by these conventions).

Moreover, conventions have to be consistent because otherwise every proposition can be proved by them. Therefore, by Gödel's second theorem, any conventions which yield much of logic or mathematics must presuppose a good deal of mathematical knowledge. Carnap's later switch to semantics suffers from the same circularity; the addition of the feature of arbitrariness associated with 'artificial' languages does not help in the grounding of mathematics, since mathematics determines the right 'artificial' language that is capable of deriving it, and not the other way round.

From these considerations it follows that those who accept (C1) and (C2) must reject (C3) and replace it by (2b), or at least some (weaker) variant of it which ceases to deprive all analytic propositions of their 'content.' In order to simplify my line of reasoning a little, I would like to consider, instead of the somewhat weaker assertions to which Carnap's position directly commits himself, the following three altered and more definite propositions which are, I believe, true and also in agreement with Gödel's position:

(G1) Logic includes set theory and, therefore, also mathematics.
(G2) The true propositions of logic and mathematics are analytic.
(G3) Analytic is to be understood in the sense of (2b) so that analytic propositions need not be void of content; indeed, mathematics (and logic) have 'real' content.

(G1) is a little stronger that (C1). But, for the purpose here, the three propositions can be taken to be (C1), (C2), and (some weaker variant of) (2b) just as well. In what follows I shall, for brevity, use the three G propositions as representative of the three types of assertion.

These propositions taken together give a roundabout proof of proposition (A). One could have chosen a more direct proof of (A) by observing simply that mathematics has more content than is accountable by empiricism, either of the Carnap or of the Quine variety. What neither of them could accept is (G3), because they are fully aware that it is incompatible with their (different brands of) analytic empiricism. In the case of Carnap, since he accepts (G1) and (G2), he seems committed to (G3) also, and this fact proves proposition (A) for his type of empiricism. In the case of Quine, the matter is more complex because he, while rightly and forcefully rejecting the combination of (C3) with (C1) and (C2), is rather ambivalent about (C1) and (C2). In particular, he is, therefore, not as directly committed to (G3) as is Carnap.

For example, Quine changes his views about (G1). His most recent view seems to reject (G1) and accept (1a), i.e., that logic is simply first order logic.[12] For the present purpose this poses no great problem because we could substitute 'set theory' for 'logic.' But Quine's view on set theory seems to change also. For many years he used to talk as though set theory were more or less arbitrary conventions; recently he appears to concede more intuitive content to standard systems of set theory.[13] One could still leave out set theory and directly think about good old mathematics. But even here, we are denied a clear issue because we come across one more instance of Quine's fondness for obliterating basic distinctions, in this case between mathematics and natural science.[14] To most of us, however, the line between pure mathematics and the special sciences would seem clear enough. In any case, as I shall argue below, the inadequacy of Quine's view can be shown by elementary examples which, even Quine has to agree, fall squarely within the (indeterminate) range of pure mathematics.

A better-known instance of obliteration, directly related to (G2) and (G3), is Quine's attitude toward the distinction between analytic and synthetic propositions (or rather 'statements' according to his preference for the tangible):[15] 'That there is such a distinction to be drawn at all is an unempirical dogma of empiricists, a metaphysical article of faith.' This is more consistent than Carnap's position and leaves room for nonempiricists to make such a distinction in some such manner as in (2b). Indeed, Quine's refutation of the distinction proceeds by implicitly accepting (C3) and denying (2b) as a meaningful specification of the analytic; he goes on to conclude, however, not that (C2) is false, but that it has no clear meaning.

Quine's brand of empiricism is sometimes called a holistic pragmatism. On one level this agrees with an aspect of moderately educated common sense and cannot be faulted because human knowledge is in a loose sense connected as a whole and we do most of the time make progress in science (and other cultural pursuits) and in daily life by local 'pragmatic' considerations. When we, however, try to determine its implications for the philosophical concern, for example, of understanding the undeniable fact of our having conceptual knowledge and of separating out what is fundamental or great in music or literature or science, we find that Quine's empiricism has very little to say. It is particularly puzzling that Quine arrived at such a position by way of an intensive study of the philosophy of logic and mathematics. Indeed, it is, in my opinion, exactly in these areas that Quine's holism is most clearly inadequate. Hence, I may as well concentrate on these areas, especially since my concern here is to establish the plausibility of proposition (A), which asserts the inadequacy of empiricism for an account of mathematics.

Quine's changing conception of set theory seems to me to be moving along the right direction but to remain ambivalent and indefinite. Elsewhere I have considered this matter at length;[16] here, I shall confine myself to examples in areas where our intuition is stronger and less disagreement is involved. The most elementary example is the principle of modus ponens which was used by Quine as his prize weapon to refute conventionalism in logic.[17] Exactly in this principle we have an indubitable instance of conceptual knowledge based on our logical (or mathematical) intuition, about which Quine's holism could give no reasonably satisfactory account except the remote and undifferentiated one: by an appeal to its yet to be specified place in the total accumulated human experience. It is not surprising that under this perspective of Quine's, all major distinctions become a matter of differences 'in degree.' (Of course analytic empiricists shun the concept of intuition like the plague and many other philosophers are disturbed by an appeal to intuition. I shall return to say something on this at the end of this section.)

In the theory of integers we have a number of remarkable discoveries by conceptual analyses which depend crucially on our mathematical intuition of the integers. An early example is Dedekind's discovery, by an educated reflection on the concept of arithmetic truth, of what are known as the Peano axioms, as explained in his letter of 1890.[18] An empirical (not to say empiricist) approach would have completely failed to achieve anything nearly as conclusive as Dedekind's analysis which shows that the axioms are separately necessary and jointly sufficient. In Gödel's two letters to me,[19] he points out the decisive importance of the nonfinitary concept of arithmetic truth for his discovery of the incompleteness theorems; indeed, this nonfinitary concept is, in addition, also important for a sound (intuitive) *understanding* of the theorems and their proofs. (Gödel also points out that the crucial step in his discovery of constructible sets was to take as given the highly non-constructive and indeed, for our knowledge, highly indefinite totality of ordinal numbers.) In the other direction (of going from mathematics to philosophy), the incompleteness theorems show that no (penetrable) finite rule can exhaust all truths about integers: a conclusion that favors (G3) over (C3), or at least when 'analytic' is replaced by 'mathematical.' How is Quine's holism to give a convincing account of this 'mysterious' yet stable intuition of the nonfinitary concept of arithmetic truth?

Both Carnap and Quine pay a good deal of attention to logic and mathematics; yet, in my opinion, both of them fail to take logic and mathematics seriously as clear representatives of our conceptual knowledge. This is not surprising since the commandment of empiricism is dominant for both of them and when it conflicts with the other commandment of the centrality of logic, they are forced to adapt and modify the latter to suit the former. As a result, we see in both of them an ambivalent attitude toward logic (and mathematics): logic is one of the two pillars of their philosophies, yet it is not permitted to possess any measure of autonomy for fear of impinging on the monopoly of fact and content by (one type of) experience, that ultimately rests exclusively on sense experience of a kind which, though indeterminate, must in no way be contaminated by contact with any conceptual intuition. Indeed, the empiricist's stipulative use of the terms fact and content is a conspicuous petitio principii: by definition, there can be no mathematical (or conceptual) facts and contents. This preemptive usage has the defect of reinforcing a preconception and concealing the glaring conflict of mathematics with empiricism. The considerations outlined in this short section will, when elaborated, I believe, yield a highly plausible proof of the proposition (A).

Quine's reaction to the contradiction of (C3) with (C2) and (C1) leads to what I would like to call his 'logical negativism.'[20] In contrast, the alternative reaction of replacing (C3) by (G3), in my opinion, does more justice to human knowledge. It also retains a more positive (in the sense of optimistic) attitude toward the power of reason, at least with regard to the exact sciences and philosophical reflections on them. By giving up the first commandment of (analytic) empiricism, one is in a position to view the wealth of the less concrete mathematical facts and intuitions as a welcome source of material to enrich philosophy, instead of an irritating mystery to be explained away. This appears to me an illustration of a broad outlook pointing to the right direction along which to look for a satisfactory liberation (and rejuvenation?) of analytic philosophy.

I believe that the considerations in this section do prove convincingly to the open-minded philosophers that neither Carnap nor Quine has a remotely adequate account of mathematics, or that, whatever mathematics is, it is not what their theories say it is. A much harder question is to say positively what mathematics is. This is a question to which I have nothing approaching a complete answer and cannot even sketch my highly incomplete views here. But it is necessary to say something about the appeal to our logical or mathematical intuition in connection with modus ponens and the integers, since I expect many philosophers have already shut their minds at the mention of such intuitions.

Gödel said to me more than once: How strange (is it) that the positivists (and empiricists) do philosophy by cutting off parts of their brain (in excluding conceptual knowledge)? Around 1955 he spent several years in writing six versions of a paper entitled: Is mathematics syntax of language? It was to refute the conception of mathematics favored by his teachers H. Hahn, M. Schlick, and Carnap. In the end he did not publish it and told me on several occasions that he did not publish the paper because he had no adequate answer to the positive question what mathematics is.

For the purpose of proving the proposition (A), it is of course not necessary to give a full account of mathematics; it is enough to exhibit some basic aspect of it that is unaccountable by empiricism. The examples of modus ponens and the integers are a very solid part of what we know, and philosophy has an obligation to do justice to what we know. Hence, even avoiding the dangerous term intuition, the examples do illustrate the basic inadequacy of the philosophies of Carnap and Quine. Let me, however, turn briefly to the matter of intuition, for the purpose of rounding off the picture.

It may help clear the ground if we remove first some implicit associations with the concept of intuition. There is no implication that intuition cannot make mistakes or that it cannot be improved by discipline or by the cooperative effort at advancing human experience. Hence, an appeal to intuition need not exclude, indeed to some extent often depends on, evidence from consensuses and pragmatic consequences. All these are clear from common usage and explicitly stated by Gödel in his writings and conversations. And I agree with him. Once these implicit associations, which appear to be widespread among philosophers, have been corrected, the reluctance to accept selective and careful appeals to intuitions should disappear or at least decrease. When faced with an appeal to intuition, the natural response is not to reject it offhandedly on the ground of unclarity, but to ask oneself whether one does share the intuition and how strongly and detachably. In the ultimate sense we have no absolutely certain knowledge at all, and a careful reliance on intuition is absolutely indispensable in daily life and in all intellectual pursuits. There is no reason why, and indeed it is curious that, anybody should, only in doing philosophy, choose to dispense with explicit and conscious (public and private) appeals to intuitions.

There remains an uneasiness, a sort of prejudice resulting from the dominance of empiricism, that conceptual intuitions must in some sense be reducible to sense experience (and sense intuitions, if they are accepted). For the proof of (A), I do not have to refute this possibility because I believe I have shown that neither Carnap nor Quine has achieved such a reduction. It is rather for the purpose of moving toward a positive account of what mathematics is, that one appears to have to face the epistemological problem of accessibility of mathematical objects (primarily the sets) or, more broadly, of concepts. I can only speak briefly on this matter here, leaving a more extended account for the future.[21]

Many people, including Hermite, early Russell, Gödel, and Quine, have suggested analogies between mathematics and physics. The analogy means different things for Gödel and Quine. For Quine it is a part of his holism which appears to say that philosophy must not look at anything closely for fear of unwisely intruding into the territory of science. Gödel's comparison has more content. In a famous passage[22] he compares physical objects with sets (mathematical objects) and says that 'even our ideas referring to physical objects contain constituents qualitatively different from sensations or mere combinations of sensations.' He also says that sets and physical objects both have the function of 'the generating of unities out of manifolds': this is clearly the essence of sets and in the case of physical objects we have the Kantian idea of generating '*one* object out of its various aspects.' In conversations, Gödel speaks of sets as 'quasi-spatial' objects.

For the purpose of this section, I need not delay over Gödel's question whether 'synthesis' of the two kinds is subjective or objective. (Contrary to Kant, he believes and would like it to be objective, in a stronger sense than Kant's mind-determined 'objectivity.') The relevant point here is rather that both Kant and Gödel are struck by a basic aspect of physical objects which gives a more definite meaning to the more widely shared belief that they are not quite 'reducible to' sensations; in other words, to see an object over and above sensations, it requires the assistance of an 'intuition.' It follows, therefore, that empiricism in its traditional formulation cannot even account for physical objects (a point of Kant's). Indeed, it is known from studies in child psychology that 'shape-detectors' and 'object-detectors' are actualized in the brain only gradually in the child's development: this appears to be an empirical evidence for the separability of the perception of shapes and physical objects from crude sensations.

It is certainly plausible that the perception of small and simple physical sets (such as the set of the five fingers on my right hand) is sufficiently analogous to (and apparently less complex in some aspects than) the perception of simple physical objects. In this way a process of extension gets started in mathematics, moving toward more abstract and more complex sets. This is parallel to but different from the process in physics, as we move from tables and chairs to viruses, galaxies, electrons, positrons, etc. Of course the move from simple physical sets toward a set F consisting of all finite 'pure' (i.e., excluding nonsets altogether) sets (a plausible substitute for the integers) and thence to a set which is the totality of all subsets of F, etc., poses fascinating questions to be investigated in the philosophy of mathematics; but certainly we need not go into them here.

What I say in this section does not, I believe, contradict Gödel's views in any way. Indeed, I am inclined to think that I have added nothing to the substance of what is explicit or implicit in his sayings. On the other hand, I am not depending on certain of Gödel's stronger assertions of his strong position. I do not wish to discuss here where I either disagree with or fail to understand him. Rather it is my hope and belief that the weaker assertions of this section are easier to accept and may already suffice to cause some fundamental rethinking (at least in the 'analytic' tradition,[23] particularly in the science-centered portion) that would lead to some change of direction in philosophy from what I take to be a path filled with unfortunate misuses of very fine analytic powers.

Notes

1. Quine 1951. Quine formulates the first dogma as 'a belief in some fundamental cleavage between' analytic and synthetic propositions; he devotes his attention, not to logic or mathematics, but to the notion of synonymy in which he says that 'the major difficulty lies.' This, in my opinion, is a shift of emphasis from the primary to the secondary issue and reverses the sensible approach of consolidating first regions where we have more solid intuitions. Hence, my reformulation of the first dogma, I believe, gets closer to the heart of the matter. (Compare Carnap's formulation of the central concern of the Vienna Circle in note 3, which seems to support my interpretation.)

2. In this section I mention also some points to be treated more fully in the book under preparation, as described in note 21.

3. This basic dilemma of empiricism was very much on Carnap's mind. For example, after equivocating on the 'tautological' character of mathematics (see notes 8 and 9), Carnap goes on to say: 'What was important in this conception from our point of view was the fact that it became possible for the first time to combine the basic tenet of empiricism with a satisfactory explanation of the nature of logic and mathematics' (*IA*, p. 47).

4. See B. Russell, *History of Western Philosophy*, p. 860.

5. BP, p. 230.

6. This does not imply that philosophy is only concerned with finding analytic propositions. Indeed, I believe there are nonanalytic propositions (such as what I call the 'principle of necessary reason' elsewhere in this book) which properly belong to philosophy.

7. In particular, not in Poincaré's special sense of 'conventionalism' for geometry and not in Quine's contrived sense of 'nominalism.'

8. See report in Moore 1955, pp. 1–4.

9. *IA*, p. 47. The quotation in note 3 follows the quotation here, which is preceded by a summary of Wittgenstein's ideas about tautology and an acknowledgment of modifications: 'At any rate, he did not count the theorems of arithmetic, algebra, etc., among the tautologies.'

10. R. Carnap, *The Logical Syntax of Language*, 1937. The account is given, somewhat sketchily for Carnap's style, on pp. 121–124 and p. 141. In particular, the treatment of the axiom of infinity on p. 141 is elusive and has been questioned by various people, including me and H. Bohnert. 'I found several possible interpretations for the axiom of infinity,' recounts Carnap on pp. 47–48 of *IA*, 'of such a kind that they make this axiom

analytic. The result is achieved, e.g., if not things but positions are taken as individuals.' I believe we have here another example of Carnap's confusion between (C3) and (2b), as well as of his unfulfillable wish to get mathematics out of physical experience alone.

11. Op. cit., p. 121.

12. For example, on p. 388 of Schilpp 1963, Quine says: 'The further part of logic is set theory.' Yet in his *Philosophy of Logic*, 1970, he argues at great length that logic is just first order logic (e.g., pp. 64–70; compare also his *Roots of Reference*, 1974).

13. Quine's influential view of the arbitrariness of set theory is too familiar to require citations. For example, 'Conventionalism has a serious claim to attention in the philosophy of mathematics, if only because of set theory' (see Schilpp 1963, p. 392; compare also p. 348 and p. 396 for more of the same). What may be less familiar is his apparent change of heart more recently. For example, in the 1980 foreword to his *From a Logical Point of View* (1953, 1961, and 1980), he subscribes to the general opinion that familiar systems of set theory correspond closer to our intuition than his own deviant systems.

14. See, e.g., *Philosophy of Logic*, pp. 98–100. In his *Mathematics in Philosophy* (1983), Charles Parsons questions this position of Quine's with extensive observations, both in the Introduction and in Essay 7.

15. BP, p. 358.

16. *MP*, Chapter 6 (this chapter is also reprinted in the second edition of BP as the concluding essay). These considerations are continued in my article 'Large sets' (1977).

17. BP, pp. 342–344. The argument goes back to Lewis Carroll, 'What the tortoise said to Achilles,' *Mind*, vol. 4 (1895), pp. 278–280.

18. Published for the first time in my 1957 article.

19. *MP*, pp. 8–11.

20. The negativism refers not only to the wealth of Quine's negative theses (relativity, indeterminacy, inscrutability, etc.) but also to what I take to be the negative effects of his amazingly successful (in being influential) doctrines on the state of analytic philosophy. By refusing to give up empiricism despite his own acute and largely correct insights into Carnap's doctrine, Quine was, I think, driven into a structureless make-believe position which for me is a reductio ad absurdum of analytic empiricism and, owing to its predominance, seems to discredit the whole analytic approach by dimming its promise to clarify our important larger intuitions in different areas.

For those who are, for one reason or another, more inclined to basically different (nonanalytic) approaches, Quine's work could be seen as a positive step toward an emancipation in philosophy. (See note 23.) However that may be, since Quine is himself committed to the general attitude covered by the umbrella conception of analytic philosophy, and there are better 'analytic' responses to Carnap, I believe I am justified in considering Quine's impact negative.

21. I am working on a book, tentatively entitled *Reflections on Kurt Gödel*, in which I intend to separate out where I agree and where I disagree with

what I take to be Gödel's philosophical views. On points of agreement I plan to give an extensive exposition, as well as further developments (which Gödel, given his choice to concentrate on the 'beginnings,' has probably left largely open) based on it; and on points of disagreement I shall expound my own views. There will certainly be longer discussions in it of the points raised in the following few paragraphs. In order to add a check against my misinterpretations and failures to appreciate his significant ideas, which will undoubtedly be many, I shall include as detailed a record of my conversations with him as I am able to reconstruct from my rather incomplete notes. In any case, such a public record is of value in itself. Of course eventually his massive Nachlass will be deciphered and become more accessible to scholars.

22. BP, pp. 271–272; these pages were written in 1963. Elsewhere Gödel mentions an analogy of the assumption of sets to that of physical bodies (or objects) in his Russell paper (1944); see BP, p. 220. Quine speaks of 'The analogy between the myth of mathematics and the myth of physics' in his 1948 paper on 'ontology' (see BP, p. 195) and again of sets as myths, epistemologically 'on the same footing with physical objects and gods, neither better nor worse except for differences in degree' of their usefulness (in his 'Two dogmas' of 1951; BP, pp. 363–364). I have always found Quine's deliberate misuse here of the words 'myth' and 'differences in degree' disconcerting. The apparent similarity between Gödel's and Quine's analogies is, in my opinion, only on the surface.

23. There is a tendency to equate analytic empiricism with analytic philosophy, even though the latter caption certainly permits and indeed invites a broader interpretation. This historically conditioned tendency is unfortunate because it tends to deprive nonempiricist works in the analytic spirit of a natural designation, as well as to create a source of conceptual confusion and terminological awkwardness. For example, I would include under analytic philosophy, but definitely not under analytic empiricism, the famous work of John Rawls in political philosophy (centering on his *Theory of Justice*, 1971), as well as the much less widely known work of Howard Stein in the philosophy of physics (in his dispersed articles) and my own work in the philosophy of mathematics (as represented by a major part of my *MP*). Indeed, these examples may be taken as silent (and not so silent in my own case) responses to analytic empiricism resulting from a belief that it is a mistaken course of development.

   I now agree with Gödel that his all too few published philosophical essays and much of his philosophical Nachlass also belong to analytic philosophy. (There were occasions when I spoke negatively of analytic philosophy, meaning by it analytic empiricism, and Gödel protested on behalf of the use of analysis in philosophy. If I had had the distinction then, the matter would have been cleared up to mutual satisfaction.)

   I should emphasize that the distinction between analytic empiricism and analytic philosophy is closely associated with the different conceptions of 'analysis,' as is clear from the contrast between (C3) and (G3) [or (2b)]. In other words, in my opinion, there is no impartial reason to restrict analysis, conceptual or logical, to the limited type that is primarily 'linguistic,' and especially in the more specific sense of conventionalism, according to which analysis can produce 'analytic' propositions only in the sense (C3). Hence, the distinction is closely connected with different conceptions of logic and different attitudes toward conceptual knowledge.

'Analytic empiricism,' as I construe it (and, I believe, appropriately and correctly), includes also a narrow conception of analysis that is intimately connected with its first commandment, viz., that of empiricism, which is based on a narrow conception of experience. There are broader conceptions of linguistic analysis which go beyond the bounds of (C3). But I believe them to remain an inadequate explication of or substitute for our intuitive idea of logical or conceptual analysis, unless they are so equivocated as to include also analysis as characterized by (G3). This, however, is a more involved issue and it transcends the intended scope of this book.

Richard Rorty paints a sad picture of 'Philosophy in America Today.' He summarizes the current state by a memorable image: 'The best hope for an American philosopher is Andy Warhol's promise that we shall *all* be superstars, for approximately fifteen minutes apiece' (*Consequences of Pragmatism*, 1982, p. 216). Surely Rawls has been and will continue to be a superstar for a much longer duration than fifteen minutes. Stein and I have never attained the status of superstars and probably never will; but for the small circles of kindred spirits our work is surely of interest for much longer than fifteen minutes.

Indeed, Rorty does immediately admit the work of Rawls to be an exception 'whose importance and permanence are deservedly recognized on all sides.' It, however, lies 'in moral and social philosophy' but not 'in the so-called "central" areas of philosophy.' He then runs into the terminological awkwardness which I have just tried to resolve by distinguishing analytic empiricism from analytic philosophy. 'But analytic philosophy cannot draw any comfort from this fact when it looks for a self-description which preserves and updates Reichenbach's [in his *Rise of Scientific Philosophy*, 1951].' 'It is not a triumph of "analytic" philosophizing.' In my opinion the combination 'analytic empiricism' does conveniently capture both the preconception and also the style which Rorty has in mind when he qualifies analytic philosophy by bringing in Reichenbach and puts 'analytic' in quotes to pin down the distinctive style of philosophizing.

In his *Philosophy and the Mirror of Nature* (1979) Rorty puts Quine's (and W. Sellars') work to use in a manner which was, I believe, not intended by these philosophers. It is taken as a decisive advance in wiping out artificial constraints and thereby restoring to philosophy a lost freedom. Where I part ways with Rorty is when he seems to me to equate analytic philosophy with analytic empiricism, taking a 'deconstruction' of the latter as also one of the former.

I am certainly not among those who believe that analytic philosophy is the only appropriate way to do philosophy, even though, despite my serious efforts to broaden myself, it happens to be the only one in which, up to now, I can philosophize with some assurance. Perhaps my ambitious wish to find a way of combining insights attained from fundamentally different approaches is somewhat unrealistic. But at least on a more modest and less speculative level, Rorty and I are, I believe, in agreement: whatever distinct approach one may be better suited to follow with effect and satisfaction, we agree that the state suggested by Warhol is a morass to be avoided by philosophy (or any other subject). It follows that, apart from more internal criteria, work which helps philosophy to move away from the Warhol state is more valuable than work getting philosophy more deeply into it. Even only on this slender common ground alone, I believe that Rorty can have some sympathy with the alternative response to analytic empiricism sketched in this section.

While I find the broad sweep of Rorty's work appealing, I have great difficulty in grasping his own positive views. Sometimes he seems to propose to make or remake philosophy into a highbrow culture in the following peculiar sense: 'The kind of name-dropping, rapid shifting of context, and unwillingness to stay for an answer which this culture encourages runs counter to everything that a professionalized academic discipline stands for' (1982, p. 65). It should be clear that, while I also revolt against the familiar forms of specialization, I have no sympathy with such a conception of philosophy as highbrow culture; indeed, I am eager not only 'to stay for an answer' but also to look for agreement after reflection and discussion.

3. Contractions of philosophy

Subjects, from physics to psychology, which used to be included under philosophy have gradually detached themselves from it. Even logic, traditionally a central branch of philosophy, has half moved into mathematics. This phenomenon is the more obvious and more easily understandable aspect of the contraction of philosophy. It naturally suggests the question whether there remains any territory that has not and cannot be occupied by isolable disciplines each of which covers only some special aspect of human experience. One likely candidate is the quest for an appropriate worldview.

For worldviews centered on morality, the traditional central place of religions has been partially taken over by ideologies (in a nonpejorative sense and sometimes containing some characteristic aspects of religion) in modern times. Ideologies tend to involve a closer association to politics and collective morality (as well as a looser connection to ethics and individual morality) than religions. They, therefore, leave a larger or smaller empty space for doctrines bearing more directly on individual morality. Related to the decline of religion has been the advance of science and the accompanying attempts to develop 'scientific' worldviews. The contrast of science with morality gets us entangled with the related but distinct large contrasts between reason and instinct, necessity and freedom, universality in physical nature and particularity in human nature, etc. In addition to science and morality, there is also the important but elusive esthetic dimension of human experience, which both demands a place in an adequate worldview and may supply a necessary link for its completion.

The emphasis on science leads to the quest for an account of why science is so specially successful and the search for a scientific worldview gets intimately connected with such an account. It seems to me that from Descartes to Kant to Husserl to Gödel, and from Locke to Hume to Mill to Russell, their philosophical work may all be viewed as centering on this sort of approach toward a scientific worldview. The work of Marx seems to me to center on morality and could be called 'scientific' only by further extending a broad sense of science (= Wissenschaft). No matter whether one emphasizes and begins with science or morality or esthetics, the common goal is a worldview which somehow comprehends the three components.

3.1. Philosophy as worldview

But if the task of philosophy is to develop a worldview, then it is not clear today either that it can possibly be accomplished in its plenitude or that philosophy in its traditional form is necessarily the most fruitful way to get at central aspects of the whole or the totality. The 'mode of production' in the main philosophical tradition is to use nonnarrative prose. Even leaving aside radically different media and modes such as films, television, dance, music, painting, architecture, and so on, why should poetry or novels or history not be better vehicles for attaining and communicating insights or views about the whole or some of the important wholes? Moreover, if a comprehensive and adequate outlook is unattainable (in the foreseeable future), then there remains the possibility of concentrating on some important and large aspects of the totality to look for a 'synthesis,' either as a preparation for the more remote end or as a self-contained finished product or preferably as both.

Quantitatively populations (in general and in special segments) and cultural (material, intellectual, spiritual, and esthetic) production, as well as the total amount of leisure, the ranges of awareness, and the contents of life, have increased tremendously over the past hundred years. The social functions and internal contents of philosophy have, over this period, undergone a process of disintegration in several directions. The quantitative increase of everything has introduced a division between technical and nontechnical philosophies; the former is no longer capable of speaking directly either to the common people or even to the narrower audience consisting of the (vaguely defined) intellectual community or a fairly large segment of it. For example, we have the idea of the novelist (or playwright) as philosopher who is in a better position to grapple with life in its entirety; an arbitrary list might include D. H. Lawrence, Thomas Mann, Gide, Brecht, Camus, Sartre, Solzhenitsyn, and Beckett. Harold Bloom speaks of the social function of teaching 'the presentness in the past': 'The teacher of literature now in America, far more than the teacher of history or philosophy or religion, is condemned to teach the presentness of the past, because history, philosophy and religion have withdrawn from the Scene of Instruction' (*A Map of Misreading*, 1975, p. 39).

The increase of awareness is, not surprisingly, both a cause and an effect of specialization, which is probably the single most important factor causing changes of the nature of philosophy, and particularly contractions of the domain of academic philosophy. In this century we no longer have sweeping systems of perennially influential philosophy comparable to those of Kant, Hegel, and Marx. (Marx was of course not an academic philosopher and has largely been excluded from the philosophical curriculum in America. For many years it has been a standard complaint that there is a shortage of qualified teachers of Hegel. Even Kant is only taught in a one-sided way, usually limited to less than the first half of his first *Critique*.)

The increased awareness comes from both the increase of cultural material (caused largely by specialization) and the improvement of the means of communication in quantity and speed. Particular examples of explicitly broadening our awareness include the work of Marx, Nietzsche, and Freud. In different ways each of them challenged the traditional conception of human consciousness by unmasking concealed instincts and motives. Even for those who are not disciples of any of them, it cannot be denied that each of them pointed to a gray area where something important is going on and where our understanding is very inadequate. All three philosophers are very much alive today (including, unfortunately and perhaps inevitably, exaggerated applications of their insights), undoubtedly because they remain both relevant and more or less undigested. These unmaskings also suggest the need to pay more attention to the process of child development if only to get a better understanding of the interplay between instinct and social conditioning.

With specialization various aspects of human experience which are of central concern to philosophy have become the foci of concentrated attention for special subjects which, therefore, are in a more authoritative position to speak about them. For example, it is familiar that fundamental mathematics and physics can come close to philosophy. Indeed, Sommerfeld attributes to Hartnack the saying: 'People complain that our generation has no philosophers. Quite unjustly: it is merely that today's philosophers sit in another department, their names are Planck and Einstein' (Schilpp 1949, p. 99). Related to but different from this observation are the influence of Einstein's work in physics on philosophy, on one hand, which is conspicuous from the flood of philosophical books on it, as well as the importance of philosophy for his study of physics, on the other. He does say, 'Epistemology without contact with science becomes an empty scheme, Science without epistemology is— insofar as it is thinkable at all—primitive and muddled' (ibid., p. 684). Most physicists today, however, probably don't care about the first statement and find the second statement old-fashioned or merely temperamental; in any case it is doubtful whether even the best physicists today consciously think of epistemology in doing research. A less ambiguous specimen of 'philosopher-scientist' than Einstein is Gödel, who actually spent as much of his energy in doing philosophy as in doing science. Gödel not only speaks of the importance of his philosophical views on his mathematical work but also uses his mathematical conclusions to argue for his philosophical thesis (of conceptual realism).

Generally it is not easy to determine explicitly how a person's philosophical thoughts interact with his work in a specialized discipline. It is easier to illustrate how specialized reflections can contribute to philosophical studies than the other way round. For example, Freudian psychology and political theory are each in its own manner relevant to a study of the concept of self (or person). And, particularly in moral and political philosophy, much depends on one's beliefs as to what the future should and could bring, and history would seem to be the chief guide to the formation of such beliefs. Even in architecture we encounter suggestive reflections on the nature of space and time. In the other direction, G. E. Moore's *Principia ethica* (1903), as the gospel of the Bloomsbury Group, may have influenced the artistic practice of some members of the group. Schrödinger's essay 'What is life?' (1944) may be construed as a philosophical work, which apparently had some influence on the development of biology. The impact of the reflections on the concept of justice by Rawls on political and economic theory as well as jurisprudence is widely recognized and surprising at a time when philosophy is generally thought to be futile.

There remain gaps between the goals of existing specialized disciplines and the goal of philosophy as a 'view of the whole.' Attempts to fill some of these gaps may lead to new disciplines such as the sociology of science, cybernetics, the psychology of invention (or discovery or creation), systems science, the 'science of science,' artificial intelligence, etc. Other gaps may be considered yet unexplored parts of philosophy. These include the much debated relation between the 'two cultures,' issues considered in books such as *The Possible and the Actual* (1982, F. Jacob), *So Human an Animal* (1968, R. Dubos), *Ideology and Utopia* (1929, K. Mannheim), and of course many others, as well as Dewey's call for the integration of specialized results as a practical need. In his words, philosophy should contribute to the satisfaction of this need:

'The need for direction of action in large social fields is the source of a genuine demand for unification of scientific conclusions. They are organized when their bearing on the conduct of life is disclosed' (Dewey 1929, p. 312). According to this view, philosophy should presumably also contribute to the questions about science and public policy, as well as the elusive relation between basic research and its applications (say in medicine).

Philosophy as an academic subject today appears on the whole very remote from the type of quest for worldviews suggested above. Indeed, there is a general impression that it is isolated from all serious concerns. On different occasions I have come across broad-minded intellectuals with an interest in philosophy who express their puzzlement along the following line: 'It is easy to wonder at the activities of contemporary professional philosophers, to contrast the struggles of philosophers of the past with the most profound questions concerning the world and the place of human beings in it, with what often appears to be barren argumentation about arid technicalities by a group of strident sophists.' How to sort out what is true or false in such an impression is a complex task to which parts of this book may be thought to be a contribution.

It may be of interest to look at a few examples to illustrate how society at large in the West views philosophy in this century. In this regard of the apparent relative place of philosophy it would appear that there has been an overall tendency of decline. On the level of popular attention, the awarding of Nobel Prizes is a convenient indicator. Philosophy is not one of the subjects included and so far it has been absorbed into literature so that only a special type of philosopher, a type which coincidentally has a wide appeal, is considered. Four philosophers have been recognized in this way: Rudolf Eucken (1846–1926) in 1908, Henri Bergson (1859–1941) in 1928, Bertrand Russell (1872–1970) in 1950, Jean-Paul Sartre (1905–1980) in 1964 (which he declined). Certainly this is not an indication that they were the best philosophers of their times but probably corresponds more closely to the popular fame they enjoyed then.

According to one story, when the Institute for Advanced Study at Princeton was being planned around 1930, the founder went around soliciting opinions about which subjects should be included. It is said that mathematics and history were found to be the only two of the central subjects in which there was something like a consensus on who were the best practitioners. That was, so the story goes, why initially there were only these two schools. The story need not be construed as evidence for a belief that philosophy was thought to be less central, except that the lack of a consensus might be taken to be a negative feature for subjects like philosophy. From my limited experience, Oxford seems to be the only place in England and America where philosophers do not feel defensive toward their colleagues in any other field. Elsewhere, Paris is possibly another place.

Not long ago a collection of extended 'perspectives' on all the major cultural domains was published (Ashmore 1968). Included are twelve domains: (1) nature, (2) human nature, (3) the technological order, (4) the legal order, (5) mathematics and logic, (6) the social order, (7) the economic order, (8) the political order, (9) education, (10) linguistics, (11) the fine arts, (12) religion. Apparently contemporary philosophy receives more than negligible attention only under linguistics! The 1984 *Who's Who in America* sponsors an election of Americans to receive 'achievement awards' under five categories: (a) arts and communication; (b) entrepreneurship; (c) life sciences; (d) social structures, social sciences, and social policy; (e) technology, mathematics, and physical sciences. The conspicuous absence of anything near philosophy from this list, I believe, illustrates quite well the peripheral and inconsequential place of philosophy in the minds of one powerful group of the American elite.

In 1979, Ricoeur compiled an ambitious volume to survey the 'main trends in philosophy' of the world today. Apart from some brief mentions of Asian philosophies (represented by India and Japan), the book divides the main trends into three which are roughly represented by: dialectic realism, analytic philosophy, and continental philosophy. More flexibly, he summarizes the three trends as follows.

(A) Philosophy is a Weltanschauung; it is to build up a systematic representation of reality, at both the natural and the social levels. It 'seeks to create a unified view of the world out of the facts ascertained by science and the values that emerge from the social experience of mankind.' Four species are listed: (1) Marxism as inherited through Engels and Lenin; (2) derivatives from Hegelianism; (5) philosophies of scientists calling for a synthesis of cosmology and anthropology; (4) derivatives from the Aristotelian-Thomist synthesis.

(B) According to this conception, 'science alone provides an image of reality, an image to which philosophy is quite unable to add.' Its deliberately modest modes of philosophizing are 'reductionist and therapeutic.' They are generally linked with an investigation of language (and its grammar), as well as a use of analytical techniques. They may or may not expect 'symbolic logic to provide a model for the reformulation of ordinary language.' This 'stream is represented most notably by English and American analytic philosophy.'

(C) This trend is refined into two principal factions: subjectivity and beyond. According to the first faction, the responsibility of philosophy is 'to preserve, to make explicit and to coordinate other forms of experience than objective knowledge.' It is notably influenced by the young Hegel, Kierkegaard, the young Marx, and certain developments of phenomenology. The second faction is often presented as 'post-philosophy' or 'metaphilosophy' and influenced by Nietzsche and Heidegger. It emphasizes reality like (A) and language like (B), but for members of this faction, 'both reality and language turn out as more archaic, more poetical and more fragmentary than they do as seen by' (A) and (B).

This summary of Ricoeur's useful summary suggests to me one way of describing what my own vague conception is. Like (A), it looks for a worldview. I would like to begin with a broader and more natural 'analytic' approach than is depicted under (B) and hope also to do justice, in some sequel to this book, to our 'other forms of experience than objective knowledge,' thereby sharing a goal with the first faction of (C). In this book, I am more concerned with developing a better conception of analytic (or rather 'exact') philosophy than the familiar but historically contingent one depicted under (B). The two leading initiators of 'exact' philosophy in this century would seem to be Husserl and Russell.

For the last thirty years of his life, Husserl (1859–1938) attempted to deepen and broaden the ideas of Descartes and Kant; he spent most of his energy in the struggle for securing a 'true beginning.' The indiscriminately applied pejorative term 'foundationalism' is a quite appropriate label for his work. The success of his own program is hardly encouraging, and it was not his disciples but rather those who departed from his spirit that became conspicuous: certainly Heidegger and Sartre, and, with lesser departure, Merleau-Ponty. A more relevant example for my purpose is Gödel, who shared Husserl's ideal (at least as a crucial step for his own program) but seems to me to get more liberal when he considered more specific issues. By extending what I take to be more or less implicit in Gödel's practice (rather than his ideal), I believe it is possible to work toward a more liberal and more rationalistic sort of 'analytic philosophy,' which may be called 'phenomenography,' and thought of as a much less radical version of what Gödel calls his 'rationalistic optimism.'

Russell's early work also influenced Gödel, who has improved Russell's early concept of logic and gone far beyond it. But the more manifest influences of early Russell on contemporary philosophy are seen through the work of Carnap and Quine, which also serves as a frame on which to hang most of my reflections in the present book.

3.2. From Russell to Quine: a case study of contraction
Philosophy has undergone a great contraction from Russell to Carnap and Quine. Before 1910, Russell and Poincaré carried on a lively and

instructive debate on the foundations of mathematics. In 1913, Russell began a friendship with Joseph Conrad which was specially dear to him for years to come. In 1915 he had a brief and stormy friendship with D. H. Lawrence. There was the Russell–Einstein manifesto on the nuclear peril on the eve of Einstein's death in 1955. Long before that, Einstein had written an essay to honor Russell, saying that 'I owe innumerable happy hours to the reading of Russell's works' (Schilpp 1944). Sartre respected Russell and joined his Vietnam Tribunal in 1966. Arnold Toynbee and Herbert Read acknowledged their debt to Russell's work. While within professional philosophy Carnap and Quine at times enjoyed a reputation almost as solid as Russell's, there is nothing in their thought and action to come near to Russell's place in the intellectual scene at large. Moreover, compared with Quine's 'negativism,' Carnap's philosophy had a greater appeal in its day and an attractive though limited optimism. I do not believe that this example of philosophical contraction can be fully explained by the different historical periods and the different capacities of these philosophers.

I consider the years from 1910 to 1914 the crucial transition period in Russell's philosophical development. Before that period he had done the most solid and enduring part of his work in logic and philosophy. During that period his interests shifted from the foundations of mathematics to the foundations of physics and a general theory of knowledge. He could not find a sufficiently definite large program. His adherence to the spirit of British empiricism and to the model of mathematics, combined with a complex of factors in his personal life, had led him to abandon his pursuit before the war came and took him into an interlude (from August 1914 to the end of 1917) of more political writings.

His suggestion of a 'logical construction' of the external world from sense-data and more generally the decisive importance of technical logic for philosophy (in the spring of 1914), which afterwards exerted a determinative influence on Carnap's lifework, was, I believe, a hasty and casual substitute for a more meaningful and more thought-out project which he had looked for but failed to capture. This opinion is, I think, borne out by his strivings just before offering the suggestion and by the fact that he himself did not return to its execution later on. This appraisal is an illustration of my broader thesis that Carnap and Quine began with some of the less serious suggestions from Russell's fertile pen and accentuated rather than corrected their tendency to lead into the course of contraction. In my opinion, the gain of added definiteness in the form of the work of Carnap and Quine has failed to balance off the increase in artificiality.

Russell himself followed a different course, even when he was doing theory of knowledge. He was rather disappointed in philosophy; and he neither gave it up nor concentrated on it for any extended period. At different times he allowed one or another of his varied interests and abilities to take command over his 'superabundant vitality,' according to what occasions and circumstances appeared to require. Santayana spoke of him as a failure 'on the whole, relative to his capacities.' Russell's reflections on his eightieth birthday also give an impression of his own different sense of failure.

Certainly such a judgment does not apply to Russell's work before 1910. It is when we come to his work since 1910 that the judgment becomes hard to evaluate, except by using some highly speculative assumptions. It might be claimed that if Russell had found the appropriate approach to philosophy and concentrated on it, he would have made a greater total intellectual contribution. But what if he could not have found the right approach, on account either of his own defect or of an intrinsic impossibility of his historical time, but had concentrated on philosophy? One might possibly view the actual course he had taken from 1914 on as his personal manner of resisting the encroachment of contraction on philosophy and on philosophers.

Of Russell's numerous general books after 1914, the topics as suggested by the titles mostly fall under philosophy in its broad sense: justice, social reconstruction, political ideals, freedom, bolshevism, atoms, relativity, education, marriage, morals, happiness, organization, religion, authority, individual, ethics, politics, etc. But he did not treat these topics in the manner of professional philosophy. Apart from the two popular expositions of physics, the ranges cover principally politics and education (centered on the idea of freedom), as well as ethics and religion. He probably valued more highly his professional reputation than his popular fame. In the late 1950s, when a brand of linguistic philosophy supposedly derived from later Wittgenstein was in fashion and detested by Russell, he expressed his concern for recognition with a generous sense of humor. 'It is not an altogether pleasant experience to find oneself regarded as antiquated after having been, for a time, in the fashion. It is difficult to accept this experience gracefully' (*PD*, p. 214).

Carnap spent several years trying to carry further the projects suggested in Russell's *External World* and used the teachings of Frege and the Hilbert school to improve formally on *PM* in formalizing syntax and semantics in various books. He became also the most authoritative spokesman of the Vienna Circle. Compared with Russell, he and Quine seem to me to have a less adequate conception of mathematics, physics, and logic, relative to the state of the subjects at their own time. They are more concerned with a precarious formal precision. In this regard Quine has the safeguard of adhering to well-established areas (set theory and elementary logic), while Carnap constructs and develops artificial systems, often without the necessary thorough prior scrutiny to make sure that they indeed capture important concepts in a substantially correct way. They both have a tendency to pay more attention to being formally precise than to the significance of the content about which one is being precise; but Carnap carries this practice further into a systematic principle: 'Let us construct a system first and then see what happens.' This attitude of Carnap's seems to play an important part in the debate on ontology and analyticity between Carnap and Quine.

The willingness to combine local precision with global indefiniteness takes different forms with Carnap and Quine. In both cases their practice seems to me to invite and encourage a type of specialization which, in my opinion, does more harm than good in philosophy. Isolation of concepts and problems in philosophy is not as clean as in mathematics (or any mature branch of science). Larger intuitions about connections with vague but more familiar concepts and problems have to be consulted frequently to safeguard against the danger of wrestling with insignificant artificial issues. (I hope the concrete examples in the body of the book will clarify these admittedly ambiguous remarks to some extent.)

While this book centers around a discussion of the work of Russell, Carnap, and Quine, I consider in it also the place of the tradition of the Vienna Circle in American professional philosophy up to the present day. But my own purpose is primarily to help myself see a little less darkly what I really look for in philosophy and to attain some dialogue with the philosophical community on my unorthodox views, by way of the shared familiarity with the range of work discussed in this book. A word of explanation may be in order for the fact that I cover Quine's work at greater length. Quine's work is the most recent and, I conjecture without study, presumably of the greatest current interest. Moreover, there exists no comparable comprehensive treatment of his work, especially not from my type of perspective. In addition, I have been exposed to a larger portion of Quine's work than of Russell's or Carnap's; hence, it is less hard to be fairly comprehensive. In particular, my discussion of Quine's work in mathematical logic fills a gap in the literature.

After I came into direct contact with Quine in 1946, I went through a period of enthusiasm over his approach to logic and philosophy. Familiarity with works of Gödel and others in logic made me feel that Quine's approach is not sufficiently natural and substantive. In philosophy I could not relate his approach to my preconceptions of what philosophy is supposed to offer, preconceptions which were to a considerable extent conditioned by my Chinese background (including a greater respect for history and literature and some acquaintance, acquired in China, with the history of Western philosophy). When I saw the central place which Quine's philosophy occupied in the professionalized discipline, I realized that my disagreement was with a pervasive tendency of which Quine's work formed a distinctive part.

Over the years I have attempted to do philosophy in a different manner but could not give a coherent and convincing account of my own conception of philosophy. I have also voiced my negative sentiments toward current academic philosophy in very ineffectual general terms, particularly in my *From Mathematics to Philosophy* (1974), which contains also Gödel's several brief but pregnant contributions. To my surprise and disappointment (and Gödel's, too) the book has pretty much been completely disregarded by the philosophy establishment. Meanwhile, my conception has grown a little clearer. In spring 1972, Schilpp invited me to contribute a paper to a volume dealing with Quine's philosophy. The invitation was revived in 1981 by Lewis Hahn, the new editor. The idea occurred to me that if I try to use my conception to examine well-known work in the field, I may be able to focus my uncontrollable thoughts better and my views may have more chance of receiving some attention and at least some responsible critical comments. In the process of executing this idea, I have been led to broader considerations which have helped to clarify my own views and their relations to the prevalent ideas. The results are partly reported in this book.

My central theme is that philosophy should pay more attention to what we, the human species, know and believe (and feel) at present. That, in my opinion, must be the base of any serious philosophy. The difficult question is only how philosophy can most effectively take into consideration the vast and diversified range of what we know (or merely believe) and how we feel. To attempt an answer to this question seems to call for looking at current philosophy with the question in mind and, of course, actually doing philosophy from such a perspective. It is for the dual purpose of making the conception clearer and doing some philosophy according to it that I have planned a series of three books, of which this is the first.

Russell's work before 1910 had also, in quite different ways, exerted great influence on Gödel and Wittgenstein, who had each absorbed Russell's influence in his own manner and gone beyond it in significant ways along different directions. I have included a digression on Wittgenstein's work in this book, largely dealing with his *Tractatus*. Also some contexts in this book invite brief expositions of some of Gödel's ideas on logic and mathematics which have influenced me. A more extensive account of his philosophical views is planned for the book *Reflections on Kurt Gödel,* which is in progress. While I do not fully agree with his philosophy, I feel it is right on many questions. The task is to find a right framework in which appropriate places for it can be located in a natural manner.

Since 1972, I have studied Marxism, Chinese philosophy, the philosophy of biology, artificial intelligence, some psychoanalysis, some political theory, and a little hermeneutics. I have even written in several of these areas; the published material is listed in the table of references. I feel that all these and a few other subjects each have something to contribute to a comprehensive philosophy.

The obvious danger is of course eclecticism, which I certainly intend to avoid. With this threat we come back to the question of how to effectively take into consideration what we know. With the view of absorbing at least a few of the areas which I consider of importance, I am planning for the series a third and concluding book, to be entitled *Purity Is Not Enough,* or *Phenomenography: Tasks and Illustrations.* I have every intention to complete the series in a few years. It is my hope that at that time I shall have gained enough clarification to be able to begin pursuing systematically the large project of a philosophy based on what we know or believe and how we feel.

It is, therefore, obvious that this book and indeed the whole planned series of three all are very much reports of work in progress. A more vigorous and self-confident mind would probably not proceed in this way. But I find the explicitly stage-by-stage advance more congenial. In this way when things go wrong, the mistakes will not be forgotten or concealed (and thereby mislead and mystify). Moreover, it is not excluded that at some stage some people will get a better conception of progressing further than what will in fact be done by my own efforts.

3.3. The idea of phenomenography
We recognize reality through human experience, the context of which may be said to be phenomena. When a physicist speaks of phenomenology he means 'that division of any science (physics in this case) which describes and classifies its phenomena.' If this is extended to the whole of human experience, it appears that my conception of philosophy might be called 'phenomenology.' But the way Husserl has used the term contains two components which I find both disagreeable and unnecessary. He begins with the subjective so that not only objectivity but also intersubjectivity appear to me to be no longer attainable, while, in my opinion, they are among the most basic data which we begin with. In addition, he looks for the absolutely certain or synthetic

a priori foundation once and for all, while I feel such a quest for an unattainable goal is doomed to failure, however useful and interesting its by-products might be.

I have not found the word 'phenomenography' in the dictionaries, but the combination seems quite reasonable and the association of the '-graphy' ending with descriptive sciences appears appropriate. The contrast with Husserl's phenomenology permits it to dissociate from the two aforementioned negative (for me) components of the latter. Moreover, for example, the analogy of geography, as contrasted with geology, would seem to suggest the intended quest for a structured comprehensiveness rather than the more concentrated attention to limited aspects or domains required of specialized disciplines.

To endow the word with more definite contents is more difficult. All I have now are vague ideas which promise (perhaps falsely) to lead to sharper components which at some stage will miraculously fit together to yield a fruitful skeleton backbone for reality as seen through human experience.

One leading idea is to study where we agree and why we disagree (when we disagree). By bringing out, consolidating, and expanding the areas where we agree, and by looking more closely at why we disagree, we concomitantly broaden the areas where we agree to disagree, without compulsion or resentment. Of course it is often very difficult to find out why we disagree, and there is a serious doubt whether this is a fruitful area for systematic study. Individuals disagree, groups disagree, and one disagrees with oneself not only from one time to another but even at the same time (in the form of 'internal' conflicts). A source of great complexity is the intricate interplays (the dialectical relation) between the agents that disagree with each other, as well as between the different types of disagreement. There is no doubt that the area of disagreements and their causes is rich, important, and sufficiently broad and varied to have the quality of centrality and universality.

One important feature of this century is a greater appreciation of the diversity of individuals and groups in their material conditions and in their scientific, ethical, esthetic, political, and religious consciousness. It is much harder to be comprehensive or to be significantly universal, particularly in matters having to do with human values. The diversity of 'forms of life' does make it possible for an 'insider' to say more meaningful things to (or even about) his or her group (say of German farmers or French youths or American liberals) than an 'outsider,' by starting (implicitly) from shared sentiments and beliefs. But I believe it is possible to approach universality not only in mathematics and physics but also elsewhere if we can find the appropriate specification of particularities (of dominant purposes and stages of development, etc.) and qualifying conditions (of which a simple example might be the bondage of existing biology to terrestrial life).

The 'metaphilosophical' question 'why people disagree' helps us to get closer to universality, which is of course closely interrelated with the philosophical interest in totalities and in what remains invariant in a totality. Contrary to some interpretations of Wittgenstein, he wrote in 1940: 'If we look at things from the ethnological point of view, does that mean we are saying that philosophy is ethnology? No, it only means that we are taking up a position right outside so as to be able to see things *more objectively*' (*CV*, p. 37). This example also bears on the question: What constitutes a 'systematic' study of disagreement? Certainly physics is not the appropriate model. While Wittgenstein's later work strikes one as extremely unsystematic, it could also be construed as a systematic study of what he calls 'language-games.' While I do not envisage a treatment largely limited to painting only particular examples where I 'really' see clearly, I do appreciate the importance of examples. For instance, I often regret that most philosophers (certainly including me) cannot communicate in a manner which more fully secures the advantage of presenting alternative viewpoints as naturally as is done in novels and in detailed work in the history of ideas. Few philosophers possess Plato's literary talent, as revealed in his dialogues.

Attention to why people disagree does not imply what Carnap calls the 'principle of tolerance' (in his *Logical Syntax* and in many entries in the index of Schilpp 1963) but does promise to clarify the matter of determining who the friends and enemies are. Often people are discouraged from examining closely why people disagree for fear of weakening the will to fight, but certainly in the long run such examinations are worthy of recommendation. The relation between difference (or rather its recognition) and disagreement is closely related to the creation of a second level agreement to disagree. This of course depends on the particular nature of the difference, which may either eliminate competition or intensify or moderate conflict.

It appears to me that philosophy has paid more attention to why we agree than where we agree. The preoccupation with why tends to lead to the quest for an absolute beginning and a 'linear' mode of justification which shifts the attention away from the search for a mutually supporting frame that confronts the desire to understand as an organic whole. A closer examination of where we agree serves both to extend its range, for example, by deductions, and to help to localize the factors causing disagreements.

On several occasions Gödel speaks of 'the separation of fact and force (which takes the form of wish particularly in human beings)' as the 'meaning of the world.' Clearly wish in this case is construed in a broad sense to include drives and instincts which often have more force than articulate or even just conscious (but inarticulate) wishes. With such a beginning, knowledge takes a derivative place as the basic means of apprehending fact, in the service of the wish to reduce or eliminate the separation between fact and wish. This idea seems to me to assign knowledge its appropriate place in the world so that, even when we concentrate our attention on knowledge (as a crucial step in our larger pursuit), we have in mind a more adequate frame within which there is space for considering the relation between knowledge and the rest of human experience.

A first attempt to interpret the all-important place of the separation of fact and wish takes the form of articulating wishes into feasible ends which call for ends in view (or 'subgoals') and means to attain them. In this interpretation we have to find a place for the wish for esthetic experience which for G. E. Moore was the major (or even the only, if understood to include also affection of good people) intrinsic good (see his 1903). The role of the esthetic appears to be auxiliary to each fragment of life yet pervasive and overarching in life as a whole. The sense of fitness or appropriateness points to the teleological. It implies something extra (beyond what is necessary) as, for example, when we speak of a person as being not only good but also beautiful (in a moral sense). There is also the element of play and a rest from the 'battle of life' which is dominated by constant concerns over finding means to attain ends.

Part of the fact is the presence of different and often conflicting wishes, which are the basic source of disagreements. The distinction between wishes and needs is notoriously ambiguous, unstable and elusive, but remains nonetheless, in my opinion, of great importance. In particular, the cultivation of wishes, which benefit or at least do not harm others directly or indirectly, becomes easier as a way is found to simplify one's needs and leave room for productive labor to occupy a large position among the needs. Freedom is a generalized wish in that it need not be tied completely to any wish to attain a specific concrete end. Its content is not exhausted by the negative stipulation of accepting and doing what is seen to be necessary. Rather, its basic meaning seems to be the association with the availability of (real or merely imagined) choices.

An important contrary to freedom appears to me to be crowdedness, in space, in time, and more broadly. It is related to but seems to cover a wider range than competing for what is scarce. For example, to find and create more free time and to make fewer commitments (in order to fulfill each better) all are ways to reduce crowdedness and increase freedom. Crowdedness is an 'ensemble' property which goes beyond the close examination of the properties and the functioning of each individual item. Perhaps it can be compared with the difference between statistical mechanics and the study of how each molecule behaves individually.

Central to the universal wish to overcome the separation of wish and fact is the derivative universal wish to unify knowledge and action (or theory and practice in the political domain). To fulfill this wish may also be taken as a central perennial purpose of philosophy. Such a unity solves for each person the unsolvable problem of the best way to live according to his or her ability and awareness. For a group (a family, a profession, a country, or the whole of humanity), the matter of unity is more complex since the 'theory' is interpreted differently and accepted to different degrees by members of the group, and the 'practice' has to vary with their different places in the group. In practice, strenuous efforts to attain a semblance of such unity have led to large-scale make-believes, concealments, and deceptions, including secrets and outright lies. A theory is supposed to apply under certain conditions and to yield certain results when followed correctly. If a society does not satisfy the conditions, both the theory and the facts are twisted to give the impression that the society indeed fits the theory. When the desired results are not forthcoming, it is necessary to conceal and distort the real situations in order not to discredit the theory and those who have been in charge of its application in practice. Since most people have their own motives and interests which need not coincide with the common interest, it becomes difficult or impossible to distinguish between the two kinds of motive in the actions executed in the name of common interest. Not surprisingly, the more broadly appealing a theory is, the more room there is for the authorities to misuse it for the benefit of their own undeclared purposes.

It is of course possible that there is an unbridgeable gap between theory and practice, since theory implies some degree of neatness while collective practice is inevitably messy and complex beyond any complete theoretical account. For every attempt to give an adequate theory claiming that the real situation is 'nothing but' what it captures, there appears to be always a subsequent realization that there is 'something more.' Hegel's fascinating idea of 'concrete concepts' (in his *Smaller Logic*) suggests a unification of the abstract and the concrete (or the universal and the particular), which appears to be an unattainable limit not unlike the more mathematical wish for an 'intellectual intuition' or Husserl's synthetic a priori intuition of the 'essences.'

A fundamental disagreement in the political sphere is between those who wish for radical changes and those who do not. This disagreement is probably more basic and more forceful than the one between the believers in the 'scientific culture' and those in the 'literary culture.' It tends to be associated with the contrast between revolt and upholding existing authority. Revolt involves the need to look for and locate the 'dynamic force' and to create some form of leadership and organization. And, for example, to overthrow some entrenched cultural form requires something forceful to take its place. The extreme position of destroying first in the belief that anything afterwards will be better seems to have been discredited by recent historical experience. The open-minded questioning of widely accepted norms of rationality and even sanity is congenial to but different from such an extreme position. Even in the seemingly simpler task of consciously trying to modify one culture with another, existing culture as a model usually fails on account of an unavoidable ignorance about what constitutes the necessary, material and other, preconditions which made the 'model' culture possible.

There is a considerable gap between the issues raised so far in this section and the main topics discussed in this book, which mostly deals with a part of where we agree, or, in other words, of objective knowledge and shared beliefs which are not refuted by special beliefs of any existing particular group. The range of where we agree includes not only logic, mathematics, and natural science, but also selections from history, everyday knowledge, and all other cultural areas. One task is to choose and somehow categorize what we take to be relatively certain irrespective of particularities of special groups, as well as to look for large principles which appear to have a 'regulative' function. The range is extended by adding suitable qualifications to (bodies of) beliefs shared by large groups but denied by other groups. The qualifications may take several forms. Within a body of beliefs one may try to separate the undeniable parts from those parts which are conditioned by special circumstances, determinable by looking more closely into the differences between those who share the beliefs and those who do not. A theory or doctrine can be studied as a 'model,' with a view of examining its relativity to special conditions to determine its range of applicability. These types of analysis can hardly exhaust the content of strong beliefs (such as those associated with 'national characters') shared by special groups and will inevitably leave gaps or residues which neither the insiders nor the outsiders can fully capture in an articulate manner. But this is nothing exceptional, since in different degrees all attempts at understanding have a similar limitation.

Toward the end of his life Wittgenstein recognized a type of empirical propositions which have a special status in that they 'are solid' and 'stand fast' for us (published in *OC*, 1969). Examples are: there is a brain inside my skull, I am a human being, my friend hasn't sawdust in his body or in his head, motor cars don't grow out of the earth, the earth has existed for many years past, no one has ever been on the moon, etc. (see 281, 4, 279, 411, 108, 106). If one speaks of a proposition of this type as an assumption, it sounds strange. 'But in the entire system of our language-games it belongs to the foundations. The assumption, one might say, forms the basis of action, and, therefore, naturally, of thought' (411). It is possible that reflecting on what makes up and characterizes the main kinds of the whole range of this type of proposition might assist us in determining the area of where we agree and weeding out the more precarious beliefs (such as the example of moon travel). But I have no idea how this is to be done, and doing this in a 'systematic way' is, I am sure, not in the spirit of Wittgenstein.

According to Gödel, everyday knowledge is more basic than scientific knowledge which is based on it, and its analysis is more central to philosophy. I believe he has in mind the analysis of concepts like time, cause, force, substance as they are understood in everyday thought. This belief alone does not, I think, imply that we should concentrate primarily on reflections about everyday concepts and beliefs. The total range or union of our accumulated awareness includes the more structured fruits of specialized studies and magnifies what gets distilled into everyday awareness which is a sort of intersection or shared minimum of the broad range. It contains more conspicuous indicators, more checks against mistakes, and more room for modifying wrong conceptions. Hence it is a more modest rather than a more ambitious enterprise to pay more attention to the broad range rather than to burden the mind with the apparently impossible task of discovering the primitive concepts and their axioms by the sheer power of pure thought to reflect on our shared everyday awareness. In addition, like Gödel, I feel that the history of philosophy has something to offer for the study of phenomenography.

The work of Newton in physics, Adam Smith in economics, Darwin on evolution, and Mendel in genetics, or even Shakespeare in literature, Kant in philosophy, and Beethoven in music suggests the idea of discovering and creating a 'backbone' for an area of study. Even though there have been either improvements on their work or new directions in their fields, there remains something astonishingly stable and solid. In particular, their work and the whole field of mathematics suggest that universality need not be bought at the price of vacuity of content. And by analogy, it also appears possible to me that we can look for broad and meaningful principles in philosophy.

For example, the hierarchical view of the world in Aristotle seems to have given way to a general regulative principle of equality: Other things being equal, stars or physical bodies or persons should be equal. What I propose to call the 'principle of necessary reason' says that sameness implies sameness; it is briefly discussed in section 4.4. This example illustrates the sort of general principles I would like to look for in trying to extend the range of the 'formal' beyond mathematics and that of the universal beyond physics.

In contrast the idea of overcoming the separation of wish and fact is most intimately felt in the individual. We have two sets of data for a solid beginning: the rich concreteness of the experience and consciousness of the individual at one end, and the remote universality of physics and mathematics at the other ('accidentally' obtained by the human experience through abstraction and idealization). For the development of philosophy we have to work out an appropriate blending (or dialectic) of them. At present I look for guidance from a few broad observations (compare also section 19.4).

There are a number of flexible generalities which we do not doubt. Changes occur in the world, and not haphazardly but with a certain regularity. The regularities admit of fluctuations and variations within certain indeterminate limits. Only in a restricted sense of nature can we, surprisingly, handle relations of functional dependence with mathematical precision. The wide gap between physical time and time as experienced is the favorite indicator of wider concepts of nature (and human nature). As we move from physics to biology, we find imagined interplays between instruction (as typified by the genetic code) and selection; but they are far from capturing the 'individuality' of an individual and, in particular, selection remains an umbrella concept covering much that is yet to be explored.

Our experience (and correspondingly our knowledge) includes many categories: perception, introspection, skill, habit, esthetic experience, 'lived experience,' maturity, historical experience, etc. Generally cognitive, affective, and volitional acts coexist in our consciousness. Each moment of consciousness, as Husserl and others stress, involves also the past (retention) and the future (protention or anticipation). End (wish, will) points to the future, while value centers on the feeling of an affective enjoyment of the present that works out a compromise between wish (the pleasure principle) and fact (the reality principle). Parts of an individual life (viewed as a whole) get 'meaning' by conditioning and illuminating one another, as revealed by memory (recognition of the past).

In its particularities this perspective on the world leads (through autobiographies, biographies, ensemble biographies, etc.) to history. Art and literature attend to types, while the social studies atend to the regularities. However, even combining this subject-oriented approach with the more impersonal knowledge, a huge area of ignorance remains, which has to be recognized as the central fact in the pursuit of philosophy.

Chapter 1

Russell and philosophy in this century

The astonishingly long and vigorous life of Russell (1872–1970) is a phenomenon to wonder at. Within philosophy, his work plays a central role in its actual development in England and America, and his gropings point to several possible alternative approaches to it in this century. More generally his life provides an exceptional example to illustrate the idealized question of finding the best course of action for an intellectual with unlimited resources. There appear to have been four not necessarily exclusive alternatives open to him, all of which he pursued with more or less energy and success: scientist, politician, philosopher, and writer. He spent more energy and was more successful in being a philosopher and a (largely though not exclusively philosophical) writer. His work in the other two fields is peripheral or sporadic. In science he made some mathematical contribution to logic as a by-product of a philosophical project and wrote some books to popularize logic and physics. In politics he stood for Parliament thrice and protested against war around 1916 and toward the end of his life.

Within philosophy he worked in the 'analytic' tradition but had contacts with other trends. He studied socialism in 1895, which led to his very first book (published in 1896), and he visited Russia in 1920, which disappointed him and yielded his book on bolshevism. Before 1914 he criticized the philosophies of Bradley and Bergson and William James. During World War II he wrote his book on the history of Western philosophy. Unlike most analytic philosophers (in this century) he had a good command of general history and was knowledgeable in many other areas as well. But most of his books produced in his role as a writer are philosophical in a broad sense. I am concerned here, however, more with his technical philosophical work.

It is common to use 1910 as a dividing line between the more concentrated work of his early stage and the diversified pursuits during the rest of his life. From historical data uncovered in recent years, I have arrived at the thesis that the period from late 1909 to the spring of 1914 was a determinative transition period in Russell's philosophical development. Circumstances during this period combined to create in him a decreased confidence in the importance of philosophy (in its technical and for him fundamental sense) and in his own ability to make decisive advance in it. The crucial factor in the latter aspect was his contacts with Wittgenstein, whose criticism of his unfinished book in 1913, in particular, dealt him a serious blow.

A great virtue of Russell's work before 1910 was, in my opinion, to take as given the rather stable body of knowledge in ordinary mathematics and Cantor's set theory, and look for a natural axiom system in which they can be derived (recovered). This approach of beginning with what we know gave way to the familiar concern with how I know after 1910, which, for brevity, may be labelled 'egocentrism' (along the line of the 'egocentric predicament' in Lewis 1946). He consciously returned to his early mode only thirty-five years later to work on his *Human Knowledge* (published 1948).

There is another contrast between Russell's work at different stages, which is connected with Russell's strong and almost inborn inclination toward the basic doctrines of British empiricism. This was to a considerable extent suppressed in his early work, undoubtedly as a result (at least in part) of his immediate concern with doing justice to what we know in mathematics. In his *Principles* (1903), he was pretty much a realist about mathematical objects. With his efforts to resolve the paradoxes and the success with his theory of descriptions, he began to develop a 'no class' theory, which was congenial to his empiricism but led to various confusions and equivocations. The many philosophically unfinished features of *PM* may in part explain the forming of his strange conception of mathematics later on, which he declared, surprisingly, to be a reluctant conversion to the view of the *Tractatus*. The adherence to empiricism affected not only his work when practicing egocentrism but also his *Human Knowledge*, which appears to leave out conceptual knowledge altogether and to sever arbitrarily the actual link between mathematics and physics.

Apart from the issues of empiricism and egocentrism, there are, I believe, two other central issues in this century's philosophy which may be misleadingly abbreviated to 'linguistism' and 'inhumanism.' Inhumanism in philosophy excludes the richer human experience beyond objective knowledge from the concerns of (serious) philosophy. It may be thought to be either too hard or too sacred or too private or too secondary or even too easy to permit or warrant or be accessible to philosophical investigations. Philosophers upholding this position either do not write about this area or confine their writings on it to the popular (or, as a third alternative, to the private) domain. Clearly Russell belongs to the secondary category. The dominance of the concern with (formal or informal) language is too conspicuous to require be-laboring. Linguistism is usually associated with a desire to cling to the more concrete and a distrust in our ability to deal fruitfully (in a direct manner) with obscure things such as concepts, intuitions, and things in themselves. While Russell does remark on the importance of looking at language and grammar (as of assistance to philosophy), it seems clear that he never believed that the study of language is the central concern of philosophy.

It is clear that I would like to adopt a position which is not constrained by any of the four restrictions. The emphasis on doing justice to what we know seems to rule out directly the restriction to egocentrism and indirectly the restrictions to empiricism and linguistism. The wish also to have philosophy do justice to what more broadly we are aware of is a proposal to reject inhumanism in philosophy. The last restriction is, however, different from the other three in that it limits our area of investigation, while the others limit our means of investigation. It seems plausible to believe that by abandoning the three restrictions on what we can use, there is a good chance we can extend the range of what we can fruitfully study.

The work of Russell has been considered so extensively and in so many directions in the literature that I shall in this chapter confine my attention to a general evaluation of his work with special attention to those parts which, in my opinion, center on what we know. The first section discusses Santayana's suggestion of an updated Baconian project for Russell. The second section makes some general comments on Rus-sell's development. The last section reviews his work in logic.

Various ideas are suggested but not worked out in this book. The influence of Russell's work up to 1914 on Carnap and Quine is relatively transparent and, I believe, adequately treated in this book. But a full study of Russell's early conceptions of logic and their influences on Wittgenstein and Gödel is not attempted here. The scattered obser-vations seem, however, to point to many interesting conceptual and historical details of interest, which, I believe, will undoubtedly be in-vestigated by specialists. In particular, aspects of the more specific issue of the relation between Russell's 1913 manuscript on the theory of knowledge and Wittgenstein's contemporary pursuit have been con-sidered by Pears (1977) and Blackwell (1981), but the broader matter of what each of them thought to be their common pursuit at the time seem to involve at least an account of the place of logic in (our knowledge of) the world (and, in particular, Russell's early conception of logic and what Wittgenstein took it to be).

The *Tractatus* stimulated two alternative revisions of *PM* by Russell (the ramified type theory in the introduction to the second edition of

PM) and Ramsey (the simple type theory slightly later). I believe that relative to Russell's perspective then, the problems left open in his ramified theory may be said to have been solved by my system Σ_ω, which will be described later in this book. Similarly, the problems left open in Ramsey's simple theory may be said to have been solved by systems of set theory based on the iterative concept of set, which also suggests a richer concept of logic. The richer concept seems to possess most of the virtues Russell initially looked for in logic and to permit us to restart on a new level the quest for all the great things Russell had expected from logic: for example, it should be capable of serving philosophy as mathematics serves physics.

4. Russell and a Baconian project

In my opinion, a faithful and comprehensive attention to what we know would reveal the limitations of empiricism and, in addition, yield significant large structures even if empiricism is not consciously abandoned. That is why I am struck by the positive element in Santayana's regret that Russell missed an opportunity to update Bacon's project. He states this regret and at the same time deplores Russell's irrevocable adherence to empiricism. Either he believes that in pursuing such a project Russell will learn to overcome empiricism or he believes that the outcome will be important even if Russell does not shake off his empiricism.

A natural stage in Russell's career to begin such a project would seem to be the transition period from 1910 to 1914. He did indeed begin a large project but atypically did not complete it. A successor to the project would seem to be his *Human Knowledge*, published thirty-five years later. This book, which was probably unknown to Santayana, may perhaps be taken as a step toward the Baconian project. It appears to be both suggestive and deficient exactly in its empiricist foundation. It is of course likely that if Russell had begun such a program thirty years earlier and continued it with his inexhaustible energy, the outcome would have been very important, with or without empiricism.

4.1. Santayana on Russell
In his old age Santayana (1863–1952) offered an evaluation of Russell's achievements (1953, p. 27):

> He had birth, genius, learning, indefatigable zeal and energy, brilliant intelligence, and absolute honesty and courage. His love of justice was as keen as his sense of humor. He was at home in mathematics, in natural science, and in history. He knew all the

important languages and was well informed about everything going on in the world of politics and literature. He ought to have been a leader, a man of universal reputation and influence. He was indeed recognized as a distinguished man, having made his mark in mathematics and logic. . . . Yet on the whole, relative to his capacities, he was a failure. He petered out. He squandered his time and energy, and even his money, on unworthy objects.

This is a plausible view very well put, whether one agrees with it or not. It brings out the ideal question of how best to choose a career when equipped with almost unlimited resources. In particular, was it still possible even in his day to do justice to his capacities by being a philosopher? Indeed, in the 1950s he said in an interview that if he had been young again, he would choose to be a physicist or, if lacking the ability, a political propagandist. It is hard to know how serious he was, and in any case such counterfactual conditionals are notoriously elusive. There does remain, however, the question whether he could have done better as a philosopher, which continued to be his principal occupation even after 1910. On the whole Russell is regarded as a more important philosopher than the living philosophers today not only in the world at large but even within the strange world of academic philosophy where greater overall capacity nowadays often seems to hamper rather than help. Compared with Russell's case, the opposite phenomenon is more frequent: relative to the philosopher's capacities, he is a success.

What alternative courses did Santayana have for Russell? 'I can imagine two ways in which Bertie might have proceeded to prove how great a man it was in him to be.' One was to become Prime Minister, 'to exert the power of government for the heroic purpose of diminishing that power,' to lead a 'party true to democratic, anti-military, anti-imperialistic, anti-clerical powers,' and to give England 'a maximum of liberty and a minimum of government.' The other was to accomplish in a modern setting what Francis Bacon set out to do but did not complete.

> He might have undertaken an *instauratio magna* of scientific philosophy. He could have done it better than Bacon, inasmuch as the science at his command was so much more advanced; and the *Principia mathematica*, a title challenging comparison with Newton, seemed to foreshadow such a possibility. Why, then, didn't Bertie proceed in this course?

Santayana answers himself thus: 'He seemed to practise criticism only sporadically, caught and irresistibly excited by current discussions.

His radical solutions were rendered vain by the conventionality of his problems. His outlook was universal, but his presuppositions were insular. In philosophy he couldn't entertain the hypothesis that Berkeley, Hume, and Mill might have been fundamentally wrong.' It does seem that Russell was to a considerable extent bound to this empiricist tradition since 1906 when he began to develop his 'no class' theory, or at least since he had turned from logic to epistemology after 1910. Indeed, the complex issue of the role of this tradition in Russell's philosophy has been examined by Pears in *Bertrand Russell and the British Tradition in Philosophy* (1967); but the influence of Cantor, Frege, Peano, Meinong, and Poincaré and Russell's deeper involvement in mathematics would appear to call for an extension of Pears' book.

This empiricist presupposition, with minor variations such as changing from phenomenalism to physicalism and holism, has been shared by Carnap and Quine as well, indeed more devotedly. I would have thought that we have long passed beyond the exclusive alternative of allegiance to empiricism or rationalism. The task is, as I see it, rather to find the appropriate dialectic of the intricate interplays of the empirical and the rational components. Moreover, since philosophy aims at being comprehensive and universal, it is only natural that the rational element plays a larger role in the actual development of a philosophy. For me, the important data for philosophy are not sense data or observation sentences but the corpus of human knowledge and understanding.

Santayana's evaluation of Russell's work suffers from two major, interrelated abstract presuppositions. First, philosophy was assumed to be Russell's central, if not exclusive, vocation. The real problem for Russell from 1910 to 1914 was of course how best to live his life as an intellectual. His doubts about the value of philosophy and the complexities in his personal life (including his romanticism, particularly toward Lady Ottoline and Wittgenstein) all contributed to diverting his attention away from extended concentrated efforts on philosophy. This situation was both a cause and an effect of his not finding a more satisfactory (to himself and to the world) conception of philosophy.

Second, many people have to choose between more assured short-term attention and less assured long-term accomplishment. Certainly Russell was in the exceptional situation of being well suited to undertake an ambitious project, in terms of both external circumstances and his own preparations (his capacities as well as his work already done at the time). But the necessary motivation and single-mindedness appear to require more detachment and perhaps less versatility than he had. In my opinion, the transition from 1910 on (or indeed from the onslaught of the confusing no class theory in 1906 on) had, not just coincidentally, generated enough uncertainty in his mind to allow his submerged faith in empiricism to assert itself. This led him from attention to 'what we know' to concern with 'how I know,' in the realm of what he took to be fundamental philosophy, which was the theory of knowledge.

4.2. The transition period (1910–1914)

Since Santayana seems to consider *PM* a good beginning for the Baconian project, it seems natural to look at the period immediately following its completion. Indeed, this was a period when Russell was looking for an area in which he could do another large-scale piece of work.

Russell's philosophical work up to 1910 centers on logic and is generally considered his more solid contribution to learning. The manuscript for *PM* was completed toward the end of 1909, and in 1910, Russell helped with political campaignings for election and began his five-year lectureship at Trinity in the autumn. A mistake was found in January 1911 by Whitehead in a part of *PM* about to be printed, which took the authors nearly five months to repair. Russell began his affair with Lady Ottoline Morrell the same spring, which was to last a long time and to have the effect of broadening his interests. Late in July he finished *The Problems of Philosophy* (the 'shilling shocker') and remarked shortly before: 'Doing this book has given me a map of the theory of knowledge which I hadn't before. From that point of view it will have been a great help in my own work' (quoted in Clark, p. 153). The book may be said to contain several basic elements of the type of philosophy Russell and his successors were to develop later; in particular, the term sense-data was used, probably for the first time in print.

There followed, after his 'shocker,' a short digression into the 'essence' of religion. In December he wrote: 'All the historic problems of philosophy seem to me either insoluble or soluble by methods which are not philosophical, but mathematical or scientific. . . . But as a stimulus to the imagination, I think philosophy *is* important. . . . I think it is more important to write popular than technical philosophy' (Clark, pp. 164–165). Before this, he had met Wittgenstein in October, who was important for Russell's work during the next few years.

In 1912 Russell, among many other things, also tried his hand at creative writing and finished on July 2 *The Perplexities of John Forstice*, a novella that describes in a disguised way his intellectual pilgrimage. Opinions were sought from the Whiteheads, from Lowes Dickinson, and from Joseph Conrad. He eventually decided not to publish it in his lifetime, and it was only published posthumously. The reason for the excursion was, as he wrote in March, that he had so little belief in philosophy and really couldn't think it very valuable (Clark, p. 178). In November he wrote that since the completion of *PM*, he had done little really hard thinking and now the necessity was revived. He had apparently recovered from the strain of his work on *PM* and wished to embark on another big project. Also at about this time he finally agreed to a three-month visit to Harvard to begin in March 1914.

Around the end of 1912 he began to plan a big project on the theory of knowledge (also to be used for his Harvard visit). According to Blackwell 1981, the book was to have two divisions: the analytic and the constructive. The first was to consist of three parts: acquaintance, judgment (atomic propositional thought), and inference (molecular propositional thought). The second was to move from knowledge of logic to knowledge of sense and thence to knowledge of science; as well as, finally, so to state the existence of certain sense-data and certain principles of inference that science would follow. He began to write on May 7, 1913, with his usual high speed. Shortly afterwards he began to discuss the work with Wittgenstein, who was very critical of it. Russell was disturbed by the criticism and wrote on May 28: 'Well well—it is the younger generation knocking at the door—I must make room for him when I can, or I shall become an incubus' (Blackwell, p. 16).

He carried on writing, but without enthusiasm. By June 6 he had written 350 pages which made up the first two of the three parts of the first division, and decided to leave the rest for later. (This manuscript has recently been published as volume 7 of Russell's collected works.) By June 20 he was reporting about his successful effort to be honest and saying that it had been difficult to be honest about Wittgenstein's attack 'as it makes a large part of the book I meant to write impossible for years to come probably' (Clark, p. 206). Of Russell's later work his 1918 lectures on logical atomism use some of the ideas, but what comes closest to a return to the interrupted project (with a more modest flavor) is, according to my bias, probably *Human Knowledge* (1948), his last substantive philosophical writing. R. Crawshay-Williams reports in his *Russell Remembered* (1970) that Russell was proud of the book and was much disappointed because it was not taken seriously.

The Lowell Lectures (for the Harvard visit but separately in Boston) were essentially written from September 1 to November 15, 1913, with interruptions by a visit from Wittgenstein in between. They got published in 1914 as *External World* and contain propaganda for the use of (his) logic and the outline of a program of reaching empirical knowledge by logical constructions out of sense-data. Carnap was greatly influenced by the book and carried the program further in his *Aufbau* (1928); Quine speaks of his own 'liberated epistemology' as a modification of the same program. Hence, this less ambitious book has been more central to the work of Carnap and Quine than the unfinished, more comprehensive project. In contrast to more localized recent works with close connection to actual science, all these projects strive after universal 'foundations.' For quite a few years after 1914 Russell wrote no extended work in philosophy, and it seems reasonable to say that the transition period was completed in 1914.

I feel that the transition period contains the elements for an answer to Santayana's question on the great instauration. *PM* was a sufficiently appealing and definite project (at least for its time); but it is not easy to find or run across major philosophical projects which are comparably definite. Russell was interested in many things and pursued them with energy and speed. Hence, it appears that he had little chance to reflect on his presuppositions or deliberate on the choice of programs and plan out their execution. He seems to look for a kind of certainty and conclusiveness not available in philosophy and was as a result disappointed in the value of philosophy.

Moreover, the influence of Wittgenstein on him is hard to understand. There was a strangely esoteric atmosphere surrounding his dealings with Wittgenstein. 'I couldn't understand his objection,' for instance, he said, 'but I feel in my bones that he must be right' (Clark, p. 204). Given Russell's famous clarity of style, it is strange that he could not even locate more explicitly the obstacles, yet was willing to give up his project. One can only surmise that there must be something very elusive and ill-defined about the project itself which probably involved a few ill-posed problems and had no moderately clear purposes. (In my opinion, the influence of Wittgenstein, with his very different motivations, was harmful rather than beneficial to Russell's work.) The abandoned project (on the theory of knowledge) seems to ask for a once-for-all homogeneous justification of all (scientific) knowledge. It is now common to give up the justification side. The homogeneity side is also questionable, but Carnap and Quine both appear to me to retain this side.

4.3. Updating Bacon's unfinished instauratio magna

There are fundamental differences between Russell's project and Bacon's great instauration of the sciences which was to contain six parts:

(1)   The division of the sciences: a summary or general description of the knowledge which the human race at present possesses;
(2)   The new organon, or directions concerning the interpretation of nature;
(3)   The phenomena of the universe, or a natural and experimental history;
(4)   The ladder of the intellect or the thread of the labyrinth:

'actual types and models, by which the entire process of the mind and the whole fabric and order of invention . . . should be set, as it were, before the eyes,' or a scale of ascent in proven knowledge, from lesser to greater axioms;

(5)   The forerunners: pieces of knowledge experimentally derived but not yet placed in the new synthesis;

(6)   The new philosophy, or active science

(Bacon 1620, pp. 17–29 and xxvii–xxxiii, where a list of Bacon's incomplete writings under most of the headings is also given).

The two projects are empiricist in very different senses. While Bacon wrote nothing under (6) and his project contains no counterpart of the analytic division of Russell's plan, Russell seems to be primarily concerned with heading (6). While the need of extended work for Bacon's plan is transparent, Russell's seems to be ambitious in a different way, viz., in requiring little factual information. It is tempting to speculate on what project Santayana had in mind for Russell.

Bacon (1561–1626) was a contemporary of Galileo and thirty-five years older than Descartes; he was the optimistic leading spokesman for an important aspect of the spirit of his time, a more or less unique juncture of history when the rise of modern natural science was the most powerful intellectual force. His message of studying nature in order to control it ('knowledge is power') expressed what was moving the hearts of thousands in his time. In contrast, Russell could not identify his philosophy with any comparable major historical trend, and he was much influenced by later thoughts initiated by Descartes and Locke. Science had come a long way between Bacon's and Russell's time. Hence, the Baconian respect for existing natural knowledge must now take on a different shape. For example, his parts (3) and (5) have been absorbed into the special sciences which have become much more autonomous since Bacon's time. Bacon thought that his method was also adequate to dealing with the knowledge of man. As we know, his method is defective even in the natural sciences, particularly in underestimating the importance of mathematics. Even if we assume that his part (2) is replaced by something more adequate to the natural sciences, there remains the familiar question of looking for additional components appropriate to the special complexities of the human studies.

Hence, we may leave out parts (3) and (5). What is intended for the first two parts seems fairly clear, but parts (4) and (6) are less explicitly described. Let me try to construct a current version of Bacon's plan of instauration. Take logic (or the principles of inquiry) in a broad sense as a revision of part (2); it is to include mathematics, 'scientific method,' some 'dialectics,' as well as (the avoidance of) the idols and other suggestions in Bacon's new organon. Part (1), the summary idea, remains the same with the 'at present' relativized. This is not a passive task. As Bacon says, 'I do not propose merely to survey these regions in my mind, like an augur taking auspices, but to enter them like a general who means to take possession.' For example, 'I take into account not only things already invented and known, but likewise things omitted which ought to be there.'

What would such a summary look like? For example, the fifteenth edition of the *Encyclopaedia Britannica* (1975) includes one volume to classify all the entries and three volumes on 'perspectives' (Ashmore 1968) that consist of a dozen long essays summarizing major areas of learning. These are useful. But the classification volume is crude and mechanical; the perspectives are by different authors and do not form a coherent whole. If Russell had devoted a number of years to such a project, he certainly would have gotten an end product much closer to Bacon's ideal. Santayana must have felt it very regrettable that Russell, with his rare qualifications for this task, had not chosen to undertake it.

The bland concept of summary can mean so many different things in its execution that its content is rather thin unless its fruits are put into some imaginative framework. I suppose the main idea is first to take seriously available human knowledge (or experience) as it is and not to jump too quickly to some a priori conception with the belief that it will lead to a neater and more correct picture of human knowledge. The accumulated human knowledge supplies the most important part of accessible data which to a larger extent constitute the criterion for determining whether a philosopher's scheme is adequate rather than the other way round. Hence, how good a summary is depends on how it is to be used, and there is a question of how far one can separate it from the other three remaining parts of Bacon's project. Philosophies which pay attention to the summary aspect are of course also of quite different qualities, as can be seen from the examples of Aristotle, Hegel, Marx, Auguste Comte, Herbert Spencer, Nicolas Hartmann, and Mario Bunge. As I see it, even Kant's idea of beginning with mathematics and physics as a given fact to be accounted for leans toward the preference of first paying attention to the summary aspect.

It is to be expected that if anybody of Russell's calibre pursues seriously the project of 'summary,' it would be intricately related to and greatly improve the development of the other three parts. For example, it would help the construction of a broader structure of logic with components of varied degrees of exactness. I take Bacon's part (4) as a program to refine and bring more order into the summary with the help of the logic part. Finally part (6) would be a worldview, as stable and well founded as is humanly possible for a given historical stage. Such a great instauration has the advantage that the need to modify any part spreads its influence out in a comparatively clear and distinct way. Moreover, the creation of the more philosophical part enjoys a safeguard against the natural tendency to oversimplify and get into blind alleys. In contrast to Russell's radical changes of his philosophy over the years, the instauration project would have more of the virtue of being cumulative.

As it was, Russell did not move in this direction during his transition period and even gave up his relatively ambitious project on the theory of knowledge. Instead, he opened up a narrower path in his *External World* which was not appealing enough to himself for him to do any extensive work on it. The path suited Carnap better, who took over the torch and solidified the path in various ways. He and others of like spirit joined forces to make a restrictive but confident movement. Quine followed Carnap's approach and then revolted against some aspects of it. As a result of the failed expectations from Carnap's program, Quine's revolt hastened its disintegration, which is one of the principal causes that Anglo-American philosophy is currently in a state of chaos and anarchy. Quine himself has chosen a contraction of Carnap's vision (as Carnap did to Russell's) but has found nothing as broadly appealing as the old Vienna Circle to join forces in. It is about time to reverse the process of contraction, I hope.

I have resisted the temptation to go into aspects of Russell's well-documented full and varied life. Instead, I have singled out some relevant details and included them in a combined chronological table of Russell, Wittgenstein, Carnap, and Quine. Allow me to discuss briefly Russell's *Human Knowledge* (1948).

4.4. Human Knowledge *and human knowledge*

The novel aspects of *Human Knowledge* are largely contained in the last two of the six parts, which deal respectively with probability and 'the postulates of scientific inference.' Russell gives five postulates about the 'make-up' of the world, which he takes to be tacitly presupposed in scientific work and which he believes to be sufficient though not so surely all necessary. They are to confer on putative generalizations that initial probability (or credibility) which is a precondition for the application of induction to increase or decrease their meaningful probability.

The five postulates are:

(1)   Quasi-permanence: The world is composed of more or less permanent 'things.'

(2)   Separable causal lines: The causes and effects of an event are confined to a limited part of the (preceding or following) total state of affairs.

(3)   Spatio-temporal continuity: There is no action at a distance (in time or in space).

(4)   Structural invariance: When structurally similar complex events are ranged about a center in nearby regions, they usually belong to causal lines originating from an event of the same structure at the center.

(5)   Analogy: If A-events and B-events are observed together and there is reason to believe that A is an essential factor in causing B, then observing A makes it probable that B, even if in principle unobservable, occurs (this is to justify particularly the belief in other minds).

Russell seems to say that infants and higher animals have innate dispositions to form inferential habits conforming to these postulates, as a result of evolution and adaptation to environment. But deliberate thinking and action, which is in fact in accordance with these postulates, can occur only in mature and suitably trained human beings.

As Russell says, he does 'not lay any stress on their exact formulation.' It would of course be a long way to get from these postulates to science as it is known today, and in their given form it would be hard to distinguish correct and incorrect applications of them. One question is whether postulates which are closer to existing scientific or other principles may not be more stimulating and more likely to acquire less indefinite content. For instance, I have recently written down the following thoughts which suggest a somewhat different emphasis from Russell's.

One of the most attractive goals of the intellectual pursuit seems to me to be the search for broad principles which imply a variety of consequences but remain true even if they turn out to be mistaken in many details as initially set forth. Darwin's evolutionary theory is a striking example. In the realm of philosophy it seems possible to find similar principles, further removed from detailed facts, which are not necessarily true come what may, but rather *come what may within a wide range of allowed for surprises*. The transformation of Aristotelian physics to the Galilean suggests what I would like to call the 'principle of necessary reason.' In other words, there must be special reasons for differences: sameness implies sameness. This principle underlies Galileo's law of inertia (Newton's first law), which supplanted Aristotle's hierarchical view of the universe. It also accounts for the central importance of conservation and symmetry laws in contemporary physics. In the human sphere, 'one person one vote' and 'equal pay for equal work' can be taken as normative instances of the principle of necessary reason. As is clear from these examples, the use of the principle in each instance requires careful consideration of relevant factors which are to supply the convincing detailed evidence and arguments. Biology suggests the 'principle of precarious sufficiency' in the sense that what survives in nature and in society requires only the satisfaction of certain relatively minimal rather than any abstractly optimal conditions. One interest of this principle is our natural tendency to forget it and, as a consequence, find many phenomena puzzling.

Russell sometimes speaks of his disappointments in philosophy and in his own pursuit of it, stressing that they do not satisfy his feelings or, rather, that they have failed to resolve the conflicts between his intellect and his emotions. On the whole, he looked for certainty (or agreement) in important matters but could not find it. About ethics, he explains his position as not inconsistent and goes on to say: 'But in feeling I am not satisfied.' About religion, he considers 'some form of personal religion highly desirable' but cannot accept any well-known theology and thinks that most churches 'have done more harm than good' (Schilpp 1944, pp. 724–726). 'When I was young I hoped to find religious satisfaction in philosophy; even after I had abandoned Hegel, the eternal Platonic world gave me something non-human to admire.' 'I have always ardently desired to find some justification for the emotions inspired by certain things that seem to stand outside human life and to deserve feelings of awe.' 'And so my intellect goes with the humanists, though my emotions violently rebel' (ibid., pp. 19–20). Could this be because things human are so changeable and uncertain or merely they are so full of meanness and treachery? Elsewhere he does say: 'To teach how to live without certainty, and yet without being paralysed by hesitation, is perhaps the chief thing that philosophy, in our age, can still do for those who study it' (*History*, p. 11). It would, however, appear, I think, that much of current professional philosophy has little to offer to the teaching of how to live with uncertainty.

A natural question to ask about Russell's five postulates is, how do we apply them to empirical data to arrive at, say, the Newtonian system of physics? I have not examined the matter but believe that we are a long way from getting even an approximate answer to the question, which appears to me to be a good guide to a test of the adequacy of the postulates. For instance, Kant's *Metaphysical Foundations of Natural Science* appears to be an attempt to reconstruct Newtonian physics on the basis of his involved and often obscure 'transcendental' account of the human 'understanding.' However unsatisfactory we may now find this attempt, I believe that the very existence of such an attempt has been one of the major appeals of Kant's philosophy over all these years.

5. Russell's philosophical development

I have emphasized the 'internal' aspect of Russell's transition from concentration on a large project (from the *Principles* to *PM*) to what appears to be a diversification of his energy in several directions since 1910. Russell has stated at various places that the cause was a loss of self-confidence rather than the more 'external' one of World War I. For example, in 1916 he wrote Ottoline about the aftermath of Wittgenstein's criticism of his 'lot of stuff about Theory of Knowledge' in 1913: 'I *had* to produce lectures for America, but I took a metaphysical subject although I was and am convinced that all fundamental work in philosophy is logical. My reason was that Wittgenstein persuaded me that what wanted doing in logic was too difficult for me. So there was no really vital satisfaction of my philosophical impulse in that work [viz., *External World*], and philosophy lost its hold on me. That was due to Wittgenstein more than to the war. What the war has done is to give me a new and less difficult ambition, which seems to me quite as good as the old one' (*Autobiography*, II, p. 64).

Undoubtedly both factors played a part in the transition. If he had found an absorbing philosophical project before the war came, the war, astonishing as it was to him, would certainly have affected his work also, but he would have been in a different frame of mind toward philosophy. At any rate, since I have centered on the period before the war and since my interest is to use Santayana's observations to illustrate a more abstract speculation, it seems fruitless to dwell further on these specific hypothetical considerations.

Russell's philosophical development contains many components and many changes. According to him, 'There is only one constant preoccupation: I have throughout been anxious to discover how much we can be said to know and with what degree of certainty or doubtfulness' (*PD*, p. 11). But this is much too indefinite a statement to serve as a guide to view his development, which involved different influences and problems at different stages.

He 'began thinking about philosophical questions at the age of fifteen,' and discarded first free will, then immortality, and finally God. He wanted to but could not 'combine in a harmonious total seventeenth century knowledge, eighteenth century beliefs and nineteenth century enthusiasms.' By the time he went up to Cambridge in October 1890, he had, with a genuine sense of relief, 'discarded the last vestiges of theological orthodoxy' (*PD*, pp. 28–36, *MD*, p. 8). He read Mill early: 'I read no philosophical books, until I read Mill's *Logic* in the last months before going to Trinity. . . . I did not come across any books, except Buckle, until I read Mill's *Logic* which seemed to me to possess intellectual integrity' (*PD*, p. 28 and p. 35). At Cambridge he first studied mathematics and was classed as seventh wrangler in the Mathematics Tripos. He then switched over to the study of philosophy and took a first class in Part II of the Tripos in Moral Science.

The influence of German idealism dominated, and Russell gave up his 'crude empiricism' and 'went over completely to a semi-Kantian, semi-Hegelian metaphysic' in 1894. He then wrote an essay and was in 1895 elected to a Prize Fellowship of Trinity College for six free years. The essay was elaborated into *An Essay on the Foundations of Geometry*, which was completed in 1896 and published in 1897. The theory was mainly Kantian. He then proceeded to try to give a similar treatment of the foundations of physics on which he worked for two years but published little. He 'was at this time a full-fledged Hegelian' (*PD*, pp. 38–42). Early in 1899 he stood in for J. E. McTaggart (1866–1925) and lectured on Leibniz. The lectures resulted in his *A Critical Exposition of the Philosophy of Leibniz* (1900). Kant was explicitly supported in this book. [Like Descartes, Leibniz said that his general rules of thought had led him to his remarkable scientific discoveries (as quoted, e.g., by Russell in *PD*, on pp. 169–170, 283–284).]

Russell's views on Kant are a little confusing. The primary aim of *PM*, according to him in 1959, was to derive mathematics from logic. 'This was, of course, an antithesis to the doctrines of Kant, and initially I thought of the work as a parenthesis in the refutations of "yonder sophisticated philistine," as Georg Cantor described him' (*PD*, 74–75). But in his chapter on the a priori in his *PP* (1912), he went on endorsing Kant's views by giving him credit 'for having perceived that we have a priori knowledge which is not purely "analytic" ' and that 'all the propositions of arithmetic and geometry are "synthetic," i.e., not analytic' (pp. 82–84). These assertions are quite different from Frege's taking arithmetic as analytic but geometry as synthetic a priori (*Foundations of Arithmetic*, §89); L. E. J. Brouwer, by the way, denies both parts of Frege's position. I remembered being amused in the early 1950s, amid all the discussions on the analytic-synthetic contrast, by reading Russell's statement: 'It has since appeared that logic is just as synthetic as all other kinds of truth' (*Principles*, p. 457). One explanation may be Russell's familiar objection to the presupposition (in traditional logic and by Leibniz and Kant) of analyzing all propositions into the subject-predicate form. That may be why he used (inconsistently though) the quotation marks around the terms.

But independently of how Russell chooses to use the term 'analytic,' there appears to be a more substantive equivocation on his part which I can never understand. Thus, according to him, mathematical knowledge is all of the same nature as the 'great truth' that there are three feet in a yard (*History*, p. 860); or, more qualifiedly, 'to a mind of sufficient intellectual power the whole of mathematics would appear trivial, as trivial as the statement that a four-footed animal is an animal' (*PD*, pp. 211–212). But to such a mind, if there were one, most of physics and much else would appear trivial as well. 'I thought of mathematics with reverence, and suffered when Wittgenstein led me to regard it as nothing but tautologies' (Schilpp 1944, p. 19). (This statement involves in addition a historical mistake which I shall leave aside.) The equivocation I have in mind is between mathematical conventionalism and the analyticity of mathematical propositions. According to Gödel, the first is false while the latter is ambiguous but true if understood rightly, and I agree with him. It seems to me that much of the frustrating debate between Carnap and Quine over the issue of analyticity turns on this equivocation. I have already elaborated the matter in section 2 of the Introduction.

Russell was exceptionally receptive to what appear to be novel ideas on questions of his current interest and exceptionally generous in acknowledging such philosophical influences which in themselves seem to be nebulous and objectively of little persuasive force. Nonetheless, his work in philosophy was in fact undoubtedly much affected by Moore around 1900, by Whitehead around 1913, and by Wittgenstein around 1917 (and, indirectly, later as well), as he said himself. Toward the end of 1898 he joined Moore in revolting against Kant and Hegel. Moore published in *Mind* 'The nature of judgment' (in 1899), arguing that fact is in general independent of experience, and 'The refutation of idealism' (1904), which set out to refute the basic idealist proposition that to be is to be perceived. In the preface to the *Principles*, Russell says, 'On fundamental questions of philosophy, my position, in all the chief features, is derived from Mr. G. E. Moore.' Among other things his belief in classes is conspicuous in this work; for example, the definition of a number as a class 'is mainly recommended by the fact that it leaves no doubt as to the existence-theorem.'

In 1898 the project on the foundations of physics evolved into a study of the principles of mathematics, which he referred to as his 'big book' (to come). He went in July 1900 to the International Congress of Philosophy, Logic and the History of Science in Paris and read a paper on August 2 before an audience including Bergson, L. Couturat, Peano, and Poincaré. The meeting with Peano and his pupils was important for Russell. 'The most important year in my intellectual life was the year 1900, and the most important event in this year was my visit to' that congress (*MD*, p. 12). The visit was followed by intensive and satisfying work, and by the end of the year he had completed a first draft of his *Principles*. He continued with revisions and discovered the famous Russell paradox in June 1901. The book was finished on May 23, 1902, and published in 1903. Long before the completion of the book he had conceived of a mathematical sequel to it and secured Whitehead's agreement to collaborate. This was the project to write *PM* which was to occupy them for many years. I shall return to this area of Russell's work in the next section.

Judging from what is known of the division of labor and Bradley's reply to Russell (April 20, 1910; *Autobiography*, I, p. 200), the collaboration was intellectually not very fruitful for Russell. However that may be, Russell gave much credit to Whitehead's 'method of abstract extension' (probably originated around 1912) in connection with his reflections on matter and his *External World*. The idea is to construct points, instances, and particles as sets of events (*PD*, p. 103). Early in 1918, Russell gave a famous course of lectures on 'logical atomism' which was said to be 'very largely concerned with certain ideas which I learnt from' Wittgenstein. He seemed to think that these lectures had later been made obsolete by the *Tractatus* (*PD*, pp. 112–121).

From 1918 on, Russell's philosophical interest turned to the theory of knowledge. His thinking came out in four books: *Analysis of Mind* (1921), *Analysis of Matter* (1927), *Meaning and Truth* (1940), and *Human Knowledge* (1948) (*PD*, p. 128 where, however, the second is left out). Owing to the limitations of my own interest and the restricted concerns of this book, I shall leave out the first three books and I have just considered one or two aspects of the last book. An extended treatment of these and other works of Russell can be found in Jager 1972.

Judging from his review in 1943 of his previous philosophical work, he seems to begin at that time (1943) a return from 'how I know' to 'what we know' (Schilpp 1944, p. 16):

> Theory of knowledge, with which I have been largely concerned, has a certain essential subjectivity; it asks 'how do *I* know what I know' and starts inevitably from personal experience. Its data are egocentric, and so are the earlier stages of its argumentation. I have not, so far, got beyond the earlier stages, and have therefore seemed more subjective in outlook than in fact I am. . . . If I ever have the leisure to undertake another serious investigation of a philosophical problem, I shall attempt to analyse the inferences from experience to the world of physics, assuming them capable of validity, and seeking to discover what principles of inference, if true, would make them valid.

In my opinion, the phrase 'the early stages' (applied to Russell's previous endeavors) is based on a false analogy to the more successful part of basic science. The assumption is that once we have straightened out the earlier stages, they will give us a dependable basis to move beyond. The history of epistemology since Descartes has certainly demonstrated the practical falsity of this assumption. The planned project moves toward 'factualism' (or descriptivism?) with the phrase 'assuming them capable of validity.' The restriction to 'the world of physics' may presumably be taken more as a strategy of doing one thing at a time rather than as implying that nothing fundamentally new is needed to go beyond that world. There remain two ambiguous issues which can probably only be clarified with practice. To what extent do we discover the 'principles of inference' by being faithful to the (implicit) principles we actually use as a matter of fact? Can it be that a relatively transparent summary of what we do know will be a more informative and dependable basis than Russell's dualism of experience and inference?

The opportunity to carry out his new project came soon after. In June 1944, Russell returned to England and was awarded a five-year lectureship at Trinity. He chose to consider 'non-demonstrative inference' in his annual course, and the work over the next few years resulted in his *Human Knowledge* of 1948. In *PD* (1959) he reviewed the book extensively and introduced several interesting general observations. For example, 'empiricism as a philosophy must be subjected to important limitations' (p. 191); the mathematical aspects of probability are less central since the premisses themselves are uncertain (p. 193); induction 'is not among the premisses of non-demonstrative inference' (p. 200); and the method of Cartesian doubt 'no longer seems to me to have fundamental validity' (p. 207).

Very recently I was surprised to find in the same book (*PD*) a view close to my own which I take to be contrary to Russell's well-known philosophical works. In the chapter on his 'present view,' he states under the 'view to which I have been gradually led': 'It has been common among philosophers to begin with how we know and proceed afterwards to what we know. I think this a mistake, because knowing how we know is one small department of knowing what we know. I think it a mistake for another reason: it tends to give to knowing a cosmic significance which it by no means deserves' (p. 16). Moreover, 'I have come to accept the facts of sense and the broad truth of science as things which the philosophers should take as data, since, though their truth is not quite certain, it has a higher degree of probability than anything likely to be achieved in philosophical speculation' (p. 207).

I find these statements very congenial. Indeed, they seem to resemble what I have tried to say in a tortured way (under 'substantial factualism') in the introduction to my *MP*. The book as a whole was devoted to illustrating the sort of preliminary work one can do according to such a view, in the severely limited but perhaps quite central area of logic and mathematics. Of course the declarations of methodological beliefs are subject to varying interpetations which become more definite only in the process of executing what is merely envisaged. But I do feel that the spirit of the quoted statements is not very remote from not only my vaguely felt conception but also Bacon's inadequately explained project of instauration. At any rate, Russell's view as just quoted appears to me to be far more remote from the philosophical practice of Carnap and Quine. I realize that even if these two relative comparisons are true, such a fact is not in itself an argument for saying that my favored approach is more fruitful. But it does seem to support my belief that the path followed by Carnap and Quine was not the main road for Russell himself but rather a bypath initiated by a substitute or auxiliary suggestion of his. Moreover, it does seem to suggest that the evolving shift of attention from how I know to what we know is not unnatural or so uncommon.

6. Russell's work in logic

Peano's work is largely concerned with outlining how mathematical theorems and concepts can be derived from axioms and primitive concepts in the same area of mathematics with the help of symbolic logic. It shows little interest in scrutinizing further the logic being employed. The best known example is probably the Peano axioms for arithmetic, which was, by the way, anticipated and influenced by the conceptually more appealing work of R. Dedekind (compare *Survey*, Chapter 6, and section 2 above in the Introduction). There are five axioms and three primitive concepts (number, zero, successor) which make up what nowadays is called a second order theory of arithmetic.

In the summer of 1900, Russell asked for and got Peano's works. After his return from Paris in the middle of August, he soon mastered Peano's notation and 'saw that it extended the region of mathematical precision backwards towards regions which had been given over to philosophical vagueness.' He invented a notation for relations and, with the assistance of Whitehead, worked out 'such matters as the definitions of series, cardinals, and ordinals, and the reduction of arithmetic to logic.' Much of the work had already been done by Frege, but at first he did not know this (*MD*, pp. 12–13). In contrast with Peano, Frege had spent his efforts in a careful analysis of the logic part and moved rather slowly toward the derivation of mathematics. Hence, the initial project of *PM* might be thought to be a combination of Frege's and Peano's work, with the Peano portion done more carefully in the spirit of Frege. But after the discovery of his paradox in June 1901, the more challenging task for Russell became that of finding the right axioms of logic (i.e., primarily set theory) which are natural but do not imply the paradoxes.

6.1. The PM *project and its influence on Carnap and Quine*

Let me pause to make some general observations about the *PM* project. It is very much in the spirit of beginning with 'what we know' rather than trying to discover 'how I know.' This may be the instance Russell has in mind when he says that 'I reverse the process which has been common in philosophy since Kant' (*PD*, p. 16; compare the longer quotation in the last section). But, as I said before, I do not see most of Russell's work after *PM* to be in the same spirit. This may be partly because the later attempts were less successful. Physical knowledge poses a much harder and more indefinite problem for a similar approach; it calls for a change and broadening of the method, as well as a less conclusive target. As it is, even in the case of mathematical knowledge, it has taken a long process during and after the construction of *PM* before we get a fairly comfortable picture of the set-theoretic 'foundation' of mathematics. In other words, even though the starting point of what we know of the part of mathematics that is to be 'reconstructed' and the linking definitions to set theory were pretty definite and stable by 1900, it has taken a long period to arrive at a more appropriate understanding of the set theory end.

The massive work of *PM* has had a decisive influence on the direction of the efforts of Carnap and Quine. It was undoubtedly the model and inspiration of Carnap's program of 'rational reconstruction.' Early in Carnap's career (probably from 1920 to 1925), he tried to axiomatize kinematics and also study more broadly the 'foundations' of physics (Schilpp 1963, pp. 11–15). As we now know, the task is much more complex than Carnap seemed to realize; even to get a reasonable axiomatization of classical particle mechanics, many impure considerations beyond what is familiar in mathematics and mathematical logic have to be introduced (see Sneed 1971, which, by the way, is far too formal for its actual content; Howard Stein has pointed out in correspondence two defects in the work: taking motion as a non-theory-dependent concept, and making Newton's theory into a purely mathematical one deprived of any canonically intended application and therewith its intended interpretation). It is possible that, even more than with Russell, difficulties in the more controllable area of study led Carnap to shift his interests to less definite and seemingly more 'basic' problems of epistemology such as the logical construction of the world, the limits of knowledge, syntax, semantics, modality, physicalism and the unity of science, as well as probability and inductive logic. If this was indeed the case, it would be an example of believing larger problems to be easier than smaller ones.

Quine continued the work of *PM* in different directions. He strove quite successfully to improve the formal precision of *PM*. In addition he modified Russell's search for a satisfactory set theory by substituting as the basic desideratum elegance for plausibility; and he introduced one or two formally elegant but conceptually opaque systems which will be considered in detail in a later part of this book. Quine also appears to have chosen to use generally a narrower and more artificial aspect of Russell's mixed conception of Occam's razor. To sharpen the concept of the razor he has introduced a criterion of ontology which seems to me inapplicable to the cases of real interest if only because these cases are never formulable in an indisputable manner in the form required by him (viz., as a vaguely interpreted first order theory; more about this later).

6.2. The paradoxes (1901–1907)

After discovering the paradox in June 1901, Russell tried to resolve it without success and continued to finish up his *Principles*, putting an evasive solution in an appendix. This was out of the way late in May 1902. He wrote to Frege about the paradox on June 16. Frege, in his reply of June 22, said that not only his own, 'but also the sole possible foundations of arithmetic, seem to vanish.' Sixty years later, Russell still spoke of Frege's reply admiringly. 'As I think about acts of integrity and grace, I realize that there is nothing in my knowledge to compare with Frege's dedication to truth' (*FG*, p. 127). The correspondence was followed by further revisions of the *Principles* and an appendix by Frege to the second volume of his *Grundgesetze* (1903). Regarding Russell's work between 1903 and 1910, there is a renewed interest in recent years. For example, D. Lackey published a collection (*Essays in Analysis*, 1973), with notes also, of Russell's papers from this period. It seems convenient to refer just to this book which includes also the sources of the historical information. Another example is P. Hylton's long study (*Synthèse*, 1980, pp. 1–31) of Russell's substitutional theory, which was written in 1906 but only first published in Lackey's collection.

The final revisions of the *Principles* include a preliminary form of 'the doctrine of types' (Appendix B), but Russell felt that it, as it stands, would not resolve Cantor's paradox about the largest cardinal number. On May 19, 1903, he thought he could dispense with classes altogether, using only 'propositional functions,' and Whitehead telegrammed, 'Heartiest congratulations aristotle secundus.' But Russell soon noted that 'the solution was wrong' (Clark, p. 111). After more efforts in the summer, the rest of 1903 was given to the study of free trade. In April

1904 he returned to the paradoxes, continuing to January 1905. Over this period, he says in his *Autobiography*, 'Every morning I would sit down before a blank sheet of paper. Throughout the day, with a brief interval for lunch, I would stare at the blank sheet. Often when evening came it was still empty.' 'What made it more annoying was that the contradictions were trivial' (I, pp. 151–152). Moreover, this was at a time when he was very unhappy with his (first) marriage.

In late spring 1905, Russell discovered his theory of descriptions, which not only eliminated the necessity of taking 'the' as a primitive concept, as was done in the *Principles*, but has also always been considered by Russell as his first real breakthrough toward the solution of the paradoxes. It was, in addition, the occasion for him to move away from his former 'Platonic realism.'

Up to 1904, Russell had been sympathetic to the excessively liberal ontology of Alexius Meinong (1853–1920), which includes the round square and the golden mountain. 'Whatever may be an object of thought, or may occur in any true or false proposition, or can be counted as *one*, I call a *term*. . . . I shall use it as synonymous with the words unit, individual, and entity. . . . every term has being, i.e., *is* in some sense' (*Principles*, p. 43). After getting his theory of descriptions, however, Russell began to be very critical of this kind of view. The change is reflected quite clearly in the three pieces on Meinong's work included in Lackey's collection (from 1904, 1905, and 1907).

At first sight, the descriptions seem to have little to do with the paradoxes. The way Russell proceeded to apply his basic idea was to try to eliminate classes (or sets in more recent terminology) by using contextual definitions or 'incomplete symbols' (as with descriptions). In his paper on transfinite numbers, read in December 1905 and published in 1906, he suggested the three famous alternatives of the limitation of size (as in Zermelo's work of 1908), of the zigzag theory (illustrated by Quine's system of 1937), and his own favorite of no-class theory. [This was followed by his paper on the substitutional theory, a theory of 'excessive formalism' (in Whitehead's words) read in May 1906 but not published until 1973 (compare Hylton, op. cit.).] The paper provoked an interesting exchange between Poincaré and Russell in the *Revue de métaphysique et de morale* (1906).

Poincaré suggested the idea of 'vicious circle' in the context of J. Richard's paradox introduced in 1905 and Russell agreed to this idea in his reply and adopted it as the criterion for separating predicative and impredicative ('non-predicative' at that time) definitions. He also pointed out that, given the vicious circle principle, it remained a major task to construct a positive theory (for more details, compare my 1965 and *MP*, pp. 107–108). He reformulated Poincaré's suggestion in the following terms: 'Whatever involves an apparent variable must not be among the possible values of that variable' (Lackey's collection, p. 198). The fuller development of the idea emerged by the end of 1906, which was carried out in 1907 and published in 1908 (*Am. J. Math.*, pp. 222–262). (A historical question of some interest might be to examine more closely to what extent Poincaré's suggestion supplied a missing link in Russell's development of his type theory from 1903 to 1907.) By 1907, as Russell observed later, what remained for the completion of *PM* was to write it out (by brute labor).

[J. Richard's solution of the paradox of the set E of all decimal fractions definable in a finite number of words: Let N be so chosen that it differs from the nth member of E at the nth decimal place. Clearly it is easy to contrive a special definition G, with a finite number of words, which specifies such an N. But N is not in E, a contradiction. However, as Richard points out, G mentions the set E, which has not yet been defined; it has meaning only if the set E is totally defined. The Richard letter was published in 1905 and reprinted in *Acta mathematica* in 1906.

Certain historical details have been uncovered in recent years and reported throughout Lackey's collection. The need for a separate multiplicative axiom (the axiom of choice) was sensed in the summer of 1904 and recognized before 1907 (p. 15). Russell thought in 1904 that he could prove the axiom of infinity but changed his mind in 1906 (pp. 253–254). In 1907, Russell expressed the view that the theorems of set theory justify the axioms, rather than the other way round, and that set theory is nonempirical but 'inductive' (p. 255). The axiom of reducibility was probably added in 1907. The choice of negation and disjunction as primitives probably came in 1906 (p. 15). By the way, of special interest for throwing light on Russell's later conception of mathematics is his essay 'Is mathematics purely linguistics?' (probably written between 1950 and 1952, first published in Lackey's collection).]

Several aspects of Russell's work from 1900 to 1907, centering on his conception of logic (in particular, of being, class, proposition, and propositional function), are of current interest, historical or otherwise. His conceptions of logic and proposition seem to be presupposed in Wittgenstein's construction of his *Tractatus*. Relative to a later viewpoint, many things appear mysterious in their shared underlying beliefs from 1912 to 1918, in their evaluations of the *Tractatus* and its predecessors over a long period, and in how they viewed the relation of logic to philosophy. With respect to *PM*, the complex history of its development suggests that certain strange mixtures in *PM* may be clarified by looking at its predecessors from this period. A specific example is Russell's presenting two alternative ways of treating the predicate calculus (in *9 and *10). This is related to his earlier view that quantifiers are less fundamental and ought to be taken care of in some derivative manner, and also to the casual way in which the *Tractatus* disposes of the quantifiers. In a technical direction, the idea of the sharp separation of quantifiers in *9 gives the 'prenex normal form' and has a role in J. Herbrand's penetrating study of the predicate calculus in his dissertation (1930).

Another matter is Russell's ill-defined notion of Occam's razor and its influence in philosophy. Undoubtedly the elimination of descriptions is a prize example of using the razor well. But, as Russell realized, it is hard to be precise about the meaningful uses of the razor. A fairly meaningless example would be a mechanical count such as: 'Hitherto I have not succeeded in reducing [the indemonstrable propositions] to less than ten' (*Principles*, p. 15). I am inclined to think the effect of his propaganda for the razor has done more harm than good to philosophy. The meaningful uses of the razor are generally for more natural reasons than a conscious striving for economy of concepts and entities; in such cases more is gained than mere economy which, when pursued for its own sake, is often bought by paying a higher price, such as artificiality, than the gain.

According to Russell's view of the period, logic is universal and the central concepts are terms (or entities), propositions, and propositional functions. A proposition is a complex of entities (or terms) which are its constituents. The theory of descriptions serves to eliminate (some of) the fanciful entities (or 'nondenoting terms,' if one equivocates a little about the term 'term'). The next step is to eliminate classes (or sets). The universality of variables, which Russell upheld at the time, creates a difficulty for type theory which can be resolved if 'classes, etc., are merely a *façon de parler.*' Indeed, he wished 'to construct a theory in which every expression which contains an apparent variable (i.e., which contains such words as *all, any, some, the*) is shown to be a mere *façon de parler*' (Lackey, p. 206). Hence, we see here already something close to the frame of the *Tractatus*, which, as it will be recalled, proposes to eliminate quantifiers by conjunctions and disjunctions (5.2), treat a number as the exponent of an operation (6.021), pronounce the theory of classes superfluous in mathematics (6.031), and take care of mathematics by 'equations' (6.2). When the *Tractatus* is viewed in this manner, we are less mystified by the fact that Russell and Wittgenstein seem to have viewed it as a solution, elegant and final, of Russell's important problem.

6.3. Advances since 1910
As we know, *PM* was not completely successful in getting the theory Russell wanted. The axioms of choice, infinity, and especially reducibility

all appear to be ad hoc compromises. [In any case, Russell continued to hold a realistic attitude about logic in 1918. 'Logic is concerned with the real world just as truly as zoology, though with its more abstract and general features' (*IMP*, p. 169).] It is a little surprising that after the completion of *PM*, Russell did not continue to try to remove the defects which he noticed. Instead, he said (*PD*, p. 12), 'After 1910, I had done all that I intended to do as regards pure mathamatics, I began to think about the physical world.' He did not try to benefit, then or later, from alternative approaches as represented by Brouwer and the Hilbert school. Not surprisingly, however, he did try to make use of the further developments of his earlier ideas in the *Tractatus*, on the occasion of preparing a second edition of *PM*. In March 1923 he began to write a new introduction, and in September 1924 he sent a 127-page manuscript to the Cambridge University Press. Around this time Ramsey also became involved with the *Tractatus* and with improving *PM*.

In 1932, Wittgenstein spoke of, in his lectures, two basic mistakes of the *Tractatus*. The second one is that of obliterating the difference between the finite and the infinite cases. As Moore reports it (*Mind*, 1955, p. 2):

> He said he had been misled by the fact that (x)Fx can be replaced by Fa&Fb&Fc& . . . , having failed to see that the latter expression is not always a logical product, that it is only a logical product if the dots are what he called 'dots of laziness.'

In tackling a difficult problem, it is often helpful first to consider suitably simplified cases; this is a familiar way of dividing up the difficulty. Sometimes the solution of the simplified case is interesting in its own right; generally the hope is to be able to extend the solution to one for the more complex original problem. But one should not confuse the simplified case with the original: to do that would be to introduce additional implicit assumptions not satisfied by the original situation. For example, Bernays spoke of a 'quasi-combinatorial' analogy of the infinite to the finite but was fully aware of the additional complexities introduced by the analogy (BP, p. 275).

The assumption is different from saying that the world is finite. Rather, it seems to say that finite and infinite make no basic difference. This is indeed how Ramsey interpreted Wittgenstein's mistake: 'Mr. Wittgenstein has perceived that, if we accept this account [viz., the familiar one] of truth functions . . ., there is no reason why the arguments to a truth-function should not be infinite in number. As no previous writer has considered truth-functions as capable of more than a finite number of arguments, this is a most important innovation' (Ramsey

1931, p. 7). Before, however, turning to Ramsey's 'tautology theory' (developed in his paper read November 1925), I should first like to say something about the slightly earlier second edition of *PM* in the introduction of which a special acknowledgment is made to Ramsey.

There is a good deal of agonizing over the axiom of reducibility in the first edition of *PM* (1910). 'That the axiom of reducibility is self-evident is a proposition which can hardly be maintained. . . . the inductive evidence in its favor is very strong, since the reasonings which it permits and the results to which it leads are all such as appear valid' (p. 59). Hence, it is not surprising for Wittgenstein to say that 'propositions like Russell's "axiom of reducibility" are not logical propositions. . . . Their truth could only be the result of a fortunate accident' (6.1232). What is surprising is that both Russell and Ramsey undertook to rebuild the system of *PM* by appealing to (their own interpretations of) some views in the *Tractatus*, one trying to do without the axiom of reducibility and the other giving it a new reading.

Russell added an introduction and three appendices in the second edition in order to carry out what he took to be Wittgenstein's recommendation. 'There is another course recommended by Wittgenstein (*Tractatus*, 5.54 ff.) for philosophical reasons. This is to assume that functions of propositions are always truth-functions, and that a function can only occur in a proposition through its values. . . . It involves the consequence that all functions of functions are extensional' (p. xiv). The resulting new system, for what concerns us here, is nothing but what is commonly known as the ramified theory of types. The theory has familiar inadequacies, as enumerated by Russell: definition of identity, mathematical induction, Dedekind cut, and Cantor's theory of higher infinite cardinals. Russell thought he could salvage induction and devoted Appendix B to accomplishing it. It proposes to show that if induction holds for classes of order 5, it holds for classes of all orders. But, as Gödel points out in his paper in Schilpp 1944, the proof contains a gap. In fact, the statement is demonstrably untrue, since the consistency of lower-order systems can be proved in higher-order systems. In section 14.3 below I shall return to an example of a set of new systems which retains the ramified spirit but avoids nearly all the inadequacies of Russell's ramified theory. This will be one of the two answers to the main open problem of *PM* (promised at the beginning of the chapter).

What is philosophically interesting about Russell's theory are the issue of extensionality and the nature of quantification in a ramified theory. Intuitively the conceptual simplicity of the ramified theory is fairly obvious: the infinitely many values of each quantifier are all given in advance; we need only take a simple infinite conjunction or disjunction of the instances of Fx to get (x)Fx or (Ex)Fx. Indeed, Russell says similar things in the new introduction. 'A function can only appear in a matrix through its values' (p. xxix). 'Theoretically, it is unnecessary to introduce such variables as ϕ_1, because they can be replaced by an infinite conjunction or disjunction' (p. xxxiii). It may be mentioned here that Gödel was later able to combine the ramification idea with his broader perspective to introduce the interesting mixture of constructible sets (in Gödel 1939).

Ramsey's 'tautology theory' took quite a different course. 'Although he writes as a disciple of Wittgenstein and follows him in everything except mysticism, the way he approaches problems is extraordinarily different,' as Russell says in his *PD* (p. 126), where a summary of his and Ramsey's 1925 reconstruction is also given. Allow me to disregard the strange conception of identity shared by Wittgenstein and Ramsey. Ramsey uses an 'extensional' view and persists with his interpretation of Wittgenstein's (mistaken) assumption in the form that finite and infinite make basically no difference. In particular, there is, for him, no *logical* objection to the definition of any infinite set by enumeration. From this viewpoint, we arrive at what is nowadays known as the simple theory of types, and the axiom of reducibility is no longer needed or absorbed into the axiom of comprehension (which was, however, left unstated by Ramsey since he postulated all the necessary expressible and inexpressible propositional functions). Of the axiom of choice he said, 'As I interpret it, it is an obvious tautology' (Ramsey 1931, p. 59); and this agrees with the usual view according to the iterative concept of set.

The status of the axiom of infinity is left indeterminate but, according to Ramsey, it could be a tautology: 'We do not have to assume that any particular set of things, e.g., atoms, is infinite, but merely that there is some infinite type which we can take to be the type of individuals' (p. 61). For Ramsey, presumably, the 'individuals' do not have to be part of the physical world. Since around 1930, it has been customary to take the natural numbers as individuals, or begin with the finite sets built up from the empty set. If we adopt Ramsey's extensional view but pay more attention to what is expressible and overcome the superstition against going beyond the initial infinite hierarchy, we arrive at (the unfinishable large universe of) the iterative concept of set. And even richer sets of axioms than those of *PM* can be justified according to the concept (see Chapter 6 of my *MP*). This is the other answer to the open problem of *PM* (as reinterpreted by Ramsey); I shall elaborate the matter further in section 13.3 below.

If we take the step of including sets among Russell's terms (individuals, units, entities; or, simply, objects), what happens to Russell's early conception of logic? (This step is in the direction of expansion rather than contraction, which I metaphorically associate with the change from Russell to Carnap and Quine.) Russell seems to mix up use and mention in a basic way. For example, the ambiguity of 'term' and 'propositional function': a propositional function is for him both a matrix (an open sentence) and an attribute (property or relation) or concept. If we avoid this equivocation and consider what are expressed (and not the expressions), we then see that Russell agrees with Frege and Gödel in taking objects and concepts as fundamental. According to Gödel, we do not yet have a moderately adequate theory of (pure) concept. For example, even though we do not have a universal set, we may have a universal concept, but we do not have a general concept of (not) applying to itself; there are of course particular concepts which apply to themselves, e.g., the universal concept. He offers it as a conjecture that every set is the extension of some concept. One task of the theory of concept is to deal with what he calls the 'intensional paradoxes,' such as the concept of all concepts not applying to themselves.

Gödel divides the paradoxes into three classes. The extensional ones are taken care of by the iterative concept of set. The semantic ones are resolved in the manner widely accepted up to the 1960s. What remains to be studied are the intensional ones. In a sense, Gödel's conception of logic may also be viewed as pointing to another solution of the problem which the *Tractatus* was supposed to have solved. (These issues will be considered in *Reflections on Kurt Gödel*.)

Chapter 2

A digression on Wittgenstein's philosophy

This is a digression in the following sense. Unlike Russell, Carnap, and Quine, Wittgenstein (W for brevity in this chapter) is art centered rather than science centered and seems to have a different underlying motive for his study of philosophy. Moreover, this chapter is only an incomplete part of a longer planned study of W's work, which I have abandoned, at least for the next few years. Of course the inclusion of the *Tractatus* in a study concerned with the strand of analytic philosophy centered on the Vienna Circle is only natural and calls for no apologies.

I shall first make some remarks on Russell's early concept of logic which was undoubtedly important for W's work toward the *Tractatus*. This will be followed by general comments on W's attitude toward philosophy, and then the structure and the 'postulates' of the *Tractatus*. There will be occasion to mention W's later views as well. For brevity, I shall use W_1 for his views up to the *Tractatus* and W_2 for his views since 1929. It has been observed that his views developed between 1929 and 1951 so that it is possible to speak of three stages. Since, however, I am only concerned with rather broad features, it seems justifiable to merge the three into one.

7. Russell's concept of logic before 1911

A convenient place to begin to consider W's *Tractatus* is the conception of logic in Russell's *Principles* (1903), which was presumably the first book in the philosophy of mathematics studied by W. For W, logic (in different senses at different stages) is the basis of philosophy. It is of interest to examine how his early conception of logic agrees and differs from Russell's evolving idea from 1903 to 1910. For example, his principle of atomicity may be viewed as carrying to the extreme the power of logical analysis suggested by Russell's theory of descriptions (1905); while his principle of extensionality goes against Russell's early views. They shared the belief in the 'universality' of logic. What is striking is W's tendency to select a position, often suggested tentatively as a partial measure by Russell, and push it to a radical extreme. His decisiveness in carrying a view to its logical conclusions has the advantage of novelty and sharpness (as generally simplified elegant models have) but also the danger of one-sidedness.

Besides the radical position in a 'final' analysis, we see also the radicalization with regard to language and grammar. Russell finds a natural starting point of his consideration of logic in grammar (p. 42):

> In the present chapter, certain questions are to be discussed belonging to what may be called philosophical grammar. The study of grammar, in my opinion, is capable of throwing far more light on philosophical questions than is commonly supposed by philosophers. . . . On the whole, grammar seems to me to bring us much nearer to correct logic than the current opinions of philosophers; and in what follows, grammar, though not our master, will yet be taken as our guide. (The excellence of grammar as a guide is proportional to the paucity of inflexions, i.e., to the degree of analysis effected by the language considered.)

(The parenthetical remark would seem to justify regarding Chinese as the logically most advanced language.)

The chapter is entitled 'Proper names [nouns and noun phrases], adjectives and verbs.' It naturally suggests the questions about the place of other parts of speech, the place of sentences other than the declarative sentences, and, if we extend further, also the place of larger contexts than single sentences. More recently, for example, variables have been associated with relative pronouns (notably by Quine). Since 1903, linguistic concepts (such as the parts of speech) have changed, e.g., in paying more attention to context dependence; such changes may or may not play a direct role in the study of 'philosophical grammar.' The *Tractatus* certainly exalted language to a prominent position. The concern for explicitness naturally led to an initial emphasis on syntax, notably by Carnap in philosophy (in the 1930s) and by Chomsky in linguistics (in the 1950s). It was then realized that syntax was not enough, and the attention was shifted to meaning (semantics and, less conspicuously, pragmatics).

The tendency represented by Carnap (from the 1930s on) was to view syntax, semantics, and pragmatics as distinct domains to be studied, preferably, in a formal manner. In contrast, W's language-games merge these domains and assign to pragmatics a more dominant role. He modified and broadened the ordinary concept of 'grammar' in such a way that grammar becomes a successor to logic. Crudely speaking, philosophy as the study of the logic of the world has given way to the study of the grammar of language-games.

These observations remind us of the important place of what W calls 'grammar' in his later philosophy. A more direct connection is with the central position of language occupied in W's philosophy. He puts in the center of philosophy the relation between thought and the world or, more specifically, the limit of thought, and transforms it into one about language and the world, taking logic as the key to his answer. Thus we have in the *Tractatus*:

> 1.1 The world is the totality of facts, not of things.
> 2.1 We picture facts to ourselves.
> 2.181 A picture whose pictorial form is logical form [i.e., what the picture has in common with reality (which it depicts), 2.18] is called a logical picture.
> 3 A logical picture of facts is a thought.
> 4 A thought is a proposition with a sense.
> 4.001 The totality of propositions is language.

The word 'logical' in the above context has to do with 'logical space' and logical possibilities. It prepares the ground for dealing with propositions of logic (6.1). But our interest here is only to bring out W's sweeping elimination of thought by the move to language.

It would be a more intricate enterprise than I can undertake to recapture faithfully Russell's evolving views of logic over this period. My objective is a more limited one: the connections of these views with later developments by Russell and others, as well as an exposition which might reveal components of these earlier views which have not been absorbed into later conceptions of logic. What is of special interest is to take the *Principles* as an attempt to think from the beginning what constitutes logic at a time when things were much more fluid.

Russell's conception of logic could be considered under five headings: (a) the indefinables or logical constants; (b) the ultimate universality of logic; (c) the realm of being (his ontology or even 'metaphysics,' in one of the various senses of the word); (d) the intensional and the extensional; (e) set theory and the paradoxes. Of these topics, (a) seems to be the most complex because Russell used initially a large and somewhat indefinite group of primitive concepts which have undergone many changes in the hands both of himself and of others. It was also, I think rightly, thought to be the most central question by Russell. I shall limit my consideration to (a) and (b) only.

7.1. The logical constants and their axioms

On the first page of his preface, Russell calls the discussion of indefinables the chief part of logic. According to him, the number of indefinables 'appears, in fact, to be eight or nine.' These are: (1) implication between propositions not containing variables; (2) the membership relation; (3) the notion of *such that*; (4) relation; (5) truth; (6) propositional function; (7) class; (8) denoting; (9) any or every term. The last four notions are introduced to take care of the complex (and central for Russell at the time) notion of formal implication. (See p. 11 and p. 106.) (G. E. Moore's *Principia Ethica*, also published in 1903, studies the 'ethical constants' good, duty, and beauty, as well as their 'axioms.')

The six words 'all, every, any, a, some, the' are considered in the chapter on 'Denoting'; they are not taken as primitives. The concept (9) is to take care of the notion of variable (p. 94). Hence, even though it is hard to sort out how Russell proposes to define them explicitly from the indefinables, he feels free to use variables and the six words listed. Moreover, formal implication is taken to be explicated and defined in terms of the concepts (6)–(9), as explained at length in four chapters, one for each concept (pp. 53–94).

In *MP* (p. 129) I have made a tentative attempt to set up Russell's axiom system governing his indefinables. It seems clear to me that Russell makes no attempt to list explicitly and fully all the axioms on his primitive concepts (particularly the concepts of truth and denoting); rather he lists all the indefinables which appear necessary but is concerned only with an adequate axiomatization of some of them. It is likely that a more careful combing may uncover a few more primitive propositions mentioned elsewhere, since my list comes from pp. 13–26 where Russell undertakes to put his system together. That his list of indefinables is sufficient for his system may also appear doubtful, but, accepting variables and the six special words just mentioned as adequately defined by his discussions, it seems possible to establish the adequacy of his list.

His system falls into three parts. The propositional calculus uses the concepts (1) and (5), as well as formal implication, which is to be defined by (6)–(9). The concept of proposition is defined in context: 'p is a proposition' is defined by 'p implies p.' Hence, the formation rules and modus ponens can be formulated, using also (5). Since 'all' is available for propositions, conjunction, disjunction, and negation can be defined. There are altogether ten axioms of which four are the rule of modus ponens and three rules of formation.

The calculus of classes uses in addition the concepts (2) and (3), as well as explicitly (6), with identity defined in the usual manner. It has two axioms. Finally, the theory of relations uses the concept (4) in addition and has seven more axioms. The axioms of relations include: xRy is a proposition, implication and membership are relations. Relations are understood intensionally. The system contains no special axioms for the quantifiers. Moreover, the special axioms are primarily concerned with only three of the nine indefinables: implication, membership, and relation.

Nowadays we are so accustomed to listing the indefinables syntactically that it is frustrating to uncover what Russell at different stages took the indefinables to be. Even though his papers of this period, published and unpublished, are largely available today, his statements are often rather indefinite and deal with concepts rather than symbols. I can distinguish three types of problem about Russell's indefinables. First, there is the simple question about truth functions and quantifiers. Second, the contrast between propositional functions and sets (or classes, and the membership relation) was very much Russell's concern from 1903 to 1910. Third, the place of the semantic notions of truth and denoting is not entirely clear. In addition, there are also the questions about variables and Frege's concept of assertion.

In Russell 1908 (written in 1907), we find seven 'primitive ideas required in symbolic logic' (*FG*, pp. 168–169). Three of them are roughly negation, disjunction, and universal quantification; these take care of the first question. There is the concept of assertion. A difficult primitive is 'the truth of *any* value of a propositional function,' which underlies Russell's concept of a 'real variable' (in contrast to an 'apparent variable'). The apparent variable has to do with the theory of types which requires all quantifiers to be restricted; in contrast, the 'real variables' are universal. The central concepts of the system are propositional functions and predicative propositional functions. Sets and the membership relation are dispensed with. Truth and denoting are not explicitly included, but the semantic paradoxes concerning these concepts are considered, thereby implying that they are among the concepts of the system. Moreover, 'true' and 'truth' occur all through the text that describes the primitive concepts, talking also about any type, same type, lower type, etc.

7.2. The ultimate universality of logic

This is an appealing but complex idea. In one form or another it is shared by Leibniz, Frege, W (early and late), and Gödel. Hence, it is essential to determine at least some of the features of Russell's idea which are more often implied than stated. His way of stating his indefinables and their axioms reveals one feature. If truth is one of the primitive ideas, there is surely no objection to using it in the axioms, some of which are customarily taken as rules of inference. But then one would expect him to try to set down also the axioms governing truth. Also, it is not clear that a universal language cannot contain its own metalanguage or that there is no room for metatheoretic considerations about a universal logic, even though these possibilities seem to be denied in the *Tractatus*.

With regard to the (relative) consistency proof of geometrics by arithmetic models, Hilbert observed that one had to shift to a different kind of consistency proof for arithmetic itself since there is no other familiar mathematical domain to fall back on. The problem of metatheoretic considerations about a universal logic is of course harder and different, particularly because we do not have a satisfactory and clear example of a universal logic. The oversimplified model (viz., the propositional calculus) of a universal logic in the *Tractatus* is suggestive but, being so simple, offers no reliable guide to the feasibility of metatheoretic considerations.

In the *Principles*, Russell gives a few hints about the kind of ultimate universality of logic he has in mind (pp. 8–9):

> The logical constants themselves are to be defined only by enumeration, for they are so fundamental that all the properties by which the class of them might be defined presuppose some terms of the class. But practically, the method of discovering the logical constants is the analysis of symbolic logic.

If we set the task of looking for a universal logic relative to what we know today, it is not easy to see how we can benefit from the second sentence. On the formal level systems of symbolic logic seem so clear today that what we need appear to be more indefinite ideas rather than the analysis of them. The first sentence in the quotation is not convincing. Surely we can examine how coherent the class (of indefinables) is and how well the class fits whatever intuitive requirements we may have. At any rate, the phrase 'only by enumeration' seems inadequate because it surely has to be done with some guidance which ought to be specified. If the second sentence is meant to specify the guidance, then we need some additional conditions to guide us in selecting from a large group of possible different answers afterwards. One might say that Russell knew vaguely what he was looking for but could not give a more exact specification of his goal. Of course most of the interesting philosophical projects probably share this lack of complete explicitness to some extent.

With regard to the question of mutual independence of his axioms of the propositional calculus, Russell observes that the method of supposing an axiom false (and deducing the consequences of this assumption) is here not universally available (p. 15):

> For all our axioms are principles of deduction; and if they are true, the consequences which appear to follow from an opposite principle

will not really follow, so that arguments from the supposition of the falsity of an axiom are here subject to special fallacies.

This observation points more to the fundamental character of these axioms than to the universality of logic. For example, it does not apply to the axioms of set theory, which are not 'principles of deduction.' It is doubtful that one would wish to require all axioms of logic to satisfy this criterion of being fundamental. In any case, universality of logic or the peculiarity of its axioms does not imply the impossibility of independence proofs. (Of course there is now the familiar method of proving the independence of given axioms of the propositional calculus; in particular, all except one of the axioms of *PM* have been shown to be independent.) However, Russell's statement does seem to hint at the idea that logic is universal in the sense of comprehending all modes of inference.

There is no doubt that Russell wanted the range of variables to be completely universal. 'We may distinguish what may be called the true or formal variable from the restricted variable. *Any term* is a concept denoting the true variable. . . . By making our x always an unrestricted variable, we can speak of *the* variable, which is conceptually identical in Logic, Arithmetic, Geometry, and all other formal subjects. The *terms* dealt with are always *all* terms' (p. 91).

Let me conclude this fragmentary discussion by quoting Russell's specification of the 'realm of being' (p. 43):

> Whatever may be an object of thought, or may occur in any true or false proposition, or can be counted as *one*, I call a *term*. This, then, is the widest word in the philosophical vocabulary. I shall use as synonymous with it the words unit, individual, and entity. The first two emphasize the fact that every term is *one*, while the third is derived from the fact that every term has being, i.e., *is* in some sense. A man, a moment, a number, a class, a relation, a chimera, or anything else that can be mentioned, is sure to be a term; and to deny that such and such a thing is a term must always be false.

8. Wittgenstein's attitude toward philosophy

Russell visited Philip Jourdain on April 20, 1909, who reported soon afterwards: 'Russell said that the views I gave in a reply to Wittgenstein (who had 'solved' Russell's contradiction) agree with his own' (Grattan-Guinness 1977, p. 114). This oddity appears to indicate that W had begun to study Russell's writings (possibly also Frege's) by April 1909: a study that may be taken as the initiation of his work on the *Tractatus* which was completed in August 1918. The 'one thing which W willed' (in the sense of Kierkegaard?) when he was nineteen to twenty-nine was this short book of twenty thousand words. The consequential interactions between middle Russell and early W are marked by a date earlier than this (W's first exposure to the *Principles*, possibly in 1908), their first meeting in October 1911, and Russell's completion of his new introduction (and appendices) to *PM* in September 1924.

There are many remarkable features about the *Tractatus*, some of which are fascinating but hard to consider sensibly for lack of knowledge. W's upbringing (including the effects of a highly cultured and 'enormously rich' family) and personality, the social conditions of his time, the mixture of strong artistic and moral ideals with an interest in logic and mathematics: all these have undoubtedly played an important part in the style and result of his work as well as in the form and range of his influences. A few vague suggestions can be mentioned. For example, Einstein contrasts the 'more aristocratic illusion concerning the unlimited penetrating power of thought' with 'the more plebeian illusion of naive realism' (Schilpp 1944, p. 281). Others have put the emphasis on formalization to the side of the plebeian. A less elusive phenomenon is the tendency of the outsider (and the plebeian) to be more cautious: to begin with more definite and less controversial work, not to give free rein to the flight of imagination, and to spend more effort doing what is relatively routine. Obviously W did not suffer from such handicaps.

Other features are more open to inspection. How Kant, Schopenhauer, Frege, and especially Russell influenced him; how he took over Russell's problem and modified it; how he selected from Russell's wealth of suggestions, modified them, and carried them to their logical extremes; how his influences on Russell and on the logical positivists and (later) on the ordinary language philosophers are to be understood in terms of his cryptic style, serious distortions of his views, and a predisposition to certain more rigidified beliefs. A philosophically more rewarding direction is to explore new or less familiar alternative selections, modifications, reactions, and developments based on the various suggestions from Russell's early work and the *Tractatus*, in the light of more recent elucidations in related areas.

The decisiveness and confidence with which W pushed on with novel and extreme positions are truly amazing. He had an exceptional trust in his selection of what he took to be the essential aspects, thereby simplifying and narrowing down his problems to such a degree that others, who are interested in but not entirely immersed in the internal workings of his systems, would not be able to resist the felt need of examining a broader range of data and alternatives. This practice of concentrating only on what he took to be basic enabled him to get into a greater depth along his chosen paths but at the same time involved a tendency to mistake a simplified model for the real thing or to misconstrue what is appropriate to a limited area as universally applicable.

The selections or presuppositions or postulates of the *Tractatus* are particularly clear when they are explicitly stated either in the book or at later dates. Some of the postulates are shared by W_2 while others have gradually been rejected. In addition, there are certain larger conclusions which W believed and wished to establish; they were more persistent than the postulates. The basic conscious postulates and conclusions are stated quite explicitly in the preface to the *Tractatus*:

> W1. The goal is to deal 'with the problems of philosophy.'
> W2. The way to attain this goal 'is to set a limit to thought.'
> W3. The way to do this is to set a limit 'not to thought, but to the expressions of thoughts,' i.e., to language.
> W4. The reason why the problems of philosophy ('metaphysical' problems in particular) 'are posed is that the logic of our language is misunderstood.'
> W5. What 'can be said at all can be said clearly, and what we cannot talk about we must consign to silence.'
> W6 (= W_1A). W believed himself 'to have found, on all essential points, the final solution of the problems' (of philosophy).

I believe that the affirmations W1 to W5 are shared by W_1 and W_2 (the 'later W'). The place of W6 in W_2 is complex and somewhat ambiguous; I shall return to it. The concept of logic in W4 has undergone a drastic change from W_1 to W_2. What is at stake is not so much the word 'logic' but rather the underlying idea of a common form of thought which does not depend on special experience, is distinguishable from psychology and from linguistics, etc. We have here, in my opinion, a fascinating topic of study: to find x such that when x is put in place of the word *logic* in W4, it is true for both W_1 and W_2. A preliminary solution is undoubtedly the concern with distinguishing sense from nonsense. But such a solution seems to leave out certain aspects of logic in W_1 which relate it more closely to some plausible interpretation of the concept of logic, in conformity with its evolving meaning in the history of thought. For example, what is the successor to 6.3 in W_2? (6.3 The exploration of logic means the exploration of *everything that is subject to law*.)

According to W, his investigation is logic and its essence is 'that we do not seek to learn anything *new* by it. We want to *understand* something that is already in plain view' (*PI*, 89). But I see a basic ambiguity in this position. Is our concern with the intersection or the union of what 'is already in plain view' to different members and groups of the human species? He seems to take the intersection or what is plain to all (or at least all who share an indeterminate heritage, centered on his own 'world,' though not in the inescapable sense of 5.62). It could be argued that only in this way can we hope to get at the 'universal significance' pertaining to logic. I am inclined to look for this universal significance in the union of what we believe we know about the world (including people's different beliefs, dispositions, states of health, strength of will power, economic conditions, etc.). 'Not, however, as if to this end we had to hunt out new facts': this can also be accepted under an appropriate interpretation, viz., for the whole of humanity (but certainly not for any individual).

The ideal of eventually attaining first in some minds and then in all minds a reasonably adequate union of what is in plain view separately to each person is certainly complex, and impossible in many obvious senses. It certainly does not exclude different people seeing and wanting different things. Nor does it ask for any full empathy with the thoughts and feelings of others. Rather, it looks for an appropriate feasible level of mutual understanding, based on a continuing reduction of deception and improvement of communication, which inevitably depends on interrelated educational, political, and economic preconditions. But, in my opinion, it points to the right and inspiring direction of the pursuit of logic (or philosophy, or philosophy as identified with logic), perhaps as a remote ideal which, even if only attained in a very partial way, will certainly not 'leave everything as it is.' Indeed, the conception assigns to philosophy the task of clearing the conceptual ground for the inspiring quest for a reconciliation of continuity with diversity.

The postulate W1 contains in it a severe implicit limitation on the range of philosophical problems. It excludes a great deal of philosophy as impossible or failing to be genuine or pure philosophy, by cutting off the link between philosophy and other human activities. For example, philosophy of life or philosophy in the service of religion or science or politics gets excluded because it loses much of its point and life once its connection with the practical concerns is severed. This detachment from large contexts, larger than what seem to be implied in the language-games of W_2 and going beyond language in any reasonably ordinary sense, may be the main source of the puzzling and frustrating character of 'problems of philosophy.' For example, some of these problems are often asked in one's adolescence and often acquire richer meaning as more experience is obtained. Also, as concerns change personally or historically, certain problems may become separated from their more meaningful contexts; or premature problems may become more meaningful.

On one level, when an intellectual pursuit is connected with making a living or a career, there are practical constraints which have the advantage of fixing more clearly the directions and the disadvantage of probable conflicts with one's real interests. On another level, philosophy purified of its connection with large practical concerns may attempt to be universal and impartial either by seeing (the union of) all sides (to achieve understanding) or by looking for what is in common to different outlooks (their intersection) or by attending carefully to the affairs of one community (possibly, but by no means necessarily, also to illustrate a general way of dealing with all communities). But when the contexts of philosophical concerns are thinned out to the extent of retaining only the local ones of linguistic practice (surrounding a variety of particular examples), there would seem to remain missing an impure unifying link which has been gradually and increasingly lost sight of in the process of separation and detachment.

The natural tendency to discard historical contexts as irrelevant seems to be implicit in the preoccupation with 'problems' in philosophy. This tendency goes with a triple lack of interest in history: general history, the present as history (the place of philosophy in the contemporary world and the relation of philosophy to our other beliefs), and even the history of philosophy. Curiously even histories of philosophy tend to encourage rather than discourage the concentration on 'problems.' For example, W. Windelbind's famous *A History of Philosophy* (1891 and 1900) lays chief emphasis 'upon what is weightiest from a philosophical standpoint: *the history of problems and conceptions.*' But philosophy is, perhaps more primarily and more appealingly, (also) concerned with projects, systems, and comprehensive outlooks, from which we ca   separate out views on certain central concepts and problems. It is not at all clear to me that specialized concentrations on individual concepts and problems is the more effective way of bringing about 'advances' in philosophy as a 'discipline,' whatever these terms might mean for philosophy. For the individual philosopher, it certainly appears to me more attractive and more appropriate to relegate concepts and problems to a derivative position (perhaps as by-products and as auxiliary stimuli or footholds). Is this another way (perhaps even the traditional one, widely thought to be obsolete) of drawing the line between science and philosophy?

To name just a few examples: Bacon's project of great instauration (of the sciences), the Cartesian project of pure inquiry, and the project of *PM*. The two former projects have not been completed, and the last one, though completed in a temporary sense that invited and has received more advances, is hardly a project 'purely' in philosophy or comprehensive enough as a 'whole' philosophy. But even these examples of unfinished philosophies (in contrast with the 'completed' enterprises of, say, Aristotle, Kant, and Hegel) seem to render a vague idea a little more concrete: I mean the idea that these projects yield more forceful motivations and more extensive contacts with our larger intuitions, which have a tendency to generate surer and more enduring impacts (good and bad) in philosophy. For instance, I am under the impression that 'philosophical problems' handed down from Descartes are mostly of only secondary importance to his original pursuit, so that attempting a modified project (relative to additional information) would be more in his spirit than struggling with the problems born of his work.

As has often been noted, the postulate W2 is very much in the tradition of Kant (and perhaps also Schopenhauer). Kant in setting a limit to thought supplements his transcendental logic with his transcendental esthetics. W contents himself with logic alone (in different senses in W_1 and W_2). 'Logic pervades the world: the limits of the world are also its limits' (5.61). In a case where we cannot view a region from outside, it appears at first sight and upon reflection that we must say a great deal about the interior of the region in order to get an approximate idea of its limits. Setting a limit to thought seems a task bordering on the impossible, certainly one of a higher degree of difficulty than any thought we may have. Hence, we tend to suspect the presence of tricks and illusions when confronted with any proposed solution, especially an elegant and 'conclusive' one.

The task is transformed by W3 into one about language, a singularly influential move for the philosophies of this century. The shifts from the world to thought and then to language have certainly created forceful new perspectives. To get back to the world, Kant introduced the almost unapproachable Ding-an-sich. The philosophically most interesting aspect of language is also its intricate connections with the world (rather than syntax and formal semantics). The unity of language and the crystal form of logic in W_1 have given way in W_2 to the multiplicity of language-games and the fluidity of their logic (and grammar). A serious issue for philosophy is whether the divergent language-games can in any meaningful sense be put together again and how their different degrees and types of universality (and objectivity) can be arranged appropriately to make up an understandable (on a second level?) whole.

W5 is related to W's distinction between saying and showing, on which a great deal has been written in recent years. It contains also the one sentence concluding Chapter (7) of the *Tractatus*. What can be said are (all and only) propositions of natural science (6.53 and 4.11): this is central to W's conception of philosophy. To say is apparently for W to 'describe'; a typical case might be: the cat is on the mat. While he makes a sharp distinction between philosophy and natural science, at the same time he also speaks of philosophy as (purely) descriptive. One difference for him is undoubtedly that there can be no theories and deductions in philosophy, no 'explanations' over and above 'descriptions.' Yet W seems to be mainly concerned with saying the unsayable, obviously in W_1 and less unequivocally in W_2. Among his last sayings (in *OC*), we find, for instance:

> 501. Am I not getting closer and closer to saying that in the end logic cannot be described? You must look at the practice of language, then you will see it.
> 618. In that case it would seem as if the language-game must *'show'* the facts that make it possible. (But that's not how it is.)

Associated with W5 are some of W's unchanging views about the nature of philosophy such as 4.111 to 4.115 and 6.53; for instance:

> 4.112   Philosophy aims at the logical clarification of thoughts.
> Philosophy is not a body of doctrine but an activity.
> A philosophical work consists essentially of elucidations.

The elaborations of W5 are concerned with repelling the invasion of science on philosophy and do not consider explicitly the relation of philosophy to art and poetry. Since, however, they share with philosophy the attempt to 'show the unsayable,' they are probably less separate from philosophy in W's mind, if not as subjects, perhaps in the style of work. In particular, the concentration on the particular cases in W_2 (as also argued in general terms, e.g., on p. 18 of *Blue and Brown Books*) suggests a link to literature and, by way of a sort of double negation (of theory and of universality in philosophy), to Aristotle's contrast between poetry and history: 'Poetry is something more philosophic and of graver import than history, since its statements are of the nature rather of universals, whereas those of history are singulars' (*Poetics*, 1451).

The meaning and place of the belief W6 in W_1 and W_2 involve several components. Even in W_1 there is an ambiguity between having solved 'the problems of philosophy' and having established the 'correct method in philosophy' and then finding the remaining problems of elucidation not sufficiently interesting to W himself (compare 6.53). At any rate, we find W leaving philosophy after W_1 (viz., the *Tractatus*) in 1918 and pursuing it (in the form of W_2) from 1929 till his dying day. The meaning of W6 in W_2 seems to me to be entangled in the mixture of the methods and the nature of philosophy, as well as the distinction between basic and particular philosophical problems. According to

Moore's report, W said in 1932 of his own work: what mattered was that 'a method had been found' (1955, p. 26). But in 1945: 'There is not *a* philosophical method, though there are indeed methods, like different therapies' (*PI*, 133). Hence, it would seem that W could not believe himself to have found all the methods and even less to have solved all 'the problems of philosophy.' Indeed, it is doubtful that W would still think of 'the final solution.' In 1950, W wrote (*Culture and Value*, p. 86): 'Philosophy hasn't made any progress?—If somebody scratches the spot where he has an itch, do we have to see some progress?' If W_2 (say as codified in *PI*, I) is believed to have made clear the nature of philosophy as suggested by the analogy to itches, we seem to come back to the early position of 6.53. Why shouldn't W then reaffirm W6 and again leave philosophy?

W undoubtedly makes a distinction between basic and particular philosophical problems and devotes most of his attention to the basic ones, which may include the nature of philosophy and its methods as well as the nature of logic and necessity and 'following the rule' and 'certainty.' Since these can properly be studied, according to W_2, only by examining a variety of particular examples, it would then seem natural to give up any expectation of 'the final solution.' This may point to a fundamental difference between W_1 and W_2. Hence, I shall identify W6 with W_1A and take it as a basic affirmation of W_1 which is given up in W_2.

In a more concrete way the two books which W had completed for publication also reveal a difference in his views of the finality of his work. (What got published posthumously as Part I of) *PI* was (in January 1945) said to be 'the precipitate of philosophical investigations which have occupied me for the last sixteen years.' He did not stop with it but returned in 1947 to try to expand it, giving up the task before a completion to his own satisfaction.

The first book acknowledges a debt to the writings of Frege and Russell, while the second one is said to be an attempt to correct grave mistakes in the first, mistakes which W was helped to realize by criticisms (in conversations) by Frank Ramsey and P. Sraffa. The stated purpose of both books is peculiarly personal: for the unlikely outcome of giving 'pleasure to one person who read and understood it' or bringing 'light into one brain or another.' It is doubtful that any other philosopher has ever written a book for only such a purpose. In terms of a famous distinction in the Chinese tradition, his work was 'for himself' rather than 'for others.' While the first book uses a numbering system to set up an intricate tree structure, the second book is said to be only an album of sketches of landscapes. In both cases an exceptionally large amount of work is devoted to polishing pieces (paragraphs and sentences) and arranging them in a satisfactory order.

9. The structure of the Tractatus

The interrelated questions considered in the *Tractatus* can be summarized in many different ways. How is language, taken as a given fact, possible? How is logic, taken as a given fact, possible? Russell (in his introduction) formulates W's (logical) question thus: 'What relation must one fact (such as a sentence) have to another in order to be *capable* of being a symbol for that other?' 'My *whole* task consists in explaining the nature of the proposition' (*Notebook*, p. 39). The central position of propositions in W_1 is quite obvious since they make up language, and their structure, which is more accessible, mirrors the structure of the world.

If we leave out the concluding sentence (7), the six chapters may be crudely summarized thus:

(1) the relation between the world and facts;

(2) facts, pictures, and their common 'logical form';

(3) thoughts as (logical) pictures (of facts) and propositions each as a perceivable expression of thought and a unit of sense, mirroring thoughts and facts adequately;

(4) propositions, their totality making up language, seen as analyzable into truth-functions of elementary propositions which represent the yes or no of elementary facts (states of affairs or atomic facts), and as possessing a 'general form' which points to a global view of language, logic, and the world, as well as their relations;

(5) a closer look at the transparent structure thus secured of the totality of propositions;

(6) applications of the result achieved to give an account of the nature of logic (6.1), mathematics (6.2), physics (and science, 6.3); and ethics (and esthetics, 6.4), as well as the limit of language and the 'correct method in philosophy' (6.5).

Such a quick summary can at best only serve as a reference or reminder for one who is to some extent already familiar with the book. But it does give an idea of the structure of the book and bring out the central place occupied in it by propositions. Russell is often criticized for characterizing the book as concerned with the conditions for a 'logically perfect language,' which is an ideal to strive for. Of course W was not interested in the construction of ideal languages but rather in understanding the acknowledged 'perfect logical order' of everyday language (5.5563), by means of an elegant model at the time believed by him to be adequate. But Russell's statement about 'the conditions for' is not off the mark; where he misunderstood W is only his sensible presumption that W could not possibly believe the conditions already satisfied by everyday language. 'I only want to justify the vagueness of ordinary propositions; for it *can* be justified' (*Notebook*, p. 70). This remains the aim of W_2, but pursued by a totally different method.

A natural question is to look for a more adequate model, more in the spirit of W_1 than W_2, by using richer concepts of logic and language. For example, to enrich and give more structure to the objects (things) in W_1: to distinguish concepts and objects (all taken as things or entities in W_1) and to include sets among the objects. The range of logical space and logical possibilities gets correspondingly enriched so that, for instance, the formal aspect of any set or concept is what pertains only to the membership or the falling-under relation. Indeed, I believe that the idea of including sets among the objects agrees quite well with Russell's conception in 1903 (e.g., p. xix, 'the definition as a class . . . leaves no doubt as to the existence-theorem') and his suggestion (November 1905) of 'the theory of limitations of size' (Lackey, pp. 152–154). I shall try to say more about this vague suggestion.

Another way of summarizing W_1 is to choose a few aspects and present them by selections from the book in W's own forceful language.

1 The world is the totality of facts, not of things.

2 What is the case—the fact—is the existence of elementary facts (atomic facts, states of affairs).

2.01 An elementary fact is a combination of objects (things).

2.011 It is essential to things that they should be constituents of elementary facts.

3.203 A name denotes an object. The object is its denotation.

4.001 The totality of propositions is language.

4.21 The simplest kind of proposition, an elementary proposition, asserts the existence of an elementary fact.

4.22 An elementary proposition consists of names. It is a nexus, a concatenation of names.

5 A proposition is a truth-function of elementary propositions.

The perfect symmetry of these statements is remarkable. Language and the world are the sets of propositions and facts, which are truth-functions and combinatorial selections of elementary propositions and elementary facts, constituted of names and objects. Names and objects are connected by the relation of denotation. The correspondence between facts and propositions is a picturing relation (4.01), mediated by thoughts as pictures of reality (3, 3.1, and 4).

The world is fully determined by the totality of all elementary facts which render true or false every one of the elementary propositions. Elementary propositions are logically independent of each other (the postulate T1.2 to be considered in the next section). It follows that the whole world of logical inference is only concerned with nonelementary propositions, which are always 'truth-functions' of the elementary ones (according to W_1). The truth-functions are extensional in the sense that their truth-values (truth or falsity) are completely determined by the truth-values of their arguments (or components), which are ultimately the elementary propositions. The nature and number of the objects and the elementary propositions are left indeterminate because they are taken to be 'empirical matters' not among the concerns of logicians.

Given this greatly idealized framework, there remains the question of determining the logical constants, a task which W prefers to formulate quite differently (4.0312, 5.4, and 5.46). Nonetheless, I believe it possible and helpful to clarify W's 'general form of a proposition' (6), in terms of the selection of logical constants. His general form involves three components, written together as [E, S, N(S)], in which E is the totality of all elementary propositions, S is an arbitrary set of propositions, and N(S) is the negation (or denial) of all propositions in S. This is not as simple a complex as it appears. In particular, it involves implicitly the idea of collecting together various propositions into a set and selecting an arbitrary subset of a given set of propositions. This idea, as we know, permits us to build up a rich and open-ended realm of sets (of propositions in this case); we can in fact arrive at all the 'pure' sets in this manner, as can be seen clearly from the elaborations in *MP* (Chapter 6). Hence, the concept of set is presupposed by W's concept of logic. This fact is, in my opinion, an additional reason for including set theory in logic (and sets among the 'objects'), as I am urging repeatedly. What greatly simplifies W's model is his postulate of finiteness, according to which the finite and infinite cases are not essentially different (to be considered in the next section more extensively, as T2).

Propositional connectives can easily be obtained from the operation N. Thus, N(p) gives negation or -p, N(-p,-q) gives disjunction (p or q). (By the way, the appeal to fancier propositional connectives in Russell's introduction is quite fortuitous.) Quantifiers are defined (5.52) by taking S as the set of 'all values of a function Fx for all values of x,' to get -ExFx; if we take -Fx instead, for example, N(S) is (x)Fx. Essentially, these two types of application are the only uses made by W of the complex operation N. Since, however, S is an arbitrary set of propositions, there are of course many other things one can do with N. For example, we can introduce other quantifiers such as 'for infinitely many x' and 'for uncountably many x' by adding the condition on the set S associated with -Fx that it is infinite or uncountable.

On the other hand, once we apply W's postulate of finiteness, we need only be concerned with finite domains and familiarly the ordinary propositional connectives (e.g., just negation and disjunction) give us all the truth-functions. This is indeed what W_1 ends up with. The result is a logic which applies only to a world which is definite or can be made definite to have unambiguous elementary propositions and have all knowledge decomposable into truth-functions of them; as well as finite so that only finitely many elementary propositions are involved in each proposition and propositional tautologies take care of all truth-functional tautologies (including, e.g., valid formulas involving quantifiers and theorems of set theory). Such an elegant model of logic and the world can be helpful in different ways: as a basis for expansion to richer and more adequate models, as a means to get a hold on some central concepts of philosophy and their interrelations, etc.

However, W_1 does not treat this as merely a preliminary model, but as the true and complete model of the world. In particular, W_1 rejects the possibility of any metalanguage and metatheoretic considerations on the ground that they would go beyond the limit of language and cannot be 'said.' Some such idea seems to be implicitly suggested also in Russell's early conception of logic (in *PM* and before). Toward the end of his introduction to the *Tractatus*, Russell does propose the possibility of a 'hierarchy of languages' to which 'there may be no limit.' This points in the direction of the views of W_2 but of course the language-games are even more chaotic than Russell's idea of a hierarchy of languages.

In August 1919, W wrote to Russell to say that the main point of his book is the theory of what can be said and what can only be shown, 'which, I believe, is the cardinal problem of philosophy,' and 'to which the whole business of logical propositions is only a corollary.' W concludes his preface by saying, 'The second thing in which the value of this work consists is that how little is achieved when these problems [viz., the problems of philosophy] are solved.'

These observations support the impression that logic was W's tool (or even merely the necessary tool available to him) for philosophy which is mainly concerned with elaborating (or merely showing) his world picture. A major component of his world picture would seem to be the realm of the higher and the accompanying strong desire not to taint the purity of the higher by the ugly mixture of trying to say what cannot be said. 'Propositions can express nothing of what is higher [namely ethics and aesthetics which are one and the same]' (6.42). '*How* things are in the world is a matter of complete indifference for what is higher' (6.432). Granting to natural science the monopoly of saying all that can be said would seem to leave nothing for those not doing natural science to say. Talking and writing would have to serve for them different purposes than saying things. Those who are primarily interested in what can be said must put natural science at the center and those who are not interested in natural science must find something, other than trying to say things, to do. Therefore, it is not surprising that there are different responses to the *Tractatus* among those who take it seriously.

In his 'Mysticism and logic' (July 1914) Russell speaks of developing a world picture by the union and conflict of the two different human impulses toward mysticism and science (logic). The scientific impulse reigns quite unchecked in Hume's work, 'while in Blake a strong hostility to science coexists with profound mystic insight.' Heraclitus and Plato are offered as examples to illustrate the possibility of a very intimate blending of the two impulses in the work of a philosopher. While the desire to attain subjective depth would seem to strengthen the impulse toward mysticism, the desire to be objective and to share and communicate with others would seem to favor the impulse toward logic.

The complete severance of thought and will, of knowledge and virtue, and the refusal to mix or even connect them, are striking in W_1. The whole realm of practical activities is left out of the comprehensive philosophy of W_1. Even mysticism takes on a purified form, concentrated, so to say, at one point.

> 6.44 It is not *how* things are in the world that is mystical, but *that* it exists.
>
> 6.45 Feeling the world as a limited whole—it is this that is mystical.

These statements seem to be connected with the section (5.6) on solipsism, which appears to me to depend on an ambiguity. There is a sense in which solipsism has to be true (as a 'tautology'): everything I think, I do, I feel, etc., must all be in some sense a part of *me*. But, for one thing, as emphasized by Freud, there are different senses of me (the self). More, the conception of self is highly complex so that the self is integrated into the world (including other persons) in an 'organic' manner, and is indeed sometimes said to be the sum total of its social relations.

For W_1 the (philosophical) self shrinks to a point and becomes the limit of the world (5.64 and 5.641); good or bad acts of will can only alter the limits of the world (6.43). [Or, rather, the limits of the world can only be altered by such acts.] Presumably the happy person is one of good acts of will and sees 'the world aright' (6.43 and 6.54). The ethical relevance of the book is presumably, and I confess that I find this mysterious, that the transcending of its propositions makes one see the world aright and happy and have good acts of will (6.54).

Presumably the book tries to get at the mystical by helping to show (to make manifest) what cannot be said.

> 6.522 There are, indeed, things that cannot be put into words. They *make themselves manifest*. They are what is mystical.

In 1919, W wrote to Ficker about the more important 'unwritten second half' of the book. 'For the Ethical is delimited from within, as it were, by my book. . . . All of that which *many* are *babbling* today, I have defined in my book by remaining silent about it' (Luckhardt, pp. 94–95). Hence, there is no doubt that W intended to convey a moral message by his book. In addition, W speaks elsewhere of 'the darkness of this time' (*PI*, foreword) and the spirit of his work being 'different from the one which informs the vast stream of European and American civilization in which all of us stand' (*Philosophical Grammar*, p. 7). His comments on Ramsey (1931, *CV*) indicate a difference between their outlooks which may be construed as distinguishing Ramsey as an 'insider' from himself as an 'outsider.'

My own Chinese background must have conditioned me in the direction of a preference for unity (over separation), and a unity that puts everyday concerns at the center. For this reason, I find it hard to achieve a (sympathetic) understanding of the sharp separation (of fact and value) and especially the vanishing mystical in W_1; I can attain an unsympathetic understanding of the separation on account of my exposure to science but the importance of the vanishing mystical for ethics is completely mysterious to me. To my way of thinking, ethics is entirely worldly and the 'existence of the world' plays no part in ethics at all, except as a remote precondition we rightly forget in ethical considerations and in the study of ethics.

For these reasons and for the reason that I find the spirit of W_2 less remote, I shall make no attempt to speculate (more) on the 'unwritten half' of W_1. It seems unquestionable that W consistently resists the idolatry of science and (the impure) technology, not sparing the idolization of the spirit of the 'purest' fundamental science. This he does in W_1, by arguing that it leaves 'the higher' untouched; in W_2, by a kind of 'linguistic naturalism' that stresses the anthropocentric component shared by our beliefs and knowledge from the religious to the mathematical, aiming at a levelling effect that denies mathematics and fundamental science a privileged or 'qualitatively' different place on the scale of universality and objectivity. In particular, W_2 also resists and argues against the temptation to make the study of language-games 'scientific.'

I am limiting my considerations of W_1 primarily to the elegant model of logic, language, and the world, as developed in the 'written half' of W's book.

10. The postulates of the Tractatus

Once such an elegant picture of language (and thought) and the world is obtained, it is to be expected that most remarkable consequences can be drawn. A more fascinating question today is perhaps how any-body could have arrived confidently at such a simple picture and whether less simple pictures can be found that will be reasonably adequate to less ambitious but still quite exciting applications. It is for this dual purpose that an examination of the basic postulates, which are either implicit or based on defective arguments, seems in order. This also appears to be the right context to mention Russell's related ideas and their presumed influence on the book.

The most convenient place to begin is the two mistakes mentioned by W in his lectures (1932), as reported by Moore (1955, pp. 1–4). They may be called the principle of atomicity (following Russell) or definiteness and the principle of finiteness, of which much has been written on the former but, surprisingly, little on the latter. It appears that once we reject the second principle and take advantage of the infinite, we can effectively increase the range of what we can make definite, as is shown by most of the conspicuous applications of mathematics. Whether or how much a rejection of the first principle can compensate for the restrictions imposed by the second principle seems less clear, although such a combination appears not uncongenial to the spirit of W_2 which rejects definiteness but extends finiteness, in recognizing its difference from the infinite, only reluctantly to the potentially infinite, preferably only as a *façon de parler*.

T1. The principle of atomicity.

T1.1. Every statement about complexes can be resolved into a statement about their constituents and into the propositions that describe the complexes completely (2.0201).

T1.2. The elementary propositions are mutually independent (4.211, 5.134 and 5.131).

The influence of Russell's theory of descriptions is obvious and has often been mentioned. 'It was Russell who performed the service of showing that the apparent logical form of a proposition need not be its real one' (4.0031). Some (other) remarks by Russell also appear relevant to T1. 'Thus in every proposition we can apprehend,' says he in his paper on denoting (Lackey, p. 119), 'all the constituents are really entities with which we have immediate acquaintance.' In 'Insolubilia' he proposes to construct a theory in which quantifiers, descriptive phrases, and sets all are merely a *façon de parler* (ibid., p. 206).

We have an obvious contrast between the unanalyzable (the result of a final or ultimate analysis) and the unanalyzed (unanalyzable in a given context). For example, T1.1 seems natural when we think of formal systems in mathematics where we do begin with (syntactically) elementary propositions such as 'x is between y and z' in geometry. But T1.2 is not satisfied. Indeed, it is hard to think of even artificial and simple examples of language which would satisfy both parts of T1. Leibniz does compare conceptual analysis with the unique decomposition of numbers into their prime factors. In elementary probability theory, one considers the combination of the probabilities of independent events (such as the probability of two dice both with six dots facing upwards); I would like to conjecture that historically this was the main inspiration for T1.2. There is also the slightly different matter of the chemical analysis of compounds. At any rate, T1.2 is the first postulate W came to reject immediately after he had returned to philosophy in 1929 (in his lecture on 'logical form'). For example, statements about temperature can more plausibly be independent from those about color and hardness. But two statements about the temperature at the same time and place (say, the number of degrees) cannot be independent.

The relative transparency of formal systems would seem to suggest that T1.1 alone, if satisfied by a language, already does a lot of work; this may, however, have something to do with the fact that in such cases the elementary propositions, though not satisfying T1.2, are rather homogeneous and, therefore, surveyable. Of course if T1.2 can be made true, things become very elegant and its not being true invites us to go deeper in order to get to the bottom. But it remains puzzling what W had in mind when he believed T1.2. (One conjecture, as I mentioned a moment ago, is a wish to generalize the idea of independent events in the calculation of probabilities.) Another conspicuous aspect of the elementary propositions is the bypassing of the oldest central problem of philosophy: the one and the many. We are accustomed to the idea that universals play a crucial role in propositions, both for knowledge and for communication. Since W's objects lack the distinction, they have to be some neutral stuff out of which we can recover particulars and universals. In a careful study of the reasons for adopting T1.2, Pears (1981) comes to the conclusion that T1.2 is plausible if all objects are simple particulars. 'But universals are more intractable.' Hence, it seems that the two puzzles are intimately connected. In my opinion, a reasonable concept of logic has to include universals in some manner and also forego T1.2.

The postulate T1.1 is given as a comment on 2.02: objects are simple. It seems to get a process of reduction started by reducing the distance between the complexes and the (simple) objects. It seems to say that any proposition can be 'resolved into' a proposition and a set of propositions describing the complexes completely, which all presumably no longer contain the original complexes. Hence, it would seem to follow that as the process is continued, the original proposition will eventually be resolved into a set of sets of . . . sets of propositions each of which contains only concatenations of names (elementary propositions) and logical constants. If a set of propositions is taken as the conjunction of all the propositions in the set, then we can make each set into one proposition made up from elementary propositions and logical constants. The range of such propositions of course depends on what we choose to be the (simple) objects and the logical constants.

This contrived interpretation of T1.1 attempts to bring it closer to the related 4.221 and make both of them a little more explicit:

> 4.221 It is obvious that the analysis of propositions must bring us to elementary propositions which consist of names in immediate combination.

Possibly there are a smoother connection between the two formulations and a better explanation of them in W's book which could be discovered. The effort here is to separate T1.1 from the principles of finiteness and extensionality, while they may all be parts of differently merged ideas of W's. There are alternative perspectives in uncovering the axioms or postulates of W_1, taking it as one variant of what Russell aptly calls 'logical atomism'; one elegant set consists of the axioms X, Y, and Z in Pears 1971. At any rate, 4.221 only gets, in my interpretation, more specific contents as W makes more specific his choice of the logical constants, the objects, and their interpretations.

What I call the principle of finiteness selects a particular interpretation of the quantifiers which reduces them to the ordinary truth-functions. Extensionality rules out remnants of the intensional from the basic apparatus of what W takes to be the objects and the logical constants; just as T1.2 seems implicitly to leave no room for universals, the principle of extensionality explicitly excludes intensional objects and logical constants. Hence, to arrive at the strong interpretation of W's strong proposition 5, viz., 'a proposition is a [finite] truth-function of [extensional] elementary propositions,' we need, besides the principles of finiteness and extensionality, also an unannounced restriction of logic [and logical constants] to [those of] what is known as elementary logic or the first order logic.

The second mistake of W_1, as reported by Moore, concerns the treatment of quantifiers. As I understand the exposition, the stated mistake is, first of all, taking intensional contexts (using defining properties) as extensional (by enumeration): he had supposed that (x)Fx is the conjunction (logical product) of the propositions which are values of Fx and (hence) a 'truth function' of them. Hence, this is primarily a criticism of his earlier principle of extensionality. In addition, W seems to make a different point: that Fa&Fb&Fc . . . is a conjunction only in the finite case when the dots are what he called 'dots of laziness,' and he had failed to see that in the infinite case 'the whole expression cannot be replaced by an enumeration.' One might ask why W brought in the infinite case in addition to his denial of the earlier extensional reading of the quantifiers. One interpretation is that, according to W in 1932, a quantifier with an infinite range can never be taken extensionally. However that may be, W_1 certainly takes finite truth-functions as sufficient and considers them exclusively, thereby attaining a surprisingly simple picture of logic and logically true propositions (viz., the tautologies in the exact and restricted sense of the propositional calculus). Hence, it seems clear that W_1 assumes a postulate of finiteness.

> T2 The principle of finiteness. We can treat the finite and the infinite cases in the same way. Hence, it is sufficient to consider the finite case. [Whether the world (or the number of objects) is finite or infinite makes no difference to logic and to language.]

This principle is rather surprising, since W was much interested in the philosophy of mathematics, in which, as he was undoubtedly aware, the concept of infinity is of central importance. T2 would seem to cut through all the difficult issues about infinity. It is not that W_1 excludes infinity but rather that it is thought to present no new or additional problems.

> 4.2211 Even if the world is infinitely complex, so that every fact contains infinitely many elementary facts and every elementary fact is composed of infinitely many objects, there would still have to be objects and elementary facts.

Whether the world is infinite is taken to be a contingent matter and indifferent to logic, so that the 'axiom of infinity' cannot be a part of logic (5.535). If, as I have suggested, we include sets among the objects, then it becomes a logical truth that there are infinitely many objects. Indeed, the logical concept of set is, according to the view I subscribe to, an evolving one permitting different kinds of infinity.

If we adopt T2, it is, heuristically, only necessary to take finite domains as universes of discourse, since they are easier to fully conceptualize and since what are true for them are, by T2, true generally (i.e., also for infinite domains). In that case many issues change character and a number of propositions in W_1 become easier to interpret. I have already mentioned the dispensability of quantifiers in W_1. Set theory also gets trivialized with the help of the principle of extensionality. Make the simplifying assumption that there are only finitely many individuals (objects); to shorten the exposition, let there be three objects a, b, and c. Some combinations of them are elementary facts: a situation we may disregard in making up a set theory. There are only eight possible sets of them: the empty set 0, the three unit sets, the three pairs, and the set of all individuals. The phrases describing these sets can be shown to be 'incomplete symbols,' eliminable in all the basic contexts. The technical details of this observation may be illustrated briefly.

> For all y, Gy if and only if Ga and Gb and Gc.
> For all sets X of individuals, FX if and only if F0 and F(a) and . . . and F(a,b,c) (the conjunction of the eight propositions, one for each set).
> $x \in (a,b)$ if and only if $x = a$ or $x = b$.
> $X = (a,b)$ if and only if: for all y, $y \in X$ if and only if $y \in (a,b)$. [The variable X can be eliminated as before when it gets quantified.]

The idea is the familiar observation that for a fixed finite collection of objects, statements containing set constants and variables can all be reduced to more primitive statements no longer containing them. The process can be repeated somewhat mechanically to sets of sets, their sets, etc., in the manner of what is known as the simple theory of types, with all notations for higher types eliminable in context. In this manner, we arrive at a completion of Russell's project, mentioned previously (the one put forward in 'Insolubilia'), of eliminating, besides descriptions, also quantifiers and classes (as merely a *façon de parler*). In particular, the axiom of reducibility is true (when there are only finitely many individuals) and, by T2, can be taken as true for the infinite case as well; it is, therefore, a (true) logical proposition, contrary to 6.1232 and 6.1233. [This is indeed pretty much the course taken by Ramsey in 1925.] Moreover, the superfluity of classes (6.031) is seen to be true for quite different reasons than W's.

It appears clear that one can distinguish two different ideas in W_1: T2 and the idea that logically true propositions must be true independently of whether the world is finite or infinite. While T2 was implicitly assumed (by an oversight), the other idea was explicitly recognized. Hence, when there is a conflict, T2 yields. This is clear in the case of the axiom of infinity, which is false in a finite world but cannot be said to be generally false (or true) by an appeal to T2. Rather, the second idea shows that it cannot be a proposition of logic (according to W_1, as argued in 5.535).

T3. The principle of extensionality.

5.54 In the general propositional form propositions occur in other propositions only as bases of truth-operations.

I shall omit any discussion of this principle which is familiar and, for example, important for the introduction to the second edition of *PM*.

I merely wish to conclude that, once the three principles are accepted, we certainly have a very simple theory of all propositions. If we add the few assertions linking propositions to thoughts and facts, we soon arrive at a rather small set of 'axioms' from which the majority of assertions in the *Tractatus* would seem to follow as consequences. I have not stopped to examine the matter, but intuitively the three postulates certainly appear to be the strongest and most dubitable initial assumptions among all the assertions in the book. I am not sure whether it will be worth while to begin with the three postulates and look to see what minimal extensions of them will yield all or nearly all the assertions of the book. It appears that T3 eliminates psychology, T2 trivializes or makes mathematics impossible, and T1 renders it impossible to understand how we could ever get physics as we know it or, indeed, how we can actually attain any knowledge to speak of.

It may be amusing to compare 6.54, which immediately precedes the famous last sentence (7) of the *Tractatus*, with one sentence from the *Diamond Sutra* (pointed out to me by Yunzeng Wu). The sentence consists of sixteen characters only in the Chinese version:

The dharma I am preaching is analogous to a raft [which is to be discarded after use]; even the dharma can be discarded, a fortiori the nondharma.

This appears to say in fewer words the same thing as 6.54, even though the *Tractatus* is famous for its brevity. To condense 6.54 somewhat, I may paraphrase it as follows: 'My propositions' should be recognized 'as nonsensical' and used 'as steps—to climb up beyond them'; 'anyone who understands me' must 'throw away the ladder after he has climbed up it.' 'He must transcend these propositions, and then he will see the world aright.' Indeed, the message of silence is central to Chan (or Zen) Buddhism, which arose as a combination of Taoism and Buddhism. The Taoists explain Tao by saying what it is not, much as W delimits the Ethical 'from within.'

Russell's contrast of logic with mysticism overlaps with my discussion of nothing-but and something-more in section 11.5. W's concept of the mystical seems more concrete than related traditional ideals of the unattainable limit, such as Plato's Idea of the Good, Aristotle's God thinking on thinking, the concepts of Tao, Spinoza's intellectual love of God. etc.

Chapter 3

From Vienna 1925 to America 1984

I have had much exposure to 'analytic philosophy' (or rather 'analytic empiricism,' to be less misleading), yet all along, partly because of other influences in my development (such as my Chinese background), I have felt uncomfortable about it, at least in the form as it is commonly practiced. Hence, in order to clarify my own indefinite preoccupations, it may be of help to reflect on the strength and weakness of this type of approach from my viewpoint. In particular, the sort of logic most familiar to me plays an important part in the move from Russell (and Frege) to Carnap and especially to Quine's *Aufhebung* of certain aspects of Russell and Carnap. On account of this 'privileged access' on my part and the central place of Russell, Carnap, and Quine, it seems appropriate that I should center my reflections on the similarities and differences between these philosophers. Since my main interest is in broader issues, some attention to larger features of this general trend appears also in order.

What constitutes analytic philosophy is not entirely definite but, for example, G. E. Moore, Russell, Wittgenstein, Ramsey, Carnap, Reichenbach, Ryle, Austin, Waismann, and probably also Broad and C. I. Lewis, as well as many living Anglo-American philosophers, all are included among analytic philosophers. Compared with other current trends, it puts more emphasis on objectivity (or universality) and precision (formal or otherwise).

The ambiguous label of analytic philosophy suggests several alternative meanings, two of which I have distinguished in the Introduction. There is also an intermediate sense which is broader than what I call 'analytic empiricism' but remains identified with the indeterminate range of the dominant factions of English and American philosophy in this century. My explicit concern is with analytic empiricism, which occupies a central place within this range. This middle range implies principally certain methodological components such as the emphasis on language (ordinary or artificial), logic (mathematical logic or 'logical analysis'), and half the time a special attention to mathematics and physics. In the doctrinal aspect, it is primarily positivistic and empiristic, sometimes with a sympathy for pragmatism and behaviorism. Generally it contains a sharp separation from history (including the history of philosophy) as well as art and literature. The concept of analysis is rather indefinite and can take many different forms much like the concepts of clarity and precision; it seems reasonable to agree that analysis plays an important part in most philosophies anyway.

Moore and Russell led a revolt against Hegelism and idealism (idealism, not ideal-ism) in England around the turn of the century. In the process, Moore brought in an emphasis on ordinary language and Russell gradually introduced mathematical logic (as the central tool) plus mathematics and physics (as important data and as possibly providing solutions to some philosophical problems). Wittgenstein intruded with his powerful *Tractatus* which (completed in 1918 and first published in 1921) influenced Russell's conception of logic and mathematics as well as, more conspicuously, the doctrines of the logical positivists, who were also successors of Mach and excited by the emergence of relativistic and quantum physics. A parallel development was introduced by C. I. Lewis (*Mind and the World-Order*, 1929) in America, constructed from a blending of his interests in logic, pragmatism, and Kant's work.

Carnap made a careful study of Frege's and Russell's logic and, at a later date, together with the Vienna Circle, the *Tractatus*. He came up with quite exact constructions and formulations of large theses in his phenomenalistic *Aufbau* (1928) and in his optimistic *Logical Syntax* (1934). The narrow beginnings of sense data and syntax held for many people a great fascination on account of their apparent certainty and tangible reliability. Within a decade or so, the need to liberalize empiricism and add semantics to syntax was realized gradually by Carnap and a few of his comrades. And the clean sharpness of the original program was lost. Then came Quine's famous article on 'Two dogmas' (1951) which has often been taken to be the occasion for the realization that there is something more fundamentally wrong about the original program, not reparable by the remedy of liberalizing the basic viewpoint. Let me begin with a brief review of the Vienna Circle and its influences in America (adding also a few words about C. I. Lewis).

11. The Vienna Circle and its place in American philosophy

11.1. The Vienna Circle

The Vienna (or Schlick) Circle was founded by Moritz Schlick (1882–1936) in 1925; it was almost wholly dispersed by 1938 when the Germans invaded Austria. Gradually the influences spread out and the center of activity shifted briefly to England and especially to America.

Schlick was trained as a physicist but decided to pursue an academic career in philosophy, having exceptionally wide philosophical interests which included ethics and aesthetics. He published in 1918 his *Allgemeine Erkenntnislehre* (revised edition, 1925) in which he anticipated Wittgenstein in rejecting Kant's view that there could be synthetic a priori truths and in holding that all true a priori propositions, including those of pure mathematics, were analytic. This book contains the germs of many of the more elaborate developments of the Circle later on. One influential idea in this book is the expounding of the view that axioms serve as implicit 'definitions' of the concepts contained in them.

In 1922 he moved from Kiel to Vienna to occupy a chair in the history and philosophy of the inductive sciences which had initially been created in 1895 to attract Ernst Mach from Prague. Soon after Hans Hahn gave a lecture on the newly published *Tractatus* which impressed Schlick and others. Gradually a small group of people, who shared a common interest in, and a similar approach to, a set of general problems, gathered around the attractive personality of Schlick. They met regularly to discuss these problems and formed a sort of club which evolved into a more formal organization over the years. In 1926, Carnap moved to Vienna and became an active member of the group.

From outside, the members, known as the logical positivists (or logical empiricists), appear as a homogeneous group. Yet it contained a number of independent minds with a spectrum of divergent views. For many outsiders, Ayer's *Language, Truth and Logic* (1936), his first and best-known book, is a kind of manifesto of the Circle. The real manifesto appeared in 1929 with the title *Wissenschaftliche Weltauffassung, der Wiener Kreis* (for a brief summary of this and some historical material of the whole movement, see Ayer's introduction to *Logical Positivism*, 1959). The pamphlet was signed by R. Carnap, O. Neurath, and H. Hahn, but written chiefly by Neurath. They claim to be developing the Viennese tradition of E. Mach, L. Boltzmann, and F. Brentano, who flourished around the turn of the century.

In the appendix to the manifesto the membership of the Circle is listed. There are fourteen names: Schlick, Neurath, Hahn, Gödel, Carnap, Waismann, Carl Menger, Philipp Frank, Herbert Feigl, Gustav Bergmann, Victor Kraft, Marcel Natkin, Theodor Radakovic, and Olga Hahn-Neurath, who was Neurath's second wife and Hahn's sister. Ten persons were listed as sympathizers, including Hans Reichenbach and Kurt Grelling in Berlin, E. Kaila in Finland, and F. P. Ramsey in England. Einstein, Russell, and Wittgenstein were mentioned as the three 'leading representatives of the scientific world conception.' The inclusion of Gödel in the list is a little misleading. Gödel was very fond of Hahn and Schlick, and did attend a number of meetings of the Circle; but he did not find the views of the Circle congenial. In 1976 he said that he had never been a positivist but had accepted only some of their theses even at that time. Later on, he moved further and further away from them.

What is of much significance is their list of names whom they regard as their main precursors.

> (a) Empiricists and positivists: Hume, the philosophers of the enlightenment, Comte, J. S. Mill, Avenarius, Mach.
> (b) Philosophers of science: Helmholtz, Riemann, Mach, Poincaré, Enriques, Duhem, Boltzmann, Einstein.
> (c) Pure and applied logicians: Leibniz, Peano, Frege, Schröder, Russell, Whitehead, Wittgenstein.
> (d) Axiomatists: Pasch, Peano, Vailati, Pieri, Hilbert.
> (e) Moralists and sociologists of a positivistic temper: Epicurus, Hume, Bentham, J. S. Mill, Comte, Spencer, Feuerbach, Marx, Müller-Lyer, Popper-Lynkeus, the elder Carl Menger.

How is one to arrive at a coherent body of theory that would somehow contain the correct and relevant part of the contributions of each of these men to the heading(s) under which he is listed? How would one reconcile, for instance, Marx with Bentham? Perhaps the list is the union of separate lists proposed by members of the Circle. The five headings do indicate the range of the Circle's concern and aspirations. Heading (d) indicates the disproportionate emphasis on the axiomatic method, undoubtedly as a result of the desire to render implicit assumptions as explicit as possible. In the later development, heading (e) flourished the least.

Of his first book, Ayer says, 'Except in a few details, the thoughts which it expressed were not original. They were a blend of the positivism of the Vienna Circle, which I also ascribed to Wittgenstein, the reductive empiricism which I had taken from Hume and Russell, the analytical approach of Moore and his disciples, with a dash of C. I. Lewis's and Ramsey's pragmatism' (1977, p. 154). What Quine was at first so impressed with and then reacted against was a purer form of logical positivism largely as expounded by Carnap. But with the prevalence of the ambiguous concepts of logical analysis and philosophical analysis, the blending into a larger school of 'analytic philosophy' was irresistible after the war.

In 1949, H. Feigl and W. Sellars put out an influential *Readings in Philosophical Analysis* which signified the completion of such a merger. It is explained in the preface: 'The conception of philosophical analysis underlying our selections springs from two major traditions in recent thought, the Cambridge movement deriving from Moore and Russell, and the Logical Positivism of the Vienna Circle (Wittgenstein, Schlick,

Carnap) together with the Scientific Empiricism of the Berlin group (led by Reichenbach).' Apart from a few obvious names, the collection includes papers by Frege, C. D. Broad (3), C. I. Lewis (2), V. C. Aldrich (2), W. C. Kneale, K. Ajdukiewicz, C. J. Ducasse, F. Waismann, R. M. Chisholm, and C. A. Mace. Clearly the range envisaged is broader than what I call 'analytic empiricism.'

The publication of Wittgenstein's later views and the flourishing of the short-lived linguistic branch of analytic philosophy came later. This branch has something to do with the training in classics and the English tradition of distrusting generalizations and elevating common sense. Particular examples are multiplied and carefully dissected. It is empirical in the sense that Edmund Burke was a champion of empiricism.

In 1935, Roy Harrod sent Whitehead some of Ayer's writings to get his opinion on them. Whitehead consulted Quine. 'Quine can give an expert opinion. Also Quine and I have read the literature which you sent. We agree in our high opinion of it.' 'Ayer is obviously only a beginner in mathematical logic. As yet he shows no command over its techniques nor does he fully appreciate all the bearings of some of the discussions which have arisen' (Ayer 1977, p. 162). Since Ayer was and is not a logician, this comment seems to reflect a mixing of logic with philosophy or at least a view that a mastery of logic is necessary for the kind of philosophy Ayer aspired to do.

The more illuminating part of the letter reveals interesting aspects of Whitehead's attitude toward philosophy. 'I am not in my own person a Logical Positivist. The claims for it are overstated as is the case in all new movements, e.g., mathematics by the Pythagoreans. But I cannot imagine a greater blessing for English philosophical learning than the rise in Oxford of a vigorous young school of Logical Positivists. The assigning of the proper scope to their method, the discussion of the new problems which it raises or of the new light which it throws on old problems will revivify and reconstruct the presentation of the topics of philosophic thought which the new doctrine fails adequately to deal with. It will rescue the philosophy of the 20th century from repeating its complete failure in the 19th century, when history and science overwhelmed it—even theology deserted it' (p. 163). As usual, Whitehead's great sweep is impressive. Even in a somewhat negative way, the letter signifies the high hopes positivism stirred up in those days. We are now approaching the end of the century. I do not believe that Whitehead's larger prophecy is being realized.

11.2. Logical analysis and scientific philosophy
The two most favored subjects of the Vienna Circle are logic and physics. Logic is the tool for philosophy as, in Russell's words of 1914, math-

ematics is the tool for physics. Physics is the model of human knowledge and the primary area to be 'rationally reconstructed.' Given the attraction of logic and physics as autonomous fields of endeavor, the special attention paid to them by philosophers not unnaturally contains also a tendency to pull them away from philosophy.

The relation between logic and logical positivism is complex and deceptively misleading. For example, even though Gödel nominally belonged to the Vienna Circle and was very fond of Hahn and Schlick, he has been very emphatic in dissociating himself from the philosophical doctrines of the school. Once he remarked, not quite seriously, that Carnap deliberately misapplied logic in order to discredit logic (among philosophers). If we consider (mathematical) logic over the period from 1879 to 1931, we can find a common preoccupation with philosophy in one way or another. Yet there is a distinction between what might be called the substantive aspect (represented by Cantor, Hilbert, and Gödel) and the instrumental (to philosophy) aspect (represented by Frege, Russell, and Carnap). Historical force has a tendency to polarize such differences and to favor an autonomous development. Hence, there is the conspicuous phenomenon of logic gradually withdrawing itself from philosophy and assimilating itself to mathematics. As a result, philosophers have more and more lost touch with serious logic and logicians have become less and less concerned with philosophy and philosophical motivations of their technical work. The rare exception of Gödel has given some philosophical guidance to technical research on the continuum hypothesis and on the search for new axioms in set theory. He argues persuasively that his technical results had derived great benefits from his philosophical views. But his broader influence in philosophy has been rather slight so far.

Despite the close alliance between Carnap and Reichenbach, Reichenbach's conception of scientific philosophy is rather different from Carnap's. He lays less emphasis on formal precision and more on an adequate knowledge of the sciences (mostly physics in his own case) over which one philosophizes or makes 'logical analysis.' Russell is probably more sympathetic to Reichenbach than to Carnap. In 1949, Russell observed 'that logical positivism could become a new variety of scholasticism and, by concerning itself unduly with linguistics, could forget the relation to the facts that make an assertion true.' This would represent the 'danger of a technique that conceals problems instead of helping to resolve them' (Russell 1949).

There is a narrower polarization of the scientific half and the philosophical half of scientific philosophy similar to some extent to the separation of logic from positivism. There are, on the one hand, those who do not enter into physics (say) in any depth but confine their consideration to more general aspects of the methodology and philosophy of science: the nature of causal law, variants of Hume's problem of induction, counterfactual conditionals, possible worlds, convention, confirmation, etc. On the other hand, there has gradually emerged a smaller group of philosophers who have a good command of physics or mathematics (particularly the more substantial part of logic) and have undertaken limited but deeper conceptual analysis. They are not committed to positivism or empiricism as they are currently construed; in fact, more often than not they are opposed to these restrictive conceptions. The names which come to my mind are Howard Stein, Adolf Grünbaum, Abner Shimony, John Earman, David Malament, Charles Parsons, and Leslie Tharp. I am sure there are quite a few more in this category.

In the light of these more recent developments, it is tempting to ask what the original visions of Russell and Reichenbach were, and, in particular, what sort of thing they had in mind in recommending 'logical analysis' so strongly. A specially difficult question is, what distinguishes the logical analysis of physics or biology by a philosopher from that by a physicist or biologist who has, moreover, a better chance of obtaining significant new results?

Russell concludes his *History of Western Philosophy* (1946) with a chapter on 'the philosophy of logical analysis,' calling it a 'philosophical school of which I am a member.' (A critic commented that he had performed the remarkable achievement of being even more unfair to his own work than he was to Kant's [Wood 1957, p. 46].) The emphasis is on 'scientific truthfulness' and on achievements 'as solid as those of men of science.' Rereading this chapter so many years later, one cannot help being surprised by the great gap between the results listed and the vast implications attached to them. For example, Russell's own theory of descriptions is said to 'clear up two millennia of muddle-headedness about "existence," beginning with Plato's *Theaetetus.*' Frege's definition of number (probably combined with the theory of descriptions) is said to yield the result of demystifying mathematical knowledge: 'It is all of the same nature as the "great truth" that there are three feet in a yard.' These observations undoubtedly illustrate the original excitement over the great philosophical promises of logical analysis.

Three other areas are listed by Russell as having 'supplied material for the philosophy of logical analysis': infinite numbers, the theory of relativity, and quantum mechanics. Cantor's set theory is apparently regarded as a result of logical analysis (of infinity and infinite numbers). Hence, we come upon an ambiguity between using logical analysis to create new mathematics or physics and to philosophize over existing mathematics or physics. Ideally the two tasks could coincide or greatly overlap. In practice, however, those who are labelled philosophers of mathematics or physics usually do not produce significant new scientific results, certainly for the period since such labels came into common use and *qua* philosophers. For instance, Cantor's own philosophical writings were obscure and strange. We have by now indeed an extensive and respectable philosophical literature on set theory, the theory of relativity, and quantum mechanics. But it is quite different in kind from Cantor's more definite construction of set theory. Russell probably had partly in mind also the possibility of logical analysis leading to such spectacular advances. For example, on the one and only occasion I met Russell (on February 16, 1956, at his London flat), he mentioned Reichenbach's work on quantum mechanics and a new (three-valued) logic as a promising venture.

In a different direction, I have mentioned Gödel's view that his philosophical position was important for scientific discoveries. Einstein recognizes the importance of epistemology for science: 'Science without epistemology is—insofar as it is thinkable at all—primitive and muddled.' Then he goes on to say, 'But the external conditions, which are set for him [the scientist] by the facts of experience, do not permit him to let himself be too much restricted in the construction of his conceptual world by the adherence to an epistemological system. He therefore must appear to the systematic epistemologist as a type of unscrupulous opportunist' (Schilpp 1949, p. 684). This suggests the task of looking for an epistemology that is not 'systematic' in his sense.

11.3. Reichenbach and philosophy as philosophy of physics
In 1951, Reichenbach published a critical history of philosophy contrasting (the roots of) speculative philosophy with (the results of) scientific philosophy. The idea is that since speculative philosophy is a mistake, the chief task is to determine the sources or roots which are behind the misguided endeavor. In that sense those who are disappointed in 'scientific philosophy' may also wish to trace its roots. In his 'Philosophy in America today' (see Rorty 1982), Rorty examines the book in light of the development of philosophy in America over the past thirty years. I shall consider the two works together.

There are two related but distinct issues on the place of the Vienna Circle in the history of philosophy. Rorty is concerned primarily with its relation to the more concrete historical question of the dominant trends in American philosophy departments over the past thirty years. My own chief concern is in the more idealized question of searching for feasible approaches to philosophy which may offer a moderately structured and comprehensive framework in a vastly different world (say, from that around 1800) of 'information explosion' and a mass of disharmonious experience with diverse social experiments.

According to Reichenbach, the speculative philosopher 'has too often sacrificed truth to the desire to give answers, and clarity to the temptation of speaking in pictures; and his language has lacked the precision which is the scientist's compass in escaping the reefs of error' (p. viii). Moreover, in his psychological drive to search for generality, certainty, and moral directives, the speculative philosopher offers unclear and unjustified answers to questions not ripe for solution yet, and parades his answers as the 'ultimate truth.'

I agree with Reichenbach that by now we are clear on the matter of ultimate truth. Just as in the natural sciences and even more obviously in philosophy, we can only strive for truth or belief relative to what we know. Moreover, I would also prefer that Hegel had chosen to be more candid in separating a little more clearly his impressive perception of history from his leap to a more dubious grand system full of obscurities, evasions, and distortions. Within Reichenbach's broad category of rationalists, which includes not only the usual Descartes, Spinoza, Leibniz, but also Plato, Kant, and much of Aristotle, he is most sympathetic to Kant. If we take away Kant's claim to ultimate truth and correct Kant's class and provincial prejudices (elaborated on p. 61 of his book), Reichenbach's account of Kant's philosophy seems to me to present a type of pursuit which remains one good model of what philosophy can be relative to one's historical period. The difficult crucial question is rather whether a reasonable counterpart of that type of work is still possible two hundred years later.

Of Reichenbach's account of scientific philosophy I believe we are now in a position to offer some more definite judgments. If philosophy is content with playing the handmaiden to natural science, I think it is an open question whether it may not be more satisfying for philosophy and philosophers with different orientations to play the handmaiden to literature, to historical studies, etc. This question cannot be answered by the more explicit part of Reichenbach's account of the relation between science and philosophy which seems to make out philosophy to be no more than a subservient maid and, as we now see more clearly, an unappreciated and probably unnecessary one at that.

It is the less explicit part of his account which hints at a grander role for philosophy, namely, that of creating a unification and reconstruction of science on a sounder basis. This aspiration is, however, based on the familiar 'dogmas' of the Vienna Circle supplemented in the case of Reichenbach with a stronger emphasis on inductive and probability logic. According to Rorty (1982, p. 211), these positivist doctrines were, in the intervening thirty years, dismantled or 'deconstructed' by 'Wittgenstein, Quine, Sellars, and Kuhn.' This conclusion undoubtedly is in the context of professional philosophers and not that of philosophically minded scientists. Even in 1951 or before, neither Einstein, nor Gödel, nor W. Pauli, nor John von Neumann set much store by such an approach to science and its philosophy.

It is Reichenbach's more explicit account that suggests a less ambitious but more dependable kind of work which, by its very nature, is not rousing enough to achieve or retain dominance over professional philosophers. 'Just as the new philosophy originated as a by-product of scientific research, the men who made it were hardly philosophers in the professional sense. They were mathematicians, physicists, biologists, or psychologists.' 'It was not until our generation that a new class of philosophers arose, who were trained in the technique of the sciences, including mathematics, and who concentrated on philosophical analysis. These men saw that a new distribution of work was indispensable, that scientific research does not leave a man time enough to do the work of logical analysis, and that conversely logical analysis demands a concentration which does not leave time for scientific work—a concentration which because of its aiming at clarification rather than discovery may even impede scientific productivity. The professional philosopher of science is the product of this development' (p. 123). It is strange indeed that *time* should be the decisive factor!

Philosophy is or should be supplanted by scientific philosophy which, moreover, according to this passage, is nothing but philosophy of (natural) science. Out of the whole range of human experience, why should philosophy confine its attention to science? One reply seems circular and worse: only so can philosophy achieve scientific knowledge. Why should philosophy aim only at scientific knowledge? More, what is to assure us that philosophical analysis would yield scientific knowledge? In part there is an equivocation: all (real) knowledge is science, the only (real) science is natural science, and most of the time the only (real) natural science is mathematical (or exact) science, namely, physics and mathematics.

Of course much more is involved. It is thought that the basic problems in traditional philosophy are finally answered by the recent development of natural science and that the philosopher's task now is to uncover and crystallize these answers by philosophical analysis. This idea seems to be behind Reichenbach's talk of 'results' without due emphasis on their provisional character. This implied position is unscientific in itself, seeing that natural science, as the scientists stress, has not said the last word even on the questions of its immediate concern, much less on whatever philosophical problems that are related closely to existing results in natural science. There is also a bad circularity in the implication that only those philosophical problems supposed to have been solved by natural science are the real philosophical problems.

On another level there is a form of reductionism lurking barely below the surface: given our ignorance on so many fronts we had better keep quiet on most things and wait till the scientific method has conquered whatever domains we now have a psychological need to speak about (and, worse, where we now have a practical need to act and make choices and decisions). In these 'yet' unconquered areas there is typically the ambiguous appeal to resort to 'common sense' which may not be so universally common and, moreover, need not be more reliable than, for instance, what Reichenbach calls 'rationalistic' (in contrast to 'rational,' p. 31) opinions. I suppose the issue comes back to asking Reichenbach to give a clearer delineation of 'the scientific method' (a very indefinite concept indeed) and its place in rational thinking.

A practical matter more directly related to American professional philosophy today is the place of the philosophy of science in the larger universities. It experiences competition from the history of science and can benefit intellectually from a closer contact with the latter. In view of the exciting development in biology over the last thirty years or so, it is gratifying to see that philosophy of biology has been a rapidly growing field in recent years. (For example, the distinction between the 'normal' and the 'pathological' appears to straddle fact and value, as well as the natural and human sciences.) It seems difficult to understand how a philosopher in Reichenbach's sense who is thoroughly at home in a branch of science can resist the temptation to become a practicing scientist. One reason may be a distaste for the rapid changes in science and, in many cases, the necessity to work in a group. Another reason may be a loyalty to philosophy in the sense of a preference for larger perspectives. A longer-term influence of Reichenbach and what he represents is perhaps the phenomenon that for many years a slot has often been reserved for a philosopher of science in the larger departments. (By the way, just to illustrate the debilitating effect of specialization on philosophy, I may point out that Reichenbach's chapter on modern logic is surprisingly hackneyed and ill-informed.)

11.4. Philosophy in America today

Rorty's review of American professional philosophy 1951–1981 is highly stimulating. I expect and hope that there will be responses to his viewpoint. To the extent I am familiar with the contemporary scene, his portrayal of it (though not his perspective and predictions) agrees with my vague impressions. According to Rorty, the traditional image of the philosopher as the scholar cum sage gave way to the image of the scientist at large in the early 1950s, as leaders of the Vienna school got established in leading philosophy departments. By 1960 a new sort of graduate education was entrenched: logic went up, history of philosophy went down. 'Due to Sputnik and the baby boom, the 60s and the early 70s also happened to be the period in which most living American Ph.D.'s in philosophy were educated.' As a result, a substantial majority of today's teachers of philosophy in America were brought up on something like Reichenbach's version of philosophy and the history of philosophy. But things turned out quite differently from initial expectations: instead of more cooperation and more agreement on results, problems and concepts have dispersed in all directions and evaporated, only to have the same process repeated again. What remains as a common standard is the elusive concept of philosophical ability which primarily means the skill for argumentation. Hence, a new image of the philosopher has emerged as the lawyer cum sophist. 'There is no more consensus about the problems and methods of philosophy in America today than there was in Germany in 1920' (p. 216).

Rorty looks back to the early 1950s as 'a simpler, brighter, vanished world.' This may have something to do with the fact he was studying with Carnap in 1951, before 'Oxford philosophy' intruded. He states that in the fifteen years after 1951, we saw the rise and fall of 'Oxford philosophy.' C. I. Lewis was deploring the unappealing fashions and fads then (see next subsection). But things seem to have gone from bad to worse in the intervening years. Today, according to Rorty, 'Any problem that enjoys a simultaneous vogue in ten of the hundred or so "analytic" philosophy departments in America is doing exceptionally well. . . . The best hope for an American philosopher is Andy Warhol's promise that we shall *all* be superstars, for approximately fifteen minutes apiece' (p. 216).

Rorty is much concerned with the current dissension between the 'analytic' and the 'continental' philosophers in American philosophy departments. He recommends mutual tolerance but feels sorry for students who are interested in the continental philosophers and is pessimistic about their future careers in American philosophy. He suspects that by the end of the century a new discipline of philosophy will emerge in America which 'does not pretend to link up with, or even argue with what is practised under the heading of "philosophy" in other parts of the world' (p. 228).

Part of the reason for the different degrees of institutional success in America of the two European approaches to philosophy may be the fact that analytic (or scientific) philosophy is easier to transplant than continental philosophy. Rorty himself is planning to write a substantial book on or around Dewey's philosophy. He also contrasts the lawyer type with the literary critic type of philosopher. Given the social conditions in America today, the abler lawyer type has been choosing the law school while the literary critic type would probably also find some other departments more congenial, even though the issue of a better-paid job is different for the two types. Of the influential figures in recent years, Rorty selects John Rawls, T. S. Kuhn, and S. A. Kripke on the analytic side and M. Heidegger, M. Foucault, and J. Derrida on the continental side; even though they all work on different topics, the second trio, in contrast with the first, share a negative view of the 'scientific method.'

Rorty notes the contempt, expressed by Reichenbach and Quine, for history and the history of philosophy, and particularly philosophy in the nineteenth century. He speaks of 'the Hegel-Marx-Nietzsche-Heidegger-Foucault sequence' and their chosen philosophical task of 'a search for meaning in history,' as well as 'the increasing whole-heartedness with which they gave up the notions of system, method, and science, their increasing willingness to blur the genres' (p. 226). In contrast with the others in the sequence, Marx is, however, explicit in taking science as a positive force and works to extend the range of the scientific method to the 'moral' sciences. One may note that Reichenbach views Marx, in his fundamentals, as the greatest opponent of Hegel, as emphatically not an idealist, and as in the line of 'empiricism' in his historical position (op. cit., p. 71). In any case, a perspective that puts Marx in the company of Nietzsche and even Heidegger and Foucault appears to me most peculiar indeed.

11.5. Pragmatism and C. I. Lewis

Pragmatism is usually held to be the most original American contribution to the history of philosophy. C. S. Peirce (1839–1914) first explicitly set out pragmatism as a method of determining meaning in philosophy in an article on 'How to make our ideas clear' (1878). 'Consider what effects, that might conceivably have practical bearings, we conceive the object of our conception to have. Then, our conception of these effects is the whole of our conception of the object.' Peirce made many later attempts to express the pragmatic principle in a form which really satisfied him in excluding nonsense without being a 'barrier to inquiry.'

But it was the different version of William James (1842–1910) which made the doctrine famous. Dewey and George Mead further developed and enriched the tradition. Unlike logical positivism, natural sciences do not enjoy as dominant a position in pragmatism in its developed form. Moreover, there is no sharp distinction between cognition and valuation; indeed, it is maintained that knowledge as a whole is valuation. Dewey and Mead share with Marx the affirmation of the central importance of social practice.

C. I. Lewis studied with James and was sympathetic to pragmatism. He also studied logic and Kant's philosophy. He modernized modal logic before 1920 and published his famous *Mind and World-Order* in 1929 which to a certain extent paralleled some of the main theses of the logical positivists. On different occasions J. L. Austin and Isiah Berlin mentioned to me that they had jointly conducted a class on this book in 1936 at Oxford. (Compare *Essays on J. L. Austin,* 1973, pp. 7–8.) In 1965, Donald C. Williams published a very informative memoir, 'Clarence Irving Lewis 1883–1964,' which not only portrays a different type of philosopher from (say) Carnap and Quine but points out connections significant in the history of American logic and philosophy.

As an undergraduate (1903–1906) Lewis was much interested in 'the cordially contentious' Josiah Royce and William James. He completed his thesis *The Intuitive Element in Knowledge* in 1910 but stayed on for one more year 'to assist Royce in his prophetic course in modern logic.' This experience inspired Lewis to offer 'advanced logic' at Berkeley, leading to his construction of modal logic and his *Survey of Symbolic Logic* (1918), which 'was the first American book on or in the subject.' Lewis returned to Harvard in 1920 and published his 'conceptualistic pragmatism' nine years later in *World-Order*. In Williams' judgment, 'it bears traces of the public dialogue of Royce with James, of the author's dissertation of 1910, and his later private interrogations of Kant and Peirce, and of visiting appointments among the instrumentalists of Columbia and Chicago.' Instead of proceeding directly to his moral philosophy Lewis felt obliged to add more technical specificity to the ideas of *World-Order* so that this reworked basis occupies two-thirds of his longest book, *Analysis of Knowledge and Valuation* (1946), which was a significant part of the graduate study of my classmates at Harvard. As Williams observes, 'The ratio of doggedness to inspiration is naturally greater in the *Analysis* than in *World-order*.' Here we have another example of the experience that sometimes careful development renders ideas in an earlier work less rather than more suggestive and influential.

The minor farce *She Stoops to Conquer,* as some may remember, depicts the familiar psychology of being timid in front of a serious object of love. We often encounter a similar phenomenon in intellectual pursuits, doing better work in subjects which one takes less seriously. Philosophy, with its tradition of large pretensions, tends to attract such admirers more frequently. One idea is to make excessively elaborate preparations. There is also a continuous expectation that with perseverance some 'secret knowledge' will in time be revealed. More strongly, there is the natural desire to say first what can be said more clearly. For many years Lewis 'gave a course on philosophies of evolution which was a fascinating history and critique of philosophy and science since Thales; yet very little cosmology . . . appears in his published work.' 'Ethics he always believed to be the philosopher's principal and ultimate vocation; he long gave a course on social ethics'; yet he published little on moral philosophy in his lifetime and is little known in this area. 'Logic, on the other hand, its philosophy, and the critical theory of knowledge generally, he thought of as in principle ancillary and propaedeutic, yet it was just in these, doubtless for the very reason, that he did his most thorough and systematic work and won therefore his principal reputation and influence.'

There is, however, an elusive element in the philosophy of Lewis which is of greater significance than the degree of doggedness. What is involved is akin to a variant of Kantian dualism. On the one hand, he developed the ideas of phenomenalism and conventionalism (plus pragmatic tests) already in *World-Order*. On the other hand, he vehemently dissociated himself from those who stress and are limited to these and related ideas. He believed 'that James, Dewey, the positivists, and later linguists, all alike, had demoralized epistemology by their equating truth with "warranted assertibility".' 'This, he thought, meant abandonment of the idea, on which any responsible life for the intellect must hinge, of a permanent real truth by correspondence that is not the same as either the pragmatist's warranted assertibility or the idealist's coherence.' Here we of course get into highly controversial issues of interpretation and attribution. What is at stake is the longing for something more objectivistic, realistic, and even absolutistic which is not so easily accessible to his conceptualistic pragmatism, certainly calling for more elaborate explanations and constructions than Lewis had given.

I have often been struck by what might be called the dilemma of nothing-but and something-more in attempts to achieve a comprehensive philosophical position. A nothing-but philosophy tends to begin in an elegant way and then, if it attracts enough attention and criticism, undergoes stages of liberalization until it runs up by a new and different path against familiar difficulties in early philosophies. The evolution of the positions of Carnap and his successors seems to illustrate this phenomenon. In particular, vague motives such as 'ontological minimalism' lead to exercises of dubious value. On the other hand, if one begins by taking a flexible enough framework to include the something-more, the result often contains a good deal that is obscure and distorted. Indeed, it may be so difficult to penetrate the large structure that one cannot even separate out the more reasonable parts from the rest. Hegel's philosophy is an example of this type. Kant's philosophy has been so influential partly because it seems to endow the something-more with a comparatively appropriate degree of obscurity by positing the Ding an sich, discussing the antinomies, etc.

Indeed, I would like to propose an inaccurate but suggestive distinction that seems to be useful in characterizing both alternative approaches and complementary parts within an individual attempt to arrive at a philosophy. The contrast between 'analytic' and 'continental' philosophers may be summarized by such a distinction. The analytic philosophers tend to do better with the 'nothing but' part; the continental philosophers tend to begin with and to concentrate their attention on the 'something more' part. In the case of individual philosophers, J. Habermas, for instance, appears to display in public his continued efforts, unsuccessful thus far, to blend a positivist cum pragmatist element of nothing-but with an elusive something-more element along the tradition of the average German philosophers.

Beginning with Kant, there has developed a tradition of relegating the something-more to a 'dialectic' which means so many things not only to different individuals but often to the same person. Yet a central problem of philosophy would seem to be the task of giving a proper place to something-more, saying neither too little nor too much. From this viewpoint, one might oversimplify the position of Lewis and characterize his way as merely announcing emphatically that he realizes there is something more and it is all-important. (This of course also reminds one of the *Tractatus*.) Undoubtedly he had made efforts (certainly during his last few years at Harvard) to give a more adequate account of the something-more, but I do not know whether their fruits have been written down or published.

At a retirement dinner in 1953 Lewis explained to his colleagues 'that the key to his dissent from, not to say disdain for, the reigning schools of philosophy was his judgment that they lacked moral earnestness.' Seven years later he expanded this statement and brought his judgment up to date in a private letter:

> It is so easy . . . to get impressive 'results' by replacing the vaguer concepts which convey real meaning by virtue of common usage by pseudo precise concepts which are manipulable by 'exact' methods—the trouble being that nobody any longer knows whether anything actual or of practical import is being discussed; and half of them do not care. Add the bent of people too young to have learned English grammar in high school to translate problems into semantics; and philosophy looks dreary. . . . The Wittgenstein recipe of talking issues to death instead of trying for a solution simply capped the climax. . . . [But] my guess is that these tendencies have pretty well run their course.

It is all too easy to dismiss these remarks as merely sour grapes uttered by one who had been left behind by the advance of (or the next swing of the pendulum in) philosophy. But surely Lewis was an able, devoted, and fair-minded philosopher. I am inclined to think that the observations reflect to some extent both the unhappy state of philosophy (if only in bringing out the instability of what makes up philosophy) and an important difference of philosophy from, say, physics, microbiology, or mathematics.

By the way, Lewis was Quine's teacher and colleague at Harvard. But their preferences and temperaments appear quite different. Quine succeeded Lewis in the Edgar Pierce chair after Lewis had retired in 1953. Unlike Quine, Lewis seems to separate his work in logic and in philosophy more sharply. As Williams reports, 'In 1934, he saw that the principal future of logic lay in its elaboration as a mathematical science in which he respectfully refrained from trying to participate.' Of course Quine's persistent negative attitude toward modal logic is well known.

Recently there has been a revival of interest in Dewey. It is hard to predict whether this revival will also extend to Lewis. Probably not: Dewey wrote on a wider range of things and always had a broader readership; while Lewis had no 'wish to appeal over the heads of his fellow experts to the man in the street.' Although this is no reason to deter the professional philosophers, they may yet find Dewey more relevant than Lewis is to their current concerns with social practice, social usefulness, and collective interest. But 'Dewey hailed *World-order* as worthy to eclipse his *Quest for Certainty* published almost simultaneously.'

By the way, the first part (on vaguer concepts) of the Lewis complaint quoted above certainly applies to Carnap's work. I am not sure whether it might not also have been directed to some of Quine's work such as his talk of 'ontic commitment.' I think these remarks are related to some of Quine's disagreements with Carnap: for example, we are interested in 'analytic,' not just 'analytic in L'; philosophy is concerned more with common usage than with artificial languages. In other words, readers of Carnap have often found his distinctions leave out the more interesting (and more complex) concept or meaning with which one is grappling. Hence, his characteristically reasonable way of discussion can be frustrating. After reporting on the partisan pride in Carnap's performance (1935) in a match with Arthur Lovejoy, 'explaining that if Lovejoy means A then p, and if he means B then q,' Quine continues: 'I had yet to learn how unsatisfying this way of Carnap's could sometimes be' (*WP*, p. 42).

Of Lewis, Williams also reports: He had in fact always differed from the creed the Viennese were compiling, by his emphasis on both the practical motivation and control of our verificatory experience and its concrete fullness or 'fatness.' Both of these themes had been favorite themes of James and Royce.

12. Carnap's work in relation to Russell and Quine

While Carnap selected a few aspects of Russell's work partly as a basis (*PM*) for broadening out and partly to develop further (*External World*), Quine began with some parts of Russell's and Carnap's work and then made more conspicuous criticisms. The criticisms are largely of a restrictive character, appealing to behaviorism, economy, and notational precision; with regard to Carnap, there is, in contrast, a healthy reaction against his hasty idealizations of language. Carnap's *Intellectual Autobiography*, briefly *IA* (Schilpp 1963, pp. 3–84), is candid, lucid, and highly informative; it is a convenient guide to a brief review of his life and work.

The chief influences on Carnap and Quine are well documented. Let me quote some general acknowledgments first. 'Whereas Frege,' Carnap said, 'had the strongest influence on me in the fields of logic and semantics, in my philosophical thinking in general I learned most from Bertrand Russell'; 'I owe much to his work, not only with respect to philosophical method, but also in the solution of special problems' (*IA*, p. 13). Quine dedicated his *SL* (1963) 'to Bertrand Russell whose ideas have long loomed large in this subject and whose writings inspired my interest in it' and his *Word and Object* (1960) 'to Rudolf Carnap, teacher and friend.'

In 1970, Quine said: 'Carnap is a towering figure. I see him as the dominant figure in philosophy from 1930's onward, as Russell had been in the decades before' (*WP*, p. 40). Those who share Quine's conception of philosophy are likely to amend the statement by adding Quine as the dominant figure from the 1950s on.

12.1. Stages of and influences on Carnap's development
From 1910 to 1914, Carnap (1891–1970) took three courses with Frege (1848–1925) in Jena: Begriffsschrift (conceptual notation, ideography), II of it, and Logik der Mathematik. At that time he took philosophy, mathematics, and physics as his major fields. After the war he tried to combine his interests in theoretical physics and in philosophy. Around 1919 he studied *PM*, which he liked so much that he thought he could understand a concept or a proposition clearly only if he felt he could express it in the symbolic language of *PM*! He started a thesis project on the axiomatic foundations of kinematics but ended with *Der Raum*

in which he distinguished formal, intuitive, and physical space as a way of clarifying controversies over the concept of space. He studied Frege's main work in 1920.

Somewhere Russell remarks that *PM* is devoted to proving the obvious from the nonobvious. Since it contains so many elaborate constructions, it would seem natural to wish to find some applications for these fruits of extensive labor. In 1914, Russell published his Lowell lectures entitled *Our Knowledge of the External World, as a Field for Scientific Method in Philosophy*. He begins the book by talking about 'the logical-analytic method' and concludes by observing:

> The study of logic becomes the central study in philosophy: it gives the method of research in philosophy, just as mathematics gives the method in physics. . . . The one and only condition, I believe, which is necessary in order to secure for philosophy in the near future an achievement surpassing all that has hitherto been accomplished by philosophers, is the creation of a school of men with scientific training and philosophical interests, unhampered by the traditions of the past, and not misled by the literary methods of those who copy the ancients in all except their merits.

In the winter of 1921, Carnap read this book and in his *IA*, after quoting these words, he says: 'I felt as if this appeal had been directed to me personally.' Indeed, as we know, Carnap devoted himself to the polishing and the application of the new logical instrument ever since. In particular, Russell's book illustrates the possibility of imitating the constructions of *PM* to hint at an ambitious project of building the external world out of sense data, a project which greatly attracted Carnap. He began an intensive study of Russell's philosophical books.

While continuing his work on the 'foundations' of physics, the largest part of his 'philosophical work from 1922 to 1925 was devoted to considerations out of which grew' his phenomenalistic *Aufbau* (1928), a first version of which was finished in 1925. He moved to Vienna in 1926 where he was to stay till 1931. Gradually he got converted to a physicalistic attitude largely under the influence of discussions with Neurath. The first proposal to improve the system of *Aufbau* was Nelson Goodman's *The Structure of Appearance* (1951). In the meantime Carnap turned to other problems, having lost interest in the specific problems relating to the *Aufbau* on account of his switch to physicalism (*IA*, p. 19).

In Vienna he took part in an intensive discussion of the *Tractatus*, sentence by sentence. A direct influence of this study on Carnap was his monograph *Scheinprobleme* (1928) in which he elaborates the familiar contention that many theses of traditional metaphysics are devoid of cognitive content. The special feature of his treatment is to argue that the thesis of realism concerning the reality of the external world is also a pseudo-sentence. In contrast, Schlick and Reichenbach, like Einstein and Russell, 'believed that realism was the indispensable basis of science' (*IA*, p. 46). One wonders whether, in Carnap's view, his own thesis (that the realism thesis is a pseudo-sentence) is not also a pseudo-sentence.

The next major work after the *Aufbau*, or probably the most influential among Carnap's work, is the book *Logical Syntax* (1934). A vision came to him 'during a sleepless night in January 1931, when I was ill.' On the following day he wrote down the first version of the book under the title 'Attempts at Metalogic.' According to Carnap, this metalogic in a sense generalized Hilbert's idea of metamathematics. (Forty years later, the *Britannica* invited me to contribute a long 'Macro'-article on much of mathematical logic and insisted on using the title 'Metalogic' despite my protests.)

From 1931 to December 1935, Carnap had a chair in natural philosophy in Prague and spent much time on the syntax book. Gödel read a draft from 1932 and Quine also studied a draft when he visited Carnap in 1933. In a foreword dated May 1934, various stimulations are acknowledged, including those by the writings of Frege, Russell, and Hilbert, as well as by discussions with Gödel and the Polish logicians. It is announced: 'Philosophy is to be replaced by the logic of science,' which is 'nothing other than the logical syntax of the language of science.' An expanded English translation of the book appeared in 1937. Work on this book was undoubtedly Carnap's chief research occupation for his whole Prague period.

Carnap arrived at Chicago early in 1936, where he was to stay till 1952. He visited Harvard during 1940–1941, spent 1942–1944 in New Mexico on a research grant, and visited the Princeton Institute from 1952 to 1954. In 1954 he moved to Los Angeles and stayed there till his death in 1970.

Even before 1935, Carnap 'had realized, chiefly in conversations with Tarski and Gödel that there must be a mode, different from the syntactical one, in which to speak about language [viz., also to speak about the relations between language and facts, to make statements about the relation of designation and about truth]' (*IA*, p. 60). From 1935 on Carnap began to work intensively on a formal treatment of semantics which was the focus of his attention probably from 1936 to 1945. Over this period he produced four books on semantics: *Foundations of Logic and Mathematics* (1939); *Introduction to Semantics* (1942); *Formalization of Logic* (1943); and *Meaning and Necessity* (1947). In all these books, as in the syntax book, Carnap's meticulous care for formal precision is comparable to Frege's work and more thorough than *PM*. However, formal semantics is neither fish nor fowl. It has the appearance of dealing with the more important and more difficult question of meaning, but Carnap's formal method is not capable of getting at the interesting aspects of meaning. His method is more suited to syntax (or at least a restricted part of it) than to semantics; indeed, it might be said to be a method that is semantics only in appearance, but syntax in substance.

While both Russell and Carnap were influenced by Frege's work, the effects on them were rather different. Russell's main effort in this connection was devoted to developing a reasonable theory which avoids the paradoxes. He paid less attention to several additional aspects which Carnap learned from Frege: the meticulous distinction between use and mention, between sense and denotation, and the requirement to formulate the rules of logic without any reference to meaning (related to Carnap's emphasis on syntax). By the way, Carnap accepted Ramsey's reformulation of type theory and tried to show that the axioms of choice and infinity are analytic. For the axiom of infinity, he took positions rather than things as individuals (*IA*, pp. 47–48). I find the justification not convincing.

A side interest in pragmatics was acquired while Carnap was in Chicago. 'Charles Morris was closest to my philosophical position. He tried to combine ideas of pragmatism and logical empiricism. Through him I gained a better understanding of the Pragmatic philosophy, especially of George Mead and Dewey.' In 1938, Morris published a monograph, *Foundations of the Theory of Signs*, in which semiotics is expounded under the three domains of syntax, semantics, and pragmatics. It is a little surprising that Carnap moved from a more sensible attitude toward pragmatics (mainly of empirical investigations) to his typically formal mode of seeing 'an urgent need for a system of theoretical pragmatics' (Schilpp 1963, p. 861). Of course pragmatism is a larger matter than pragmatics in Carnap's sense.

In 1938, Feigl 'urged Carnap to apply his enormous analytic powers to the problems of induction and probability.' 'Carnap immediately began sketching in many hours of intensive discussion of what later became his great and influential work in Inductive Logic' (Hintikka 1975, p. xvii). More concentrated study began in the spring of 1941. By 1945 or 1946 induction and probability must have become his central, if not exclusive, concern, which was to continue for the rest of his life. Indeed, just before he entered the hospital, he had sent away a manuscript on inductive logic to the typist (Hintikka, p. xxiv). Since this part of Carnap's work is not closely related to the issues discussed in this book, I shall say nothing more about it.

Leaving out this last stage, we can indicate three stages in Carnap's work. The logical construction of the world occupied him from 1922 to about 1927; this was followed by his switch to physicalism (around 1930) and to the 'liberalization of empiricism.' The first stage or aspect of his work may be said to end with his 'Testability and meaning' (1936). The second stage or aspect was logical syntax which engaged him from about 1928 to 1936. The third stage or aspect was semantics from 1935 to about 1945. With regard to both the logical construction and the logical syntax, the initial attractive optimism was followed by liberalizations which lose the original sharpness and reintroduce old divisive ambiguities: from phenomenalism to physicalism, from translatability to confirmability, and from syntax to semantics. Let me proceed to a closer look at Carnap's work from the perspective of these two lines of liberalization.

Allow me to make a general comment on Carnap's work which applies also to major aspects of Quine's work. The philosophically more central and more difficult task is to grasp the right ideas intuitively; how far they can be or how well they are formalized is an auxiliary secondary consideration, which is admittedly very helpful sometimes. To strive for neat formalizations of inadequately conceived ideas is putting the cart before the horse.

12.2. Rational reconstruction and epistemology

In his *Aufbau*, Carnap tried to show how the whole system of concepts in science could be constructed, with the help of the logical apparatus of *PM*, on a very simple phenomenalistic basis referring to elementary experiences. The basic underlying philosophical outlook is in the tradition of Hume and Mach. It uses a single dyadic relation of recognition-of-similarity between elementary experiences; this reminds one of Russell's emphasis on the relation of similarity in his *Inquiry* (1940). Carnap states explicitly that his system is not a portrayal of the process of acquiring knowledge but should be considered a 'rational reconstruction' of the process, a demonstration of how the ideas dealt with 'could have been' derived from the original given (*IA*, p. 16).

The concept of rational reconstruction suggests a variety of tasks. While in the *Aufbau* it deals with how I know, it can also deal with how we know (as physicalism is apparently intended to do) and with what we know (as illustrated but by no means exhausted by attempts to axiomatize, more successfully in mathematics and less so in the sciences). As I have said before, I am in sympathy with the aspect of taking what is known as data for 'reconstruction.' But, given such a perspective, since our knowledge of how I or we know is among the limited and least structured, I find it an ill-chosen area (from the wide range of what we know) to concentrate on.

In his 'Theories' (Ramsey 1931), Ramsey was the first to bring out the point that scientific concepts cannot be defined explicitly in terms of observational reports as suggested by Russell and in the *Aufbau*. Particular defects of Carnap's construction have been detailed by Goodman (1951, Chapter 5) and others. For example, he uses definition by abstraction ('quasi-analysis'), which is Whitehead's 'extensive abstraction,' also adopted by Russell. But the basic dyadic relation of likeness is in general not transitive so that we cannot properly derive equivalence classes by merging all alike pairs. In assigning sense qualities to positions in physical space and time, the assignments are revised to suit the growth of experience. Moreover, as Carnap stressed later on, there are basic difficulties over dispositional ('nomological') statements. For reasons like these, the ideal of translating the sentences of sciences into terms of logic and observation (the definitional reductionism of theory to observation) was abandoned.

Carnap introduced reduction forms or sentences of a type weaker than definition in his 'Testability and meaning' (1936). A reduction pair provides a sufficient condition and a necessary one for the use of a new term; but the two do not coincide and supply no means for eliminating the new term from all contexts. Such weakened form of 'reduction' certainly loses much of the original appeal. Moreover, as Hempel points out (Schilpp 1963, pp. 685–709), it does not do what it sets out to do: there is a circularity in the treatment of dispositional statements. Hempel suggests a broadening of Carnap's method by adding new general statements which contain both the new term and some old terms; and he concludes that it 'is an oversimplification to conceive of scientific theories as establishing deductive connections' between observational sentences. Moreover, the distinction between the theory proper and its interpretative system is somewhat arbitrary. By the way, Hempel appears to share Carnap's and Quine's unrealistic identification of scientific theories with first order theories (p. 692). I take this as a source of much confusion and shall often mention it.

It is of interest to note that Carnap proposed already in the early 1930s views which were later elaborated by others and are often believed to be fundamental criticisms of Carnap's position. In 1932 he rejected the idea of a privileged class of 'protocol sentences,' which, according to him, are also subject to revisions (see Carnap 1932). He argued for a holism similar to what Quine later publicized: 'Thus *the test applies, at bottom, not to a single hypothesis but to the whole system of physics as a system of hypotheses (Poincaré, Duhem)*' (*Logical Syntax*, p. 318). Hence, the notorious disagreement between Carnap and Quine on the analytic-synthetic distinction cannot be just a consequence of their (nonexistent) disagreement on 'holism.' Rather, their particular difference seems to come from Carnap's unwillingness to go beyond idealized models, which has the consequence that he refuses to consider analyticity outside of some particular (often only imagined) formal language.

12.3. From syntax to semantics

In 1970, Quine offered an evaluation of *Logical Syntax* (*WP*, 1976, pp. 40–41):

> [In it Carnap] again vigorously exploited the resources of modern logic for philosophical ends. The book is a mine of proof and opinion on the philosophy of logic and the logic of philosophy. During a critical decade it was the main inspiration of young scientific philosophers. It was the definitive work at the center, from which the waves of tracts and popularizations issued in ever widening circles. Carnap more than anyone else was the embodiment of logical positivism, logical empiricism, the Vienna Circle.

The book benefited greatly from Carnap's knowledge and command of the work of Frege, *PM*, the *Tractatus*, as well as the work of the Hilbert school, Gödel, and the Polish logicians. Wittgenstein probably thought that his work was misunderstood and misapplied. Gödel undoubtedly felt that Carnap failed to appreciate his philosophical views surrounding his technical work. However that may be, it was an impressive and elaborate synthesis at the time of its appearance. (I remember reading the book around 1940 and thinking, rightly or wrongly, that if I could not do anything more interesting, I could certainly do work like it.)

Around 1955, Gödel spent a painfully long time on writing an article to honor Carnap, entitled 'Is mathematics syntax of language?' In the end he did not publish it. Once he told me (probably in 1972) that even though in his paper he had demonstrated conclusively that mathematics is not syntax but the more interesting question is what mathematics is, on which he had reached no satisfactory answer; that was why he decided not to publish it. Carnap would undoubtedly have said that he had long before 1955 given up the view that mathematics is syntax. But I believe there remains an important residue in Carnap's and many other people's conception of the analyticity of mathematics. The narrower conception of analyticity as linguistic conventions makes the analytic (and, therefore, mathematics for Carnap) a part of syntax. Indeed, 'semantics' remained syntactic in dealing with names and sentences, and it is circular. (Compare section 2 in the Introduction.) Hence, I do not think that Gödel was merely arguing against an obsolete position.

One conspicuous feature of the book is the 'principle of tolerance' which Carnap upheld throughout his life. *'It is not our business to set up prohibitions, but to arrive at conventions'* (p. 51). There are different levels of tolerance implied by this principle. The word 'conventions' of course reflects Carnap's preoccupation with artificial languages. Really interesting positions can rarely, if ever, be fully presented in terms of conventions; for example, legal proceedings are complex, even though society tries to make the laws explicit. If we broaden the idea a little, the advice amounts to urging one to shun controversy and to work out and convey one's own position in as clear a manner as possible. An obvious objection to this principle is: there are positions and positions. Some are so insignificant or absurd that it would be intolerable to watch someone splitting hairs over them. The context in which the principle was introduced was the quarrels of logicists, formalists, and intuitionists, which have now become part of history, as a result not so much of mere coexistence and mutual tolerance as of informed interactions and interrelating.

In Carnap's own case I believe the principle serves a congenial purpose. This has something to do with Carnap's exceptionally uniform personal conception of clarity. He is willing to exclude an exceptionally large range of things on the ground that they are 'not clear,' or sometimes, that 'everything he says is poetry.' The matter is well illustrated by the remarks of Charles Hartshorne (Hintikka 1975, pp. xlv–xlvii), who believes that 'the Carnapian criteria of clarity are too severe to make it possible to deal with this [the distinction between internal and external relations] and other important philosophical questions.' It is easy to see that tolerance in one sense fits in with the adherence to a limited sphere of 'clarity' which calls for a broader region of suspended judgments, waiting for more of it to be clarified. There is then the question of also tolerating what is considered not clear. In this regard Carnap was, compared with many other adherents to 'clarity,' relatively tolerant.

To have found a comfortable range of what one takes to be clear has the advantage of decisiveness in choosing what not to attend to and of saving much wasted energy in fruitless efforts to understand irrelevant things. But this requirement of clarity, if not devised imaginatively and applied appropriately, can also be harmfully excessive. And I believe that to some extent this is indeed the case with Carnap, as illustrated by an example offered by himself. He may not have cared about Hartshorne's problems, but his own example is different. From 1952 to 1954 he was at the Princeton Institute and had separate talks 'with John von Neumann, Wolfgang Pauli and some specialists in statistical mechanics on some questions of theoretical physics with which I was concerned.' He had expected that 'we would reach, if not agreement, then at least mutual understanding.' But they failed, despite their serious efforts. One physicist said: 'Physics is not like geometry; in physics there are no definitions and no axioms' (*IA*, pp. 36–37). If I were in Carnap's position, the experience would have made me very disturbed about my work in the particular area and seriously question my own approach to the 'foundations' of physics, including more generally my concept of clarity. I would have attempted to understand them before going further with my work in that area. But probably this is not a sufficiently objective or 'clear' issue. More, Carnap's course may have been a more efficient way of using his capacities.

Carnap's move from syntax to semantics seems to coincide with a move from a broader influence to a narrower one. His favorite work of formalization was probably more appropriate for (and adequate to) syntax than semantics. More, the work on semantics was no longer accompanied by exciting ideas such as those which he derived from Gödel and Wittgenstein in his work on syntax. From 1940 to 1941, Carnap was at Harvard and discussed at great length with Quine and Tarski the question whether there is a sharp distinction between logical and factual truth. He also talked with C. I. Lewis about the latter's systems of modal logic. Lewis regarded the system S5 as too strong and preferred weaker systems for conceptual reasons, but Carnap gave an interpretation of modal concepts that fits the strong system and thought this an advantage simply because the strong system makes more formulas decidable (*IA*, pp. 65–67). Carnap's reason is a little surprising to me, seeing that the situation was one of trying to capture an intuitive concept.

Carnap was co-inventor, with Ruth Barcan (Marcus), of modal quantificational logic, and a precursor of possible-worlds semantics (see Hintikka 1975, pp. 217–242).

13. Analyticity and logical truth

There are a number of different issues which have been intermingled in the tiresome debate over whether the distinction between the analytic and the synthetic is only a 'difference in degree.' The rigidified doctrine of the Vienna Circle, as represented by Carnap, was based on several large mistakes and misunderstandings. First, there is a tendency to confuse two senses of analyticity; roughly the narrow sense of explicit linguistic conventions and the broader and more indefinite sense of truth in virtue of meaning. This was in part a result of equivocating over Wittgenstein's concept of tautology. Second, the confusion is combined with a tendency to use the more regimented part of mathematics as a model of science, both to get a misconception of mathematics and to exaggerate the role of 'conventions' and artificial languages for 'rational reconstruction.' Third, the liberalizations of empiricism (such as Carnap's quite early endorsement of 'holism') were local responses to failures which called for larger revisions (including a different conception of analyticity and its role) which Carnap and many others failed to make; this need to revise other parts in order to be consistent was not realized by the group represented by Carnap. Fourth, just as many philosophers of an older tradition had believed that philosophy is concerned only with finding synthetic a priori propositions, there is a tendency (explicitly stated by Carnap in Schilpp 1963, p. 64) to view the task of philosophy as the search for analytic propositions.

I believe it desirable to distinguish three different aspects in considering the notion of analyticity. First, the central area of logic (including set theory and therewith mathematics) is, in my opinion, analytic in the broader sense. Second, the sort of trivial extensions by familiar linguistic 'synonymy' are of less interest and could also be considered to be analytic. Third, the more interesting case of 'meaning postulates' in the sciences (and, I believe, in other domains as well) is much more complex than Carnap thinks; it is in this area that the line between what is analytic (in the broader sense) and what is synthetic is blurred in an interesting way, which is, for example, intimately connected with the fascinating fact of the applicability of mathematics in the special case of physics.

(Related to the content of this section are the better structured presentation in section 2 of the Introduction, as well as additional considerations given in my 1955 and in Chapter 8 of my *MP*. By the way, analytic-synthetic was the topic of my first term paper, in spring 1942, and of my first publication, 1944, in philosophy.)

Let me try to elaborate these general observations and add some comparison of Quine's work with that of Russell and, more extensively, with that of Carnap.

13.1. The role of analyticity in philosophy

Kant's distinction between analytic and synthetic truths is related to Leibniz's distinction between truths of reason and truths of fact, as well as to Hume's distinction between relations of idea and matters of fact. It remains controversial what Kant means by 'analytic.' Frege thought at one time his constructions showed that arithmetic is analytic but continued to believe that geometry is synthetic. L. E. J. Brouwer held the opposite view. Both of them must have thought that they had a good understanding of what Kant meant by 'analytic.' More recent discussions of Kant's distinction are included in Beck 1965. He remarks at one place: 'I need only to point out that the positivists, who argue against Kant that he made things necessary which are in fact contingent (e.g., the Newtonian laws), seem to me to have touched perhaps a more crucial point in Kant's philosophy than those who accept eternal verities' (p. 107). In reply to my recent inquiry on Kant's treating Newtonian laws as necessary, Professor Beck told me that the matter remains controversial and informed me of the relevant writings of Kant and an extensive secondary literature including Arthur Pap's *The a priori in Physical Theory* (1946). Regarding this instructive issue of the necessity of physical laws in Kant, Charles Parsons has told me that several significant works have appeared since the book by Pap.

Since Kant, there is a large and long tradition of viewing the role of philosophy as a search for synthetic a priori propositions. For this tradition, the thesis that all a priori truths are analytic is sometimes believed to pose a real threat. For example, B. Blanshard remarks, 'In the positivist conception of reason, the necessity of an insight is no guarantee that it applies to nature or reveals anything outside the confines of meaning. . . . They [philosophical propositions] were supposed to tell us not only what words mean, but what things are. . . . That a new theory would find us with our occupation gone is no argument against it' (*Reason and Analysis*, 1962, p. 259).

This observation may be taken to be implying a presupposition of a dominant philosophical tradition, viz., that philosophical propositions must be necessary and apply to nature. Both Blanshard and the positivists agree that mathematics is necessary (whether analytic or not) and undoubtedly recognize that mathematics applies to nature. Calling mathematics analytic does not change its necessity and applicability. Hence, this does not rule out the possibility that philosophical propositions may enjoy the same privileges. Moreover, propositions such as what I have called, in section 4.4, the principle of necessary reason and the principle of precarious sufficiency are, in my opinion, philosophical ones. They are not necessary but summarize so much human experience that they are extremely flexible and constitute instances of our fundamental beliefs. In addition, there are issues obviously of philosophical significance which relate to analyticity only indirectly as a distant point of reference. For example, the paradox of small numbers suggested by me around 1957 (see Dummett 1975) points to a gray area between the analytic and the synthetic.

It is possible and desirable to distinguish between true by (verbal) convention from true in virtue of meaning. The confusion between the two may be traced in part to a mistake in the *Tractatus* (see sections 2, 6.3, and 10 above), compounded by a most peculiar wish-fulfilling adaptation by the Vienna Circle. They neither discerned Wittgenstein's mistake nor took his view seriously enough to retain a measure of faithfulness to it. The adaptation has the effect of making analytic propositions appear trivial. What happened can best be seen from an account by Carnap himself. Since the passages are so revealing, allow me to quote at length (*IA*, pp. 46–47):

> Wittgenstein formulated this view in the more radical form that all logical truths are tautological, that is, that they hold necessarily in every possible case, therefore do not exclude any case, and do not say anything about the facts of the world. Wittgenstein demonstrated this thesis for molecular sentences (i.e., those without variables) and for those with individual variables. It was not clear whether he thought that the logically valid sentences with variables of higher levels, e.g., variables for classes, for classes of classes, etc., have the same tautological character. At any rate, he did not count the theorems of arithmetic, algebra, etc., among the tautologies. *But to the members of the Circle there did not seem to be a fundamental difference between elementary logic and higher logic, including mathematics.* Thus we arrived at the conception that all valid statements of mathematics are analytic in the specific sense that they hold in all possible cases and therefore do not have any factual content.
>
> What was important in this conception from our point of view was the fact that it became possible for the first time to combine the basic tenet of empiricism with a satisfactory explanation of the nature of logic and mathematics. [My italics]

The italicized sentence involves such a big jump that it appears even more curious than Wittgenstein's overlooking the difference between the finite and the infinite. Carnap, like Ramsey before him, did worry about justifying the axiom of infinity, but he did not appreciate that the crucial point is not its justification but rather its effects. Once we accept arbitrary subsets of some infinite set, the defining conditions become very complex so that the axioms of logic are no longer transparent, whether we call them analytic or not.

From the last part of the long quotation, we see clearly the prior empiricist wish to demystify mathematics. Given the wish and the convincing account of the propositional calculus in the *Tractatus*, it is of course natural to *wish* that the same account will apply to all of logic (and therewith to mathematics). But it is amazing that the eminent group of people in the Circle, which takes pride in its high standard of clarity and precision, could overlook the glaring differences between the propositional calculus and higher logic and went ahead to draw the desired conclusions.

One often wonders whether analytic philosophers are so labelled because they are seekers after analytic propositions. The question prob-ably does not have enough definiteness to be of much interest. But it does seem to play a part in the surprising amount of energy spent in the 1950s and 1960s on debating the analytic-synthetic distinction, which Carnap equates also with the distinction between logical and factual truth. It is of some interest to find Carnap seemingly affirming the discovery of analytic propositions as the sole role of philosophers (*IA*, p. 64). 'In this way we obtain also a clear distinction between questions about contingent facts and questions about meaning relations. This difference seems to me philosophically important; answering questions of the first kind is not part of the philosopher's task, though he may be interested in analyzing them; but questions of the second kind lie often within the field of philosophy or applied logic.'

13.2. Quine and the dogmas of empiricism

Quine gave in 1934 a series of lectures on Carnap's work. Some of this material was organized into his paper 'Truth by convention,' completed in 1935 and published in 1936. It considers the 'widespread conviction that logic and mathematics are purely analytic or conventional,' less to question its validity than to question its sense. We have here an explicit statement of his underlying questionable presupposition that analytic could only mean linguistically conventional; the adjective 'purely' is quite revealing. Common sense should have told us that the whole essay is an unnecessary exercise to prove the obvious. An at-tractive feature of this early work is its neutral character in the sense that it does not presuppose Quine's own other views developed after 1935. Hence, its conclusions are weaker but more definitive.

The main points can be summarized briefly. Unlike Quine's later views, here the domain of logic is left indeterminate. The program of reducing mathematics to logic, it is said, 'has been advanced to such a point as to suggest that no fundamental difficulties stand in the way of completing the process.' It then examines the sense in which logic can be said to be true by convention. The famous dialogue of Achilles and the tortoise constructed by Lewis Carroll (published in *Mind* and, e.g., reproduced in Ralph Eaton's Harvard textbook of 1931) is applied to give a circularity in inferring logic from explicit convention. This circle is eliminated by the suggestion to 'adopt conventions through behavior.' But, Quine concludes, what remains of the doctrine is of little interest. 'In dropping the attributes of deliberateness and explic-itness from the notion of linguistic convention we risk depriving the latter of any explanatory force and reducing it to an idle label.'

During the first semester of 1940–1941, Russell, Carnap, Alfred Tarski, Nelson Goodman, and Quine were all at Harvard, and they formed a group for the discussion of logical problems. Carnap gave several talks on his attempt to define logical truth as a semantic concept. Tarski and Quine rejected the sharp distinction Carnap wished to make between logical and factual truth. These objections and their further elaborations were only published ten years later in Quine's most famous article 'Two dogmas' (January, 1951). Even then the decision to publish was in part stimulated, I would conjecture, by the unexpected publication of a report of some of the contentions. The delay in writing up the material for publication is partly related to Quine's war service in 1942–1945. But of course Quine did publish a good deal between 1941 and 1951. One cannot help regarding this long delay as yet another example of the familiar experience that the author's initial judgment as to the importance of a piece of work often differs greatly from its public reception.

This seminal and influential article is often taken as the single most effective work in dismantling the house of cards that had been built by the Vienna Circle and stood on the shaky foundation of several rousing slogans pointing to utopian projects of reconstructing human knowledge and eliminating metaphysics (which, for example, Gödel regards as the very center of philosophy). The slogans were saturated with equivocations. Mathematics is said to be analytic and the equivocation between the two senses just mentioned leads to the conclusion that no important truth can be analytic or necessary and applicable to the world. The fact that mathematics is important, one would have thought, implies that analytic truths can be important. Moreover, why must philosophy seek analytic or necessary propositions? The concept of meaning is given the normative or persuasive definition of verifiability which, as it turns out, is a highly ambiguous notion. For example, after repeated relaxations of the notion, Carnap thus paraphrases Einstein's response to him in conversation (sometime in 1952–1954): 'If positivism were now liberalized to such an extent, there would no longer be any difference between our conception and any other philosophical view' (IA, p. 38).

At any rate, while a number of people had distrusted the Vienna slogans with good reason, Quine the onetime disciple was the first one to point out that the emperor had no clothing by putting together a broad, forceful, and colorful critique of the several pillars of the Viennese architecture. Even though Quine proposed to continue the tradition with his 'empiricism without the dogmas,' my impression is, as confirmed, e.g., by Rorty's account (1982, last essay), that Quine's article played a crucial role in the process of the disintegration of the 'analytic philosophy' movement. In view of the importance of the article, for analytic philosophy and for Quine's further development, I propose to quote in full Quine's wide-ranging initial summary of the article which suggests the conclusion of one stage and the beginning of another in the history of 'modern analytical empiricism,' to borrow a term from Russell (1946, p. 862) (which happens to coincide with my proposal in the Introduction but is probably both broader and more appropriate with the addition of 'modern'):

> Modern empiricism has been conditioned in large part by two dogmas. One is a belief in some fundamental cleavage between truths which are *analytic*, or grounded in meanings independently of matters of fact, and truths which are synthetic, or grounded in fact. The other dogma is *reductionism*: the belief that each meaningful statement is equivalent to some logical construct upon terms which refer to immediate experience. Both dogmas, I shall argue, are ill-founded. One effect of abandoning them is, as we shall see, a blurring of the supposed boundary between speculative metaphysics and natural science. Another effect is a shift toward pragmatism.

The article conflates logical truths with the broader class of analytic truths by stressing their common dependence on meaning which is transformed into the matter of the synonymy of linguistic forms. It quickly drops logic and mathematics, concentrating instead on linguistics. I prefer not to follow this merger plus transformation but to cling to the simpler special case of logical (and mathematical) truths as well as the 'intuition' of the vaguer concepts of meaning and concept. I find it more informative to adhere to the natural intuitive concept (say, of set) of which a good deal is known in its own home ('one must always ask oneself: is the word ever actually used in this way in the language-game which is its original home?' *PI*, 116).

The next extended consideration by Quine on logical truth is probably 'Carnap and logical truth' written in 1954 and published (among its various forms) in Schilpp 1963 with Carnap's reply. In this paper Quine includes set theory in logic (e.g., 'The further part of logic is set theory,' p. 388). He argues that the linguistic doctrine (of conventions) is less empty for set theory than for elementary logic. He offers as support for this view his widely influential and highly controversial opinion that in set theory we find ourselves 'making deliberate choices and setting them forth unaccompanied by any attempt at justification other than in terms of elegance and convenience' (p. 394 and p. 396). (For brevity, I shall refer to this position as 'the bankruptcy theory,' following familiar usage.) A distinction is mentioned between logical truth (in a narrower sense) and a broader sense which includes truths by 'essential predication' and might as well retain its familiar label of 'analytic.' The conclusion is that logical truth (in the first sense which is Quine's own usage followed here) is well enough definable, but analyticity calls for some 'accounting of synonymies throughout a universal language' (p. 404).

Carnap now distinguishes convention from meaning and devotes most of his reply to defending analyticity 'as a semantic concept.' Part of the original reply was so long that it was published as a separate paper, 'Meaning and synonymy in natural language' (1955). Carnap agrees with Quine that a conflict of theory with observation leaves much latitude in where to readjust. 'But I cannot follow Quine when he infers from this fact that it becomes folly to seek a boundary between synthetic and analytic statements.' I remember being much frustrated in trying to think about the pros and cons as to drawing such a boundary. I now feel that the crucial issue is rather the heavy work which Carnap and his sympathizers *apparently* demand of the distinction. Since it is not easy to sort out the different components of this demand, it is perhaps not surprising that many of us have found the debate painfully elusive. Probably what is needed for clarifying this situation is not a philosopher but a historian. For example, I remember liking the spirit in which F. Waismann studied the distinction in his series of papers. But surprisingly for me at that time, these studies seem to have largely remained in obscurity. I now feel that the attempt to search out the areas of commmon agreement often fails to play a major role in philosophy unless it fits into a widely accepted large framework, indefinite and dubious as it usually is.

13.3. Logical truth and set theory

The monograph *Philosophy of Logic* (1970) sets down Quine's views on the nature of logic in a systematic way. First, we find a change of mind on the relation between logic and set theory. Does set theory belong to logic? 'I shall conclude not' (p. 64). Let me postpone for the moment a discussion of this question and consider first Quine's views on elementary logic (first order logic, predicate calculus or quantification theory with identity).

A discussion of the grammarian's goal leads into an unmotivated selection of a part of grammar called the 'logical grammar' which seems to give the formation rules of (applied) quantification in an elegant manner (followed by some philosophical discourse on time, events, adverbs, attitudes, modality, etc.). This is followed by a modern treatment of satisfiability and validity, which retains the essentials of the less formal formulations of B. Bolzano (1837) and Hilbert-Ackermann (1928). The 'logical structure' of a sentence is said to be given by 'how the truth functions, quantifiers and variables stack up' (in accordance with the logical grammar) (p. 48). Quine then gives, not surprisingly after the dice have thus been properly loaded, several neat definitions of logical truth. For example, a sentence is logically true if all sentences are true that share its logical structure; or if it stays true under all changes of its predicates; or if only truths come of it by substitution of sentences for its simple component sentences.

Identity theory is seen as belonging to logic. A subtle argument which I find unconvincing is offered on p. 31 to exclude ' = ' or any other predicate from the purely logical vocabulary. So the desired inclusion of identity is only achieved by a familiar device of defining 'x = y' by exhausting the basic contexts in which x and y can occur. This qualm over allowing any predicate at all in the purely logical vocabulary seems to contradict Quine's 1954 paper not only in the exclusion of the membership relation but also in denying his general assertion that a precise notion of logical vocabulary yields one of logical truth (p. 402 and p. 404). In any case, I am not able to see how the subtle changes in the 1970 formulation from his previous ones supply any convincing reason to affect his general device: choose the logical words first; the 'logical truths, then, are those true sentences which involve only logical words *essentially*' (ibid., p. 387).

[There are many signs that elementary logic is closed with respect to various natural extensions and can be characterized uniquely by plausible minimal conditions. Theorems along this line have been proven by Per Lindström (*Theoria*, 1969), L. H. Tharp (*JSL*, vol. 39, 1974, pp. 700–716), and probably others. For general discussions of elementary logic as a natural stopping place, see my *MP*, Chapter 4 (particularly pp. 143–163) and Tharp's 'What logic is the right logic?' (*Synthèse*, vol. 31, 1975, pp. 1–21).]

With regard to set theory I shall take as a known fact that mathematics is reducible to set theory, a conclusion which, I believe, Quine also accepts. I wish to argue for three propositions which seem to be contrary to Quine's views of 1970. First, set theory is 'one': there are different systems of set theory only in the same sense as there are different systems for the theory of natural numbers which, incompletable as they are, invite further and further extensions (e.g., the arithmetic part of increasingly stronger systems of set theory). [The interesting area of 'predicative set theory,' for instance, is from this viewpoint a segment of the larger whole that happens to possess many attractive features; one might compare it with the theory of prime numbers, which is studied as a part of number theory but could conceivably be studied by taking the primes as the basic domain.] This proposition is contrary to Quine's belief expressed on p. 65 and p. 45 of *PL*. Second, set theory is a part of logic. This agrees with Quine's statement in 1954 but is contrary to his 1970 statement, as mentioned above. Third, set theory and mathematics are analytic and necessary. This proposition is probably contrary to Quine's opinion not so much because he denies it but rather because he finds it unclear. This difference reflects what might be called metaphilosophical issues on which it is harder to reach agreement.

The position is that we have a stable enough concept of set to enjoy agreement not only in believing that the familiar axioms of ZF are true of this concept but even on many stronger axioms of infinity. In most cases we have a pretty good idea how high a 'rank' we have to go to in order to satisfy the axiom under consideration. In a few unsettled cases, it is believed that the matter will be clarified in a manner that preserves agreement. Hence, the paradoxes represent 'misunderstandings' of the concept rather than prove its bankruptcy. The meaning of the concept of set is certainly not obvious in the sense that given a proposition we can easily see whether it is true of the concept. The most spectacular example is of course the continuum hypothesis which has passed its hundredth anniversary; another example is Souslin's hypothesis. All these and more have been discussed at great length in Chapter 6 of my *MP* and in the first part of my 'Large sets' (1977). I would only like to add some historical explanation and suggest that Quine has, undoubtedly as a result of more reflections, come closer to this view since 1970.

The concept of set just mentioned is known in the literature as the iterative (or Cantor's) concept of set. It is debatable how clearly Cantor did have such a concept. For others, this concept seems to have taken quite some time to emerge more and more clearly. In other words, it had taken time and effort before the 'misunderstandings' got corrected and therefore the paradoxes were then said to be misunderstandings. In Zermelo's case, he wrote in 1908 much as Russell did on this matter. But in his paper of 1930, he expounded the iterative concept in an exemplarily lucid manner.

Of course the iterative concept is essentially just the simple type theory extended to higher and higher infinite types (or 'ranks'). Quine says in his *RR* of 1974, 'Thus I do not see Russell's theory of types as dormant common sense awakened. Still I do see it as somewhat akin to that' (p. 121). In the 1980 foreword to *LP*, Quine is more explicit. He criticizes NF and ML 'for allowing self-membership, which beclouds individuation.' He continues, 'Russell's theory of types has an epistemological advantage over NF and ML: it lends itself to a more plausible reconstruction of the genesis of the high-level class concepts. From the theory of types to the set theories of Zermelo and von Neumann, in turn, a natural transition can be made.' In fact, I feel that Quine's elaborations of the several sentences just quoted offer an alternative account of the iterative concept of set which may be more congenial to many professional philosophers.

The explanation so far may also be viewed as an argument for the conclusion that set theory (hence also mathematics) is analytic and therefore necessary. To Quine's possible objections to this conclusion, I want to say that if we do not wish to abandon the terms like 'analytic' and 'necessary' altogether, I do not see that anything can be found which is better qualified than mathematics (including set theory this time) for being (said to be) necessary. Relative to our present knowledge the iterative concept is the best concept of set (at least for developing mathematics) we have. For me one most interesting part of philosophy is to understand the richest concepts we currently possess. We have no assurance that the iterative concept will not someday turn out to be inconsistent but in speculating idly over such a possibility I cannot find anything nearly as attractive as in the work of elaborating and sharpening the existing concept to speed up its evolution.

The arguments for excluding set theory from logic in Quine 1970 do not appear convincing to me. For example, Quine points out that truth (even of the axioms) in set theory is not obvious, nor 'potentially obvious' in his special sense (bottom of p. 82), set theory has no complete axiomatization, and set theory has strong existence axioms. But I do not see these as reasons for excluding set theory from logic, nor did they seem so to Quine in 1954. In particular, the matter of complete axiomatization is an especially peculiar reason. For example, the theory of integers is in this regard like set theory, but the theory of addition of integers and the theory of real closed fields, being complete, are different. What has this to do with whether these areas belong to logic or not?

On the other hand, Quine notes important common traits between logic and mathematics (and therefore set theory): their relevance to all science and their neutrality (p. 98). Among the advantages of including set theory in logic I may mention: a greater continuity with the tradition of Frege and early Russell, a better conformity with actual practice, as well as making Quine's framework more coherent by bringing what he calls 'the locus of ontology' (the pure sets) closer to his home ground.

13.4. From Russell and Carnap to Quine
Quine first saw Carnap around the beginning of 1933 and came immediately under his spell. In 1970, Quine reviewed his intellectual relation to Carnap in these words (Hintikka, 1975, p. xxv): 'I was very much his disciple for six years. In later years his views went on evolving and so did mine, in divergent ways. But even where we disagreed he was still setting the theme; the line of my thought was largely determined

by problems that I felt his positions presented.' This judicious declaration seems to support the impression that Quine's prominence is parasitic to Carnap's work and especially the grand illusion underneath.

It may be of interest to compare briefly the work of Russell, Carnap, and Quine. There are striking differences in the style and substance of the work of these men who grew up with different social backgrounds in different cultures and historical periods. Russell not only changes his philosophical views quite often but spreads out in all directions: in education, in politics, in journalism, in social philosophy, etc. In contrast, Carnap and Quine essentially limit themselves to developing and revising continuously some central programs and ideas acquired at an early age. Carnap is primarily interested in a formal version of the philosophy of science, persisting in his efforts to apply the tools of mathematical logic. There is a clearer separation of logic and philosophy in Quine's work that applies logic more as a frame of reference for standardizing discussion by a canonical 'regimentation.' Carnap aims at, I believe not very successfully, creating and studying a formal philosophy of science as a sort of 'normal science'; while Quine tries to clarify the foundations of such an undertaking, using logic both to measure the language of science and to question distinctions fundamental to Carnap's pursuit. In my opinion, both Carnap and Quine, each in his own way, have an oversimplified view of the nature and power of logic. Quine is less fully absorbed in artificial languages than Carnap.

All three philosophers began by revolting against traditions: Russell against Hegel and Kant; Carnap against Kant and metaphysics; Quine's best-known work may be viewed as the result of revolting against Russell in logic and against Carnap in philosophy. Yet there seems to be a sense in which Quine's work is more negative, while more of Russell's and Carnap's work is devoted to carrying out positive programs. There is for Russell the monumental *PM*. Carnap revises and broadens his viewpoint as he develops under criticism; then he writes book after book to work out relatively exact ideas which do not quite answer to the more intuitive originals that we labor to get at. On the other hand, Quine's best-known work consists of negative theses and proposals. Even when he develops his ideas in a positive way, his strong critical sense seems to sidetrack him into more negative theses (indeterminacy, relativity, inscrutinizability, etc.) or artificial economy (formally simpler axioms and a mechanical examination of existence assumptions in set theory). He revealed the latent tensions in Carnap's thought in a perspicuous way. This was important in helping the average philosopher to get rid of the illusions about the promises of logical empiricism.

We all are familiar with the fascination with impossibility proofs in mathematics: $\sqrt{2}$ is not a rational number, there is no general method to trisect any angle by ruler and compass, arithmetic is incompletable, there are noncomputable real numbers, etc. In each case, we arrive at the negative result by using a clear positive delineation of the original domain. For example, we give a systematic characterization of the whole range of constructions by ruler and compass, and then we are able to see that for certain angles to trisect them calls for steps not lying in that range. It is only after Turing has found a clear characterization of computable real numbers that one sees easily there must also be non-computable real numbers.

The situation in philosophy is inevitably different. Since we do not have a clear determination of the ranges of propositions which are meaningful (or perhaps decidable by scientific method) or metaphysical, we cannot have an unambiguous proof of the claim that metaphysical propositions are meaningless. Similarly with the contrast between the empirical and the conceptual, or between theory and observation, there are various cases to be distinguished. In some cases we seem to have a clearer distinction than in others. For example, most of us are convinced that mathematical or set-theoretic propositions are not empirical. Hence, to argue for a negative result in philosophy does not give us something nearly as informative as in mathematics. A fashionable example is to ask what computers cannot do. Here again, we do not (yet) have a clear enough concept of feasible computation as we do with theoretical computability. Hence, the arguments pro and con all appear quite indefinite.

It has been suggested from time to time that Quine did to Carnap's program what Gödel did to Hilbert's program. Yet there is a difference, undoubtedly determined by the different characters of Hilbert's and Carnap's programs, which admittedly shared the defect of being too naively optimistic. On the one hand, Gödel, in discrediting Hilbert's optimism, opened a new chapter in logic by introducing new concepts and methods which have since been pursued with a more mature enthusiasm. On the other hand, in debunking Carnap's program, Quine's work created a sensation (and something of a vacuum) which had a sobering effect but yielded nothing comparable to the former (unjustified) enthusiasm many people had enjoyed in supporting Carnap's original program.

14. Ontology and theories

14.1. What is ontology?
The word 'ontology' suggests a study of being as such or being *qua*

being; it is related to the indefinite word 'metaphysics' in some indefinite way; it can also mean the totality of what is taken to exist or to have being or to be. I am not familiar with the history of its usage. A casual search of standard references has yielded only scanty information. In connection with the stoics, Windelbind speaks of 'an *ontology*, that is, a metaphysical theory as to the most general formal relations of reality' (p. 199), but does not suggest that the term was available at that time. One source traces the first use of 'ontology' to 1636 by a late scholastic writer, Rudolf Goclenius. C. Wolff (1714–1762) treats ontology as the deductive study of being as such. In his lectures of 1765–1766, Kant spoke of it as concerned with the more general properties of things, but in the *Pure Reason* he seems to deny the possibility of ontology at least as a study of thing-in-itself (Windelbind, pp. 546–548).

In this century, N. Hartmann (1882–1950) wrote a good deal about ontology, moving from the universal categories of being to more specific categories and distinguishing Dasein (being-there) from Sosein (being-thus-or-thus). M. Heidegger (1889–1976) seems to view ontology as the study of the question: What character must being (or Being) have if human consciousness is to be what it is?

Quine seems to settle on the familiar sense of ontology as the totality of what there is: this is not so much a traditional branch of philosophy as the domain, once given somehow, ontology was supposed to investigate as to the characters of what lie in it. He is interested in the choice of the domain rather than further studies of the nature of the domain once chosen. His concern is with this domain sense (rather than the subject sense) of ontology which governs his peculiar discussions about his invented topics of ontological commitment, ontological reduction, and even ontological relativity. This clever choice of the term does have an element of naturalness and even captures some aspects of Russell's emphasis since 1905 on Occam's razor and the elimination of unnecessary objects. Indeed, Russell did adopt the terminology in his 'Logic and ontology' (*JP*, 1957; reprinted in *PD*, pp. 231–238). Yet somehow the excitement surrounding Russell's elimination of descriptions and his attempt at a no class theory is missing when economy is pursued for its own sake rather than as part of some better motivated project. Moreover, when the criterion for commitment and reduction is taken in a precise sense, it does not seem applicable to the more interesting cases, and when it seems to apply to more interesting cases, the criterion becomes murky. All these factors jointly may account for the impression shared by many which is expressed by Rorty as follows: 'What on earth is the *point* of ontology if *this* is what ontology turns out to be?'

Quine's way of talking about ontology has the virtue of giving shape and a sort of dignity to an aspect not only of Russell's interests but also of certain traditional debates over nominalism, conceptualism, and realism. Moreover, it does conform to one familiar usage, which makes it easy for it to gain currency. At the same time, since there is a natural tendency to associate it with the study of ontology in the history of philosophy, one is inclined to expect from what Quine calls ontology more than it can offer.

Relative to Quine's sense of ontology there are two comparatively clear distinct notions which Quine hopes to combine by some form of equivocation. Speaking of objects of a domain, there is a clear notion of the cardinality (cardinal number) of the domain: how many objects are there in the domain? In terms of sentences and theories, there is the clear notion of first order theories which are a focus of attention for the by now extensively developed model theory. In this case, however, the theories are construed as uninterpreted sets of sentences for which there is a moderately precise notion of translatability. Quine departs from model theory by taking theories as interpreted, thereby introducing a more indefinite element, which also relates theories to languages in an ambiguous manner. Moreover, as I have said before, we do not have first order theories of physics or psychology which are philosophically interesting areas considered by Quine, for instance, in his *TT*. In addition, the combination of interpreted theories with translatability seems to trivialize Quine's ontological reduction so that he has to resort to some ill-defined repair by 'proxy functions.' I hope these general remarks will motivate and get clarified by my more detailed considerations in 14.2. The ambiguities in Quine's formulations may also be a sign that he is trying to capture some fascinating intuitive idea of his; they certainly are a cause of the extensive discussions of his views in the literature.

Using Quine's apt term 'ontology,' I would like to review Russell's 'ontological development' again, in order to fill in some missing details. In the *Principles*, Russell distinguishes between things and concepts. 'The former are the terms indicated by proper names, the latter those indicated by all other words.' (Proper names are taken in a wide sense.) Among concepts, those indicated by adjectives are predicates or class-concepts, and those indicated by verbs are always or almost always relations (p. 44). Hence, the ontology at this stage is as liberal as can be, except that unnameable or indefinable objects are not included.

The theory of descriptions (1905) eliminates terms such as 'the author of Waverley' by paraphrase (Bentham's term), i.e., by taking care of all sentences in which they occur. For example, 'Scott is the author of *Waverley*' becomes 'A person x wrote *Waverley* if and only if x is Scott.' In this way a singular description becomes an 'incomplete symbol defined in use.' In 1940, Quine undertook to extend the theory to proper names by introducing corresponding predicates. For example, instead of 'God,' we say 'the x, god(x),' where 'god(x)' means 'x is God' (*ML*, pp. 149–150).

I have earlier on reviewed Russell's ontology in the development of *PM*. Over the decade from 1910 on, Russell had a separate (less substantial) notion of subsistence in addition to existence; this may account for his preference of (subsistent) propositional functions over (existent) classes. In 1912 he said, 'Nearly all the words to be found in the dictionary stand for universals' (*PP*, p. 146). Unlike Frege, Russell tends to blur entity with expression, meaning with reference; examples can be found in his 'On denoting' of 1905, as well as in his other writings. Russell's ontology also includes facts (at least in his 'Logical atomism'). In his *Inquiry* (1940), he tried to get rid of all universals but was left with one universal, the relation of similarity. (By the way, this matter is discussed in my 1945.) This chaotic summary shows that the matter of ontology, viewed as a separate issue, becomes very messy when we look at Russell's philosophical development. Certainly Quine is much more conscientious in this regard.

14.2. Quine's views on ontology

Probably about half of Quine's philosophical publications are concerned with existence, object, reference, ontology, ontic or ontological commitment and reduction, particularly their relation to quantification and first order logic. His earliest paper, 'Ontological remarks on the propositional calculus' (1934), gets rid of propositions as denotations of sentences so that propositional calculus just became one of sentences or rather a theory of truth functions. This, e.g., is the approach later adopted in *ML*.

A paper of 1939 (preprints only), 'A logistical approach to ontological problems' (except that part of it was published in 1939 in his 'Designation and existence'), was, on account of the war, first published in 1966. It contains the famous slogan, 'To be is to be a value of a variable' (also in the paper published in 1939). 'Variables are pronouns, and make sense only in positions which are available to names.' 'We may be said to countenance such and such an entity if and only if we regard the range of our variables as including such an entity.'

The term 'ontological commitment' probably was introduced for the first time in the famous 1948 paper which also related variables to reference. 'Pronouns are the basic media of reference; nouns might better have been named propronouns.' The choice of quantification theory (first order logic) as the 'canonical notation' was stressed in 1960 (*WO*, p. 161 and p. 228). Yet another slogan is: 'Quantification is the ontic idiom par excellence' (1970). A complex explanation was offered in 1969 of the complex notion of 'the ontic commitment of a theory' (Davidson-Hintikka, p. 315); it is related to Quine's crucial concepts of theory and language. The distinction between substitutional and referential quantification became prominent in 1969 (*OR*). Related matter is discussed more extensively in *RR* (1974).

Chihara has called my attention to implicit significant changes that Quine makes in his doctrines, views, criteria, etc. Consider the several explications of Quine's 'To be is to be a value of a variable.' (1) 'We may be said to countenance such and such an entity if and only if we regard the range of our variables as including such an entity' (1939, *WP*, p. 199). (2) 'We are convicted of a particular ontological presupposition if, and only if, the alleged presupposition has to be reckoned among the entities over which our variables range in order to render one of our affirmations true' (1948, *LP*, p. 13). (3) 'Entities of a given sort are [an entity is] assumed by a theory if and only if some of them [it] must be counted among the values of the variables in order that the statements affirmed in the theory be true' (1953, *LP*, p. 103). For example, (3) is about theories, not persons, and it does not depend on what people *regard* as being the range of the variables.

I find Quine's concept of theory the hardest to grasp. He says explicitly that he does not use the term in the model theory sense of a set of (uninterpreted) sentences and that his use is not technical. He talks about a man's or an imaginary man's theory. He admits to using 'language' and 'theory' interchangeably, though not in all contexts. 'A language has its grammar and semantics; a theory goes farther and asserts some of the sentences.' He pairs the contrast between language and theory with that between meaning and belief. On his use of the term 'ontic commitment,' he does not intend to identify, as it would appear natural, 'the ontology of a theory with the class of all things to which the theory is ontically committed.' Various interpretations of the range might be compatible with a theory (with the interpretation of the predicates fixed). The theory is only committed to the intersection of the possible ranges. (Davidson-Hintikka, pp. 309–311 and p. 315.)

Putting together the pieces, I arrive at the following approximation to Quine's concept of theory. It is to be a first order theory with some fixed interpretation of the predicates and one or more interpretations of the range. The combination is a little imprecise because the interpretation of a predicate can normally be fixed only after the range is fixed. But perhaps the following example will illustrate Quine's intention and motivation. Let A be the familiar first order system ZF of set theory, and B be A minus the axiom of infinity. Any model of A is also one of B; moreover, B also has a familiar model in the domain of natural numbers (x belongs to y if $[y/2^x]$ is an odd number). Let B(E) be the theory with the primitive predicate interpreted as the membership relation; then it is only ontically committed to the finite sets, even though a (larger) model of A is also a model of it. On the other hand, B(N) with the arithmetic interpretation of the primitive predicate is a different theory.

Note, however, we could also take a different range for B(E) beginning with (say) ω in place of the empty set. In that case, the intersection of the ranges would be empty. Or, take the even more familiar example of first order Peano arithmetic. It is familiar that even after we fix the interpretation of the only primitive predicate (the successor relation), we could take any n as zero. Hence, the intersection of the possible ranges is again empty. Quine may wish to get rid of the symbol for zero by a predicate, but the device does not apply to B(E) and we do not need the symbol for zero anyway (just add an axiom saying that something is not a successor). However that may be, I would like to mention again the more serious matter of the limitation to first order theories, because we do not have interesting examples of them outside of mathematics.

The equivocation of languages and theories (in the model theory sense) has a tradition, as can be seen from Tarski's famous paper on truth where, e.g., he questioned the possibility of giving a truth definition for type theory with its infinitely many levels. In this connection I would like to tell an episode from 1950 when I was trying to carry out certain exact consistency proofs. In the process I noticed also a sharp distinction between giving a truth definition and giving a consistency proof. Roughly speaking, in order to give a truth definition in Tarski's sense for a system T (say one of the Zermelo type), we only need to handle the language of T; how strong the axioms of T are makes no difference. On the other hand, in order to give a consistency proof (or a *normal* truth definition), all the theorems of T must come out true. Hence, Tarski's assertion in his 1936 paper is false: 'In this way we are able to produce a proof of the consistency of every science for which we can construct the definition of truth' (Tarski 1956, p. 236).

I remember writing to Quine on this point, but, greatly to my surprise, Quine was not convinced by my simple observations. I often think this is connected with Quine's tendency to use 'theory' and 'language' interchangeably. At any rate, Tarski did make an admission of his mistake in an added footnote (ibid., p. 237) with a reference to my paper in *PNAS* (vol. 36, 1950, pp. 448–453). Tarski concedes, 'It is seen that in some cases, having succeeded in constructing an adequate definition of truth for a theory T in its metatheory, we may still be unable to show that all the provable sentences of T are true in the sense of this definition.' But the explanation of this phenomenon which he proceeds to give seems to miss the point. He does not seem to appreciate that, for a consistency proof by way of a truth definition, the metatheory has to contain in some form all theorems of T as theorems.

Since Tarski's work on defining truth has received so much attention, let me try to straighten out a few historical points. There is a great difference of opinion on the importance of his contribution to this area. For instance, around 1952, Turing spoke of this work to Robin Gandy and passed a harsh judgment: 'Triviality can go no further.' From the two preceding paragraphs it is clear that Tarski was not able to give anything like a definitive general formulation of what is needed. He worked with simple examples and got confused about basic points. It may also be contended that when anybody really needs a truth definition for some specific purpose, it will be constructed. Indeed, when I needed such a definition from 1948 to 1949, I was disappointed in trying to use Tarski's work as a basis. I had to start more or less from scratch to get the exact formulation presented later in my 1952. As far as the limited result of Tarski's work is concerned, Carnap also independently arrived at similar things (see §34 of his *Logical Syntax* and the reference to his 'Gültigkeitskriterium' paper on p. 336).

It appears clear now that on the essential points Gödel had not only anticipated Tarski but also understood better what was involved. Tarski explicitly acknowledged in the expanded German version (1936) of his main paper that he had obtained and added the 'indefinability of truth' theorem as a corollary to Gödel's famous paper of 1931, only in preparing the German version. But this was the very first thing observed by Gödel in the summer of 1930 before moving on to get his stronger theorems [see the report in my 1981(76)]. Moreover, a letter dated October 12, 1931, from Gödel to Zermelo, has recently been published (Grattan-Guinness 1979), in which not only is the indefinability of truth (in the system itself) explicitly stated and proved painlessly, but also is the decidability of the relatively undecidable propositions (in particular, the consistency of the given system) in 'higher systems' asserted (with a reference to the famous footnote 48a in his famous paper). Indeed, footnote 48a promises to prove the assertion in Part II, which Gödel intended to publish soon. 'The prompt acceptance of his results was one of the reasons that made him change his plan' (*FG*, p. 616).

A confusing minor matter is Quine's treatment of names and finite ontology. He does not question that names refer but uses an artifice to eliminate putative names because we are not sure they really are names (*LP*, pp. 6–9). Surprisingly he turns around to stipulate that ontology is meaningless for a finite theory of named objects because quantifiers can in principle be dispensed with (*OR*, p. 62). Thus, quantifiers began as a more reliable guide than names and then became the only soul of ontology, thereby depriving also 'real' names of their natural right to refer. This appears to me to be a counterintuitive measure which is quite unnecessary.

Quine began to consider ontological reduction in 1964 (*WP*, pp. 212–220) and continued in 1969 (*OR*, pp. 55–68). The negative starting point of the work is a fact I noticed in 1950 in connection with an arithmetical form of the Löwenheim-Skolem Theorem and a notion of translatability which is presumably similar to the notions of inner models and relative interpretation (also introduced around that time). I strengthened a result in Hilbert-Bernays to the following: If S is consistent, then arithmetic predicates can be written down so that substituting them for the predicates of S in the theorems of S, we obtain arithmetic statements derivable from Con(S) in ordinary arithmetic (*Methodos*, vol. 3, 1951, pp. 217–232). In terms of the concept of translation I introduced (*Trans. AMS*, vol. 71, 1951, pp. 283–293), this can be restated thus: Every consistent first order theory S is translatable into ordinary arithmetic plus Con(S).

This result gives us a sort of 'Pythagoreanism' which Quine wishes to block because he thinks it would trivialize ontological reduction. In the proof of the above theorem the (new) arithmetic predicates are defined very much in terms of the given theory S, and, therefore, have an air of unreality, especially if S is very strong. We can do very little directly about the arithmetical translations of the theorems of S. Hence, a natural suggestion for a more 'honest' reduction would be to require in some sense a more direct access to what S is reduced to. This may take the form of requiring that the new predicates should be introduced with no 'essential' reference to S. For instance, the arithmetical translation of the system B, mentioned a while back, would satisfy the requirement. At any rate, this is not the direction which Quine took.

Quine introduces a proxy function from the domain of theory S into the domain of theory T and the proxy function need not be in the notation of S or T. In addition, for all primitive predicates in S we effectively associate open sentences in T so that each predicate is satisfied by certain objects in S exactly when the corresponding open sentence is satisfied by the proxies of these objects. When the above conditions are satisfied, S is said to be reducible to T (*WP*, p. 218). As Tharp points out (*JP*, 1971, pp. 151–164), the function needs to be onto in order to assure that true sentences in S go into true sentences in T. Moreover, the definition permits no reduction of cardinality (at least in theories with identity) and therefore does bar Pythagoreanism. However, there is also the submodel form of the Löwenheim-Skolem Theorem which drops all but a countable part of an ontology. Quine seems willing to accept this sort of reduction but gives no convincing reason why this concession would not restore Pythagoreanism (see *OR*, p. 68, and Tharp's paper just cited).

Regarding Quine's 'proxy function' requirement for reduction, the following comments are contained in Chihara's 1973 book. (1) There are several unclarities and ambiguities in Quine's statement of the requirement (pp. 123–124). (2) Quine has not provided any good reasons for accepting his requirement: 'It is as if some board game had been ruined by the discovery of a simple procedure which enabled the beginning side to always win and the problem was to figure out a way of saving the game by changing the rules slightly' (p. 126). (3) An analysis of some simple examples suggests that Quine has given neither necessary nor sufficient conditions for a reduction (pp. 126–127).

In the lead article of *TT*, Quine merrily reduces mind to body, physical objects to (some of) the place-times, place-times to sets of sets of numbers, and numbers to sets. Hence, we arrive at a purified ontology which consists of sets only. Independently of specific qualms about Quine's definition of his proxy function, I believe I am not alone in feeling uncomfortable about these reductions. What common and garden consequences can we draw from such grand reductions? What hitherto concealed information do we get from them? Rather than being overwhelmed by the result, one is inclined to question the significance of the enterprise itself. Since we do not have a first order theory either of the physical world or of the mental states, what has happened to the 'canonical frame for theory'? What we are interested in are in some strong sense the reductions of the 'theories' from which, if accomplished, we would expect at least as much information as the (not altogether so obvious) reduction of numbers to sets.

What we are given appears to be not more than a matter of cardinality. That is to say, provided we have a sufficiently large number of objects (sets in this case), we can take care of all other objects. This is a meaningful observation which is true with enough qualifications. But after such a reduction, we would not have familiar statements about sets which serve as proxy of familiar statements about minds. We can only understand such statements about sets by first translating them back to statements about minds. This is a point which Wittgenstein argues at great length in his *Remarks on the Foundations of Mathematics* (1956) in connection with the reduction of numbers to sets. But in that case we have a much clearer picture of what we have done and consequently can make use of the reductions in many ways. At any rate, given Quine's prominence, I am sure his proposal will be examined carefully so that we can expect to get a better understanding of its significance or lack of it.

14.3. My system Σ_ω: a slight extension of the 1925 PM

In reviewing his work, Russell puts down three requisites for a satisfactory solution of the paradoxes: the contradictions should disappear; the solution should leave intact as much of mathematics as possible; and it should, on reflection, appeal to what may be called 'logical common sense.' In particular, he is not satisfied with Quine's systems 'because they seem to be ad hoc.' He goes on to recommend his ramified type theory and his vicious circle. 'I must confess,' he concludes, 'that this doctrine has not won wide acceptance, but I have seen no argument against it which seemed to me cogent' (PD, pp. 79–83). One familiar reason is undoubtedly the failure of his 1925 version to satisfy his second condition. In this regard, my system Σ_ω may be viewed as an advance in satisfying his three conditions more completely.

[The system and various extensions of it were first proposed in my 1954. They have received extensive attention in Fraenkel and Bar-Hillel 1958 and in Chihara 1973. On the technical side my paper (including the suggestion of an 'autonomous extension') has stimulated further work by C. Spector, G. Kreisel, K. Schütte, and S. Feferman, on predicative set theory. A recent example of the continuously increasing literature is Feferman's paper in *Konstruktionen versus Positionen* (1978, edited by K. Lorenz), I, pp. 68–93. On the more philosophical side, Ian Hacking, in his 'What is logic?' *JP*, vol. 76 (1979), pp. 285–319, pleads the case for ramified type theory but appears to imply that it stopped with *PM* (p. 306). I wonder whether systems like Σ_ω might not suit his purpose better.]

As early as 1939, Quine posed the question to which he returns over and over again (WP, p. 201): 'How economical an ontology *can* we achieve and still have a language adequate to all purposes of science?' His answer at that time amounts to physical objects and sets (as in set theory). Something like this persisted over the years. It was probably in 1976 that the physical objects were also 'eliminated' (e.g., TT, pp. 1–23). What remains are the pure sets of set theory. Hence, it is of central importance to Quine's philosophy to find out what sets are needed to get enough mathematics to do physics (and consequently also other sciences according to his outlook).

Given this fact plus his familiarity with *PM*, and his emphasis on 'virtual classes,' it is surprising that Quine for many years did not seem to have paid much attention to predicative set theory as a way of getting ordinary mathematics. In addition, some of his considerations of 'substitutional quantification' in 1974 seem to me to point to a conceptual framework within which the system I am about to describe is exactly what he wants. Let me first describe this system and then relate it to Quine's extended study of reference and ontology.

In the second edition of *PM* (1925), Russell attempts to develop mathematics from predicative type theory (or, as he says, type theory without the axiom of reducibility). He is even willing to give up Cantor's set theory, but he cannot even get real numbers (more exactly, Dedekind cuts). He thought he could get arithmetic (of natural numbers) but his proof of mathematical induction is mistaken. In 1953 I came upon the idea of using general variables, much as moving from type theory to Zermelo set theory (without the axioms of replacement but with the first order axiom of separation as made explicit by Skolem). In other words, I propose to use one style of variable which ranges over sets of all (finite) orders.

Russell's difficulty with induction is that a principle is needed for each order. The definition of identity of two sets has the same problem. The use of general variables removes these obstacles outright. A more interesting question is with the Dedekind cuts. The least upper bound of a bounded set of real numbers of order n is a real number of order $n + 1$. Hence, no single order suffices. Here, the use of general variables is elegant: each x (say, a bounded set of real numbers) is of some fixed finite order (say, n); therefore, $n + 1$ is also of a finite order and a set of order $n + 1$ also falls within the range of a general variable. Hence, we are able to get a form of the central parts of mathematics in such a system which, moreover, is demonstrably consistent.

Let Σ_ω be the system obtained from the empty set by iteration of the formation of predicative sets to order $\omega + \omega$ (see *Survey*, p. 571 and p. 619). This suffices for the theory of natural and real numbers and more. (For a detailed formulation of and philosophical support for this system, see Chihara 1973.) A remaining problem is to find a natural stopping place in thus moving to infinite orders. And I suggested a device that has come to be known as 'autonomous progressions.' [These ideas were presented to the Association for Symbolic Logic in December 1953 at Rochester, New York, and published in *JSL* (1954). A good deal of work along this general line has appeared in the literature since that time (in particular, I have devoted pp. 559–651 of my *Survey* and pp. 123–129 of *MP* to this subject). (Compare the bracketed paragraph above.)]

In December 1966 there was a session on Russell at the APA meeting, with Carl Hempel and me commenting on Quine's paper on Russell's ontological development (Quine 1966a). For this purpose I listed eight comments on Quine's criterion for ontological commitment. Since the length of the abstract was severely restricted, no elaboration was included (*JP*, vol. 63, pp. 670–673). Quine took the comments rather ill. Some of the comments are probably asking for too much from the criterion. Recently Quine has observed that the connection between ontology and referential quantification is trivially assured by the very explanation of the latter. 'The solemnity of my terms "ontological commitment" and "ontological criterion" has led my readers to suppose that there is more afoot than meets the eye, despite my protests' (*TT*, p. 175). But in reading *RR* (1974), I now feel that some of my vague comments can be made clearer in terms of some of the relevant passages in it.

I argued there that the ramified type theory does not commit us to the existence of sets in any opaque way because the range of variables is quite transparent. I am now gratified to see that Quine indeed makes a similar point in terms of substitutional quantification which works for predicative definitions of sets. Indeed, as I see it, the ramified theory is more or less a repeated enlargement in the manner of what Quine calls the virtual theory of classes. Hence, I feel that systems like Σ_ω should be congenial to Quine.

I do not fully understand Quine's relevant observations in *RR* and elsewhere. He seems to say that substitutional quantification and substitutional truth conditions are clear when impredicative definitions of sets are absent. 'As long as we adhere to predicative class abstracts, the circularity we just now observed does not occur' (p. 112). Moreover, in terms of psychogenesis, 'Abstract objects owe their acceptance to what is essentially substitutional quantification, cast in natural language' (pp. 112–113). What confuses me is what appears to me to be a different attitude toward substitutional quantification when he comes to number theory (p. 119). My conjecture is that he seems to say different things at different places because he has in mind also the different matter of the relation between abstract objects and infinity. Before turning to these points, permit me to make some general remarks.

Quine's appeal to the concept of individuation in evaluating NF (see 13.3) and his use of the idea of substitutional quantification in placing predicativity suggest to me an illustration of different attitudes toward the formal and the intuitive. Many people who are familiar with set theory achieve an 'intuition' that predicative set theory, having much in common with number theory, is more transparent than the impredicative, and that ZF is more 'natural' than NF; but they often have difficulty in adequately articulating these differences. In contrast, Quine's appreciation and categorization of relatively indefinite ideas seem to go together. This sort of difference must be the source of many disagreements.

Both Ramsey and early Wittgenstein used to talk about the nature of quantifiers and about whether they can be replaced by conjunctions and disjunctions (see Moore 1955 and Ramsey 1931, p. 237 ff.). As I see it, the distinction between predicative and impredicative is clearer than that between substitutional and objectual quantification. The distinction between finite and infinite is clearer than that between the concrete and the abstract. It seems to me artificial in these cases to reduce the clearer to the less clear or to discuss issues that can be done in terms of the clearer distinctions, in terms of the less clear ones.

Of course the matter of infinity is crucial, as I have often argued. Most of us find quantification over natural numbers quite clear. But according to Quine, 'A substitutional explication of arithmetical quantification brings no ontological economy to elementary number theory; for either the numbers must run short or the numerals are infinitely numerous' (p. 119). Quine appears to have in mind numerals as abstract types, so that the issue seems to change. He refers back to the 1947 nominalist construction by Goodman and him in *JSL*, where the issue is more definite. What about large numbers? Would 10^{9999} numerals be concrete or acceptable for substitutional quantification? This may also be compared with the following sorites paradox: 1 is a small number, $n + 1$ is a small number if n is; therefore, all numbers are small. (Compare Essay 15 in Dummett 1978.) I should like to suggest that the choice to stay with a finite universe rather than the choice to stay with the concrete is what is determinative. Once I argued this point at length in connection with Goodman's nominalism (*Philos. Rev.*, vol. 62, 1953, pp. 413–420; reprinted as an appendix in *MP*), and I have never been satisfied with his replies.

If the question of concreteness is put at the center, it would seem natural to connect it with the matter of substitutional quantification. I suppose we could imagine the universe infinite in space-time so that there would be every numeral. We would then presumably be justified in using the substitutional explication of arithmetical quantification. Would we then have avoided abstract objects? One would agree that envisaging infinitely or finitely many objects commits to different ontologies. Quine seems to say that when there is an infinite range substitutional explication yields no ontological economy. If that is so, does economy require restricting ourselves to finite ranges and to the question whether members of such ranges have names? In this regard, Quine's brushing away numerical coordinates (*RR*, p. 140) seems unconvincing if he is dealing with a finite range.

Perhaps Quine is not unhappy with natural numbers but merely saying that we are still committed to objects, and abstract objects at that. This interpretation would seem to agree with what he says elsewhere. 'If I could see my way to getting by with an all-purpose universe whose objects were denumerable and indeed enumerated, I would name each object numerically and settle for substitutional quantification. . . . Where substitutional quantification serves, ontology lacks point' (*OR*, p. 107). This is followed by a footnote saying in part: 'On the pointlessness of ontology at the denumerable level see also my *Ways of paradox*, p. 203.' For example, the denumerable universe of Σ_ω mentioned above may arguably serve the required all-purpose universe. How does Quine view this possibility? In other words, Σ_ω does yield ordinary mathematics on the college level and can take care of the physical objects in the manner Quine recently suggested (e.g., in the lead essay of *TT*). Would this then suffice as the desired universe for Quine? If so, what importance does such a result have?

Chihara argues in his book (1973) that Σ_ω can even be accepted by nominalists and taken as a successful execution of the nominalist's program (pp. 173–211). More recently D. Gottlieb also attempts 'a nominalist reconstruction of predicative mathematics' but is not satisfied with Chihara's claims. He goes on to say that his comments on Chihara's work are not conclusive; 'All nominalists would rejoice if these problems could be solved' (*Ontological Economy*, 1980, pp. 129–132).

Although I have no doubt the system Σ_ω is entirely transparent, I do not have any sharp conception of 'nominalism' to have an opinion on whether it has also a nominalist justification. As I see it, there are three types of possible objection to taking Σ_ω as it stands to be entirely satisfactory.

The first problem is that it invites further extensions, that it is not a natural stopping place. Since ω is quite a unique number, it could be argued that it is as natural as any other place. But, for example, since all recursive ordinal numbers can be represented in Σ_ω, why should we not use them (or rather a suitable representative set of them) as indices to extend Σ_ω? I also thought that one can use any ordinal a available in any given Σ-system and extend it to Σ_a. In this way, I thought that one could continue until reaching some closure system in which no new ordinals emerge. Not long after my 1954 paper appeared, Spector gave a result which shows that the closure is already reached with the recursive ordinals and if we take w as the first ordinal larger than all recursive ordinals (or rather ordinal types), then all ordinals available in Σ_w have ordinal type less than w (Spector 1955). Of course, there can be other natural ways of further extending the system, but it is reasonable to say that Σ_w is at least one fairly natural place to stop.

A second problem is, exactly how much mathematics (including set theory) can be obtained in Σ_ω or Σ_w? I have shown that the three difficulties with identity, induction, and Dedekind cut in Russell's system can all be solved in a natural way in Σ_ω. But how much set theory and more sophisticated mathematics can be got naturally or contrivedly is not easy to determine. A good deal of literature on problems related to this and the first issues has appeared since 1954; one survey was given by S. Feferman in 1964 (*JSL*, pp. 1–30).

The third possible objection is not so easy to formulate but is in practice the most effective. Working set theorists are quite happy with rich set theory and find it more attractive to expand the domain rather than to restrict it. Moreover, the project of predicative mathematics does not seem to promise much exciting new Mathematics and it seems not to have much direct contact with mathematical practice, except for the reverse exercise of determining, for each standard argument, the different systems in which it can be carried out. This must be the main reason why predicative mathematics, even after meeting his second requirement to his satisfaction, has not attracted as much attention (from mathematicians) as Russell might have expected.

Chapter 4
Quine's logical negativism

15. Quine's life and work

For over half a century Quine has made Harvard University his home, ever since he arrived there as a graduate student in 1930. His is a most successful and productive academic life. He has collected a maximum of honors and other recognitions available to a professional philosopher in an age when philosophy has lost much of its glitter. His friends and disciples have continued to dominate the Anglo-American philosophy departments. By my count he has so far published fifteen books (only one, *The Web of Belief*, jointly, with J. S. Ullian), of which there are various editions and translations into other languages. Many of his articles are widely anthologized. His books include nearly all his more important articles.*

15.1. His life

According to a report derived from Quine's intellectual autobiography, when Quine entered Oberlin College in 1926, he 'was of a divided mind about whether to major in mathematics, philosophy, or for its linguistic interest, classics' (Orenstein, p. 13). This third component may explain in part why, besides logic, as in the case of Russell and Carnap, language also plays a conspicuous part in Quine's philosophy. I remember serving as the assistant when Quine gave his course on philosophy of language at Harvard in 1947–1948. I believe that was the first time he gave the course. Was it also the first time that a course with such a title was ever given? 'A poker companion informed him that one Bertrand Russell had a mathematical philosophy.' 'Seeing a way to combine two of his main interests, Quine chose mathematics as a field of concentration and supplemented it with honors reading in mathematical philosophy. He started this reading in 1928.' He read *PM* and some other books by Russell.

He entered Harvard's philosophy department in 1930 as a scholarship graduate student. In 1931, when Russell came to lecture at Harvard, Quine had his 'most dazzling exposure to greatness' in seeing Whitehead

---

*His autobiography has just appeared.

and Russell on the podium together. Whitehead, who had examined Russell in 1890 and collaborated with him from 1900 to 1910, was well settled at Harvard and one of the chief attractions for Quine. Although their ways of doing philosophy seem to be strikingly different, they had a charming relation with each other. I can recall a delightful afternoon, probably in the autumn of 1949, when Quine took Mrs. Whitehead for a ride in the countryside. Margery Quine and I were in the backseat, while Mrs. Whitehead discoursed widely and impressively on many intellectual topics. Among Quine's teachers at Harvard were also C. I. Lewis and H. M. Sheffer (compare section 11.5 above). [Sheffer used to speak of Quine's logic as 'quinine logic'; I believe he would not mind using also the term 'quinine philosophy.']

Among Quine's contemporary graduate students were W. T. Parry, Paul Weiss, and my former teacher Shen Yuting. Both Parry and Weiss have spoken very highly of Shen, who soon left for Germany to continue his study of philosophy. None of the three has told me much about Quine as a graduate student. Thinking back to Harvard at that time, the little I know about it leads me to conjecture that Quine might have felt rather isolated intellectually at that time. Moreover, he probably was busy tending his own garden and did not participate much in what must have been typically vague and indefinite discussions among the students.

With his M.A. at Harvard completed in two semesters, Quine began his dissertation, *The Logic of Sequences: A Generalization of Principia Mathematica*, in the summer of 1931. This was completed in a year, and C. I. Lewis was asked to look after its publication when Quine went to Europe on Harvard's Sheldon Travelling Fellowship for 1932–1933. Quine once told me that he had at first been unhappy with Lewis over the slow progress in publication but that later he had been glad to have as a result the opportunity to revise it, undoubtedly in the light of the new horizons opened up while in Europe. The revised dissertation came out in 1934 as Quine's very first book, *A System of Logistic*.

During this first visit in Europe, Quine was extraordinarily active and energetic. He studied in Vienna, Prague (six weeks), and Warsaw (six weeks). He speaks of the period in Prague and Warsaw as 'the intellectually most rewarding months I have known.' The year brought Quine more up to date with regard to new developments in logic; he was particularly sympathetic to the extensional (and even nominalistic) view of the Warsaw logicians and philosophers. He does not seem to have had much contact with Gödel or any Vienna resident philosopher. The strongest influence (certainly in philosophy) was his close contact with Carnap in Prague (including his reading of the German typescript of *Logical Syntax*). The impact centers on the concern with the nature of a priori knowledge. The response to the extreme position of Carnap and logical positivism on this matter is related also to Quine's evolving different attitude toward verifiability and 'ontology.'

As Quine says in his homage to Carnap, 'I was very much his disciple for six years.' (Compare the beginning of section 13.4.) Presumably the six years refer to 1933–1939 when Quine was first a Junior Fellow and then a Faculty Instructor at Harvard. Indeed, it was in 1940 that he and Tarski debated with Carnap on analyticity and in 1939 that he published the slogan 'To be is to be the value of a variable.'

Not long ago I came across a memoir by Ayer (1977) in which there is some report on the Vienna Circle at the time when both he and Quine visited Vienna (1932–1933). 'The number of those regularly working in Vienna who had been admitted to membership of the Circle was fewer than twenty, and they were nearly all men of some standing in the academic world; at least seven of them held university chairs. The only person there to whom I came at all near in status was W. V. Quine' (p. 128). 'The Circle met once a week in a small room in an Institute outside the University. We sat at a rectangular table with Schlick at the head and Neurath opposite him. Menger and Hahn sat on Schlick's right, and Waismann on his left. The others present, apart from Gödel, were mostly philosophers' (p. 133). 'Quine gave us a talk on his current work in logic. Quine has an extraordinary gift for languages and I was very much impressed by his fluency in German' (p. 134). 'We hardly sought for any other company, though we took pleasure in seeing Quine and his handsome wife' (p. 137).

The year in Europe was crucial for the completion of Quine's education especially for the contact with Carnap and his work as a more definite and more congenial (to Quine) representation of the larger movement of the Vienna Circle. Immediately after this stimulating year Quine was fortunate to get three free fellowship years both to digest and reflect on the exciting new ideas just received and to prepare for his extended teaching career.

Recenty I came across a casual profile of Quine (in November 1936) which highlights several of his external traits, more or less familiar to his acquaintances (S. Ulam, *Adventures of a Mathematician*, 1976, p. 87):

> The logician Willard Quine was friendly and outgoing. He was interested in foreign countries, their culture and history, and knew a few words of Slavic languages, which he used on me with great gusto. He already had made a reputation in mathematical logic. I remember him as slim, dark-haired, dark-eyed—an intense person. During the presidential election of 1936 in which Franklin D. Roo-

sevelt defeated Landon, I met him on the stairs of Widener Library at nine in the morning, after Roosevelt's landslide victory. We stopped to chat and I asked him: 'Well, what do you think of the results?' 'What results?' he replied. 'The presidential election of course,' I said. 'Who is President now?' he asked casually. This was characteristic of many in academe.

15.2. His work

Most of his influential ideas can be traced back to the half decade up to 1940. 'Truth by convention' was completed in 1935, and by 1940 he was voicing in discussions with Carnap those qualms over analyticity which later received a persuasive formulation in his 'Two dogmas' (1951). NF ('New foundations') and its predecessor were worked out in 1936; these were followed by an inconsistent enlargement in *ML* (*Mathematical Logic*, 1940). The error was corrected by me in 1949 and the correction was incorporated into the revised edition published in 1951. The corrected version is known as ML in the literature. By the way, his only other book on higher logic, *SL* (*Set Theory and Its Logic*, 1963 and 1969), also grew out of a comparison of NF and ML with standard systems of set theory, which is quite similar to but more polished than my monograph with R. McNaughton (*Les systèmes axiomatiques de la théorie des ensembles*, 1953). Two papers on existence and 'ontology' were published in 1939 (one of them with preprints only at that time) which to a large extent anticipated the more definitive proposal in 'On what there is' (1948). This and the two papers on dogmas and on NF (with added notes on ML) were all reprinted in *LP* (*From a Logical Point of View*, 1953), which might, therefore, be said to contain all the basic ideas of his life's work.

Quine often combines his teaching with book writing. Apart from the more advanced *ML*, he had by 1950 produced three textbooks on elementary logic (1941, 1944, 1950) of which the central one is undoubtedly the latest, namely *Methods of Logic* (1950, 1959, 1972). Hence, by 1950 we can count five books (one of them is his revised dissertation of 1934), all of them in technical logic. In fact, the only other books in logic are *SL*, a collection of papers (1966), and the amphibious monograph *Philosophy of Logic* (1970). Hence, we have just enumerated eight of his fifteen books and obtained the neat conclusion that half of his books are in logic. This tedious accounting reveals a trait of obsession with order which I share to a limited extent with Quine, who once responded to my observation on Carnap's excessive orderliness by comparing Carnap with one who retains all the baseball scores over the years. The account does confirm the general impression that from

1950 on Quine's main efforts have been spent on philosophy. It also suggests the more debatable conclusion that by 1950 Quine had already formulated and written up his most influential philosophical ideas, which he has extensively developed and enlarged since then.

From the 1980 foreword to a new printing of *LP* we find a substantiation of the belief that 1950 was a turning point in Quine's diligent life of research and writing. We see from the foreword that this first collection of essays served as a temporary substitute for Quine's forthcoming central philosophical book at a time when he had completed his central books in elementary logic and set theory. 'In 1950, having *Methods of Logic* and a revision of *Mathematical Logic* in hand, I set my sights on a book of more broadly philosophical character.' This was to take nine years: *Word and Object* was completed on June 3, 1959, and published in 1960. It must be the most extended single writing project Quine has undertaken. In 1952 he foresaw the long pull ahead and became impatient. He told Henry Aiken the plan of putting out a collection of essays meanwhile. This occurred in a Greenwich Village nightspot after Harry Belafonte had just sung the calypso 'From a logical point of view.' Aiken suggested borrowing the title and Quine agreed. I suppose this caption in a sense covers all of Quine's work.

Of the three basic articles mentioned a while back, the one on NF is expanded to include an account of its predecessor and the history of ML. Hence, it might be considered a sort of concluding summary of Quine's main work in logic. In contrast, the other two articles, while also harking back to a few earlier papers, not only are known for their criticism of the bold theses of Carnap and his comrades but also contain metaphorical statements of more general positions, the development of which has occupied most of Quine's work after 1950. Quine's extensive writings on ideas related to 'On what there is' have been indicated in 14.2. Of the proposals in the sensational piece 'Two dogmas,' Quine himself offers a review of their further elaborations. According to him, the purpose of large parts of *Word and Object* (1960) and the monograph *Roots of Reference* (1974), as well as 'Essay 2, above,' is to 'pour out into utterest prose' the content of the brief metaphors of the last pages of 'Two dogmas' (*Theories and Things*, 1981, p. 180). The metaphors in question include the tribunal of experience, the gods of Homer, the experiential periphery, and statements near the periphery. Among the elaborations, we may also add *Philosophy of Logic*, which is largely concerned with analyticity.

Let me pause to complete the tabulation of Quine's fifteen books. I have mentioned thirteen of them thus far. The remaining two are more collections of philosophical and popular essays: *The Ways of Paradox* (1966 and 1976) and *Ontological Relativity* (1969). Of the seven or eight books in philosophy, *Web of Belief* is exceptional not only in being a joint work but also in giving a relaxed and popular general account of Quine's view of the scientific method. Of all these, only *Word and Object* comes close to a book (or treatise) in the academic sense; Richard Rorty views even it as more a collection of papers put out as chapters. I myself used to find it very hard to write a book rather than make a collection of essays. This not only seems inevitable in trying to say something new in technical science, but also appears to be an unavoidable consequence of a familiar manner of doing philosophy today. It is, therefore, not surprising that all or nearly all of Quine's books are either textbooks or monographs or collections of essays.

Two distinguishing characteristics of Quine's work in logic are his successful concern with formal precision and his related preoccupation with existence assumptions. These traits are combined with his great interest in language to merge into his philosophical work on logical truth, analyticity, synonymy, existence, meaning, reference, modality, translation, individuation, and language learning. The response to Carnap and logical empiricism has led to a form of 'holism' similar to Pierre Duhem's position (in his book of 1906) and a form of naturalism said by Quine to be akin to Dewey's views.

In order to view Quine's work in a larger context, I shall begin with a summary of what I take to be Quine's philosophical beliefs with critical comments and continue with a critical exposition of what I call his 'logical negativism.'

15.3. His philosophical beliefs
I am surprised to discover how often Quine finds himself misunderstood when he replies to his critics. In particular, he often emphasizes that he has not changed his position on 'nominalism,' 'posits,' 'holism,' etc., but only worked out some of the elaboration which the brief slogans and metaphors needed. As we shall see, I believe he has indeed changed his views on central issues such as logic, 'nominalism,' and set theory. I have several vague impressions of this situation. First of all, Quine's philosophy covers diverse aspects which are not grasped together by a single critic, and he often recommends new and more exact usage of familiar terms which does not quite correspond to the critics' implicit understanding of these terms. Moreover, Quine more or less deliberately leaves certain critical terms such as 'theory,' 'language,' and 'conceptual scheme' relatively indeterminate. I believe he also makes some 'assimilation of expressions' which is perhaps an essential ingredient in strikingly new philosophical observations; the use which the terms 'posit' and 'myth' are put to seems to be an example of this.

It is a familiar experience that stronger brief formulations draw much attention at first and then these are explicitly (as in the case of Carnap) or implicitly modified into a milder and less surprising position. Quine may have such examples in mind when he stresses that his basic beliefs remain pretty much the same over the years. Here again since most readers do not fully grasp his interlinked structure of beliefs and usage of terms, they are easily misled by Quine's experiments (e.g., with 'nominalism') and changes of emphasis (e.g., from phenomenalism to physicalism).

A desirable exposition of Quine's philosophy could take the form of a separation of the fixed basic beliefs from those parts of his theory which respond to the development of the subject matter and his absorption of it. For example, he has probably been all along more sympathetic to physicalism rather than phenomenalism (in the sense of using sense-data as the basic stuff) but the failure of attempts to carry out a reductionism to sense-data is an important evidence for his own view (see, e.g., *WO*, pp. 234–239). Again, he probably prefers 'nominalism' and indeed experimented with it sometimes (in his paper of 1947 with Goodman), but, in the face of evidence, he has chosen to call himself a realist or platonist who believes in sets or classes. In the case of logic and set theory, he at first believed that mathematics can be reduced to logic and seems to leave deliberately open the question what is to be included under logic (1936). Then he separated set theory from elementary logic but counted set theory under logic (1954). At a later stage he identified logic with elementary logic, treating set theory as a richer separate subject (1970). On a more substantive issue I have argued in section 13 that the development of set theory should (and may) have also induced him to change his view on alternative systems of set theory that each 'proposed scheme is unnatural,' and that 'each has advantages, in power or simplicity or in attractive consequences in special directions, that each of its rivals lacks' (*WP*, p. 18).

In order to reduce the danger of misunderstanding Quine, I propose to begin with a summary of what I take to be Quine's basic beliefs as stated in his most recent publications: the 1980 foreword (to *LP*), *TT* (1981), and *WB* (1978). I can single out four pervasive features in Quine's work. It is to be 'scientific' and, moreover, there is no first philosophy prior to natural science (naturalism or naturalistic empiricism). A basic methodological principle for philosophy is to focus attention on language (from ideas to words, from terms to sentences then to systems of sentences). Use of logic (primarily first order logic) makes 'for a deepening of insights and a sharpening of problems and solutions' (*TT*, p. 191). 'Wherever possible, Quine likes to get by with the fewest and clearest assumptions which will suffice to do the job at hand' (economy, William of Occam's razor).

I believe that for Quine, 'empiricism' in a broad sense is the correct philosophy and that real philosophy (or at least its central part) is scientific philosophy. Of empiricism he lists (*TT*, pp. 67–72) neatly 'five milestones' which began with the shift from ideas to words by John Horne Tooke in 1786 and from terms to sentences by Jeremy Bentham (in parallel with Bolzano and Cauchy, followed by Frege and Russell) with emphasis on paraphrasis or contextual definitions. The shift from sentences to systems of sentences ('holism') is traced back to Duhem (1906). According to A. J. Ayer, Otto Neurath also expressed a similar view in 1932–1933 (1977, p. 131). 'Two dogmas' (1951) drew more attention to Quine's holism which 'has put many readers off, but I think its fault is one of emphasis' (1980 foreword to *LP*). Quine now speaks of 'a moderate or relative holism.'

To many philosophers holism suggests idealism and a coherence theory of truth. But according to Quine, empiricism is not a theory of truth but one of evidence, of warranted belief (*TT*, p. 39). Here we are reminded of Dewey's 'warranted assertibility.' Do we ever get beyond warranted belief to truth? To answer no would seem to contradict much of our common beliefs and entail, according to many philosophers, idealism and an exclusive reliance on coherence. To answer yes would seem to require from Quine's brand of empiricism an account of the relation between warranted belief and truth, thereby making it also a theory of truth. Here we have of course one of the perennial problems of philosophy. My own discomfort with holism has been an inability to grasp its meaning and implications. For example, I would be more comfortable if there were a solid body of typical illustrations of how, under various circumstances, we have as a matter of fact revised our beliefs when something appears to have gone amiss. Such a body of examples would suggest to me a more definite meaning to holism and even guide my future expectations. To me, for example, set theory seems pretty well self-contained even though historically there was once a good deal of misunderstanding of the ramifications of the paradoxes as they bear on the evolving concept of set.

The fourth milestone is, according to Quine, the abandonment of the analytic-synthetic dualism leading to a 'methodological monism,' a milestone that is of course closely associated with Quine's own work. He seems to view this as a corollary to holism. 'Holism blurs the supposed contrast' so that the organizing role of analytic sentences and the empirical content of the synthetic sentences are seen as shared by sentences generally or diffused through the system. Quine does not deny that there are striking differences between logic and mathematics, on the one hand (e.g., 'their relevance to all science and their partiality toward none') and the natural sciences, on the other. But, according to Quine, it is a mistake to see a dualism here, and 'The mistake comes from responding excessively to the terminological boundaries between sciences' (*PL*, pp. 98–99).

Here we have several different issues: whether mathematics is analytic, if so in what sense, whether we can bring out suitable characteristics of mathematics to justify 'the division' which Quine deplores, etc. What I find frustrating is to assert blandly that mathematics is empirical as well because we may conceivably give it up for something else. Since this has never happened so far, I am not able to give a determinate sense to the assertion; or the special sense of 'empirical' as applied to mathematics requires a prior study. In any case, in order to appreciate the historical significance of Quine's denial of this dogma or dualism, one needs, it seems to me, to analyze a good deal of analytic philosophy before and after 1951: I have tried to do some of this in sections 2 and 13.

From quite a different approach, G. Della Volpe arrives at a similar conclusion of 'methodological monism.' 'The judgment, just because it is a subject-predicate complex, proves to be at once *analytic and synthetic*: analytic because of the specific contribution of the subject or discrete-matter (sensation, feeling, raw fact or given, etc.) and its corresponding functionality; synthetic because of the specific contribution of the predicate or universal-category and its functionality' (p. 162). Volpe's assertion is made in the context of a sustained consideration to uncover and preserve the materialist or empirical element in philosophy and the scientific method (that applies to natural and 'moral' sciences).

'The fifth move, finally, brings naturalism: abandonment of the goal of a first philosophy.' This is traced back to August Comte (1830). 'Naturalism,' Quine goes on to elaborate, 'does not repudiate epistemology, but assimilates it to empirical psychology. . . . a good deal to do with the learning of language and with the neurology of learning.' Elsewhere Quine asserts that Kant was in large part a psychologist (*TT*, p. 191). I am not able to see how one can find a way of pursuing psychology today which would make it so interesting for philosophy (or just epistemology) as Kant's work. My own inclination is rather to reflect on central scientific concepts and developments. Or, more broadly, I am among those who believe that, for the foreseeable future, we can learn more about 'scientific method,' an extremely nebulous concept, from the history and sociology of science as well as the psychology of scientific invention than from neurophysiology (a more correct name than neurology) and child psychology. Richard Rorty discusses these issues interestingly and extensively in his 1979 book (pp. 213–311). Even though I do not fully understand him and do not feel that I agree with his general position, I often wish there were more such explicit discussion of metaphilosophy by respected philosophers such as Quine.

Quine probably envisages a longer term development which, so to say, will get to the bottom of things. More, Quine seems to suggest that he is laying the foundations for such a development. He speaks of using the strategy of isolation in his thought experiments. 'A latter-day Galileo, replicating his namesake's experiment, rolls a very hard and almost spherical ball down a very hard and smooth slope in an almost complete vacuum. He excludes interferences so as to isolate one significant factor. It is in this spirit that I begin with occasion sentences,' etc. (*TT*, p. 185).

The word 'science' comes from a Latin word for knowledge. 'Much that we know does not count as science. . . . What makes for science is system, whatever the subject. And what makes for system is the judicious application of logic' (*WB*, p. 3). Hence, knowledge is much broader than science. More, to drive a car, for instance, often uses much knowledge, skill, habit, and experience; it also presupposes much social and institutional infrastructure. It cannot be denied that a traditional concern of philosophy is the relation between (and even the unity of) knowledge and action. To study this area we cannot limit our attention to knowledge or belief (at least in Quine's sense). Moreover, knowledge without 'system' (in the sense of the quoted fragment) would seem to precede science, and it is more elusive. Even the systems in science are much more informal than Quine's *ML*, and the application of logic is much less explicit and more flexible. Hence, in using the strategy of isolation, especially in a hitherto underdeveloped area, we constantly face the danger of leaving out the more crucial ingredients. In this connection Galileo's own account of his various thought experiments gives me the impression that the fruitfulness of his way of going about the matter depends on certain preconditions of stability and homogeneity which may be missing in the material studied by Quine.

Quine combines a drive for (formal) precision with a preference for gradualism that tends to blur distinctions and emphasize relativity or differences in degree. The drive for precision gives preference to reference over meaning, extensional objects over intensional objects, language over thoughts and concepts. Even though he emphatically denies that he is a nominalist (in what he takes to be the only real and exact sense of the concept), I presume there are more traditional senses of nominalism that would classify him as a nominalist. The preference for gradualism and relativism is seen not only in his holism and the related 'methodological monism' just mentioned, it also gets summarized in a number of catch phrases: indeterminacy of translation, ontological relativity, relative empiricism ('Don't venture farther from sensory evidence than you need to,' *RR*, p. 137), the inscrutinizability of reference and of ontology, and what-price-bivalence. The devotion to economy is not only conspicuous in his work in logic but also prominent in his emphasis on commitment and reduction; I feel that the same devotion is also carried over to his style of work.

One source of the endless controversy in philosophy is the indefiniteness of the meaning of many broad assertions which only receive greater determination as the implied projects of charting a map of knowledge get carried out to a reasonable extent in one way or another. More timid souls may choose to adhere at first to an examination of some specific substantial area such as mathematics, physics, biology, economics, fiction, poetry, politics, etc. But such work does not satisfy the wish to work at the fundamental part of philosophy. It requires a kind of courage to put forth even negative doctrines which purport to apply to all of knowledge.

16. Quine's philosophical system

Quine is widely known through his negative theses generalizing his criticisms of Carnap. Recently the systematic character of his philosophy has been noticed. His negativism is intimately connected with his formalistic and behavioristic prejudices which in my opinion produce in him inadequate and not particularly fruitful (from a detached viewpoint) conceptions of science (including logic, mathematics, and physics) and philosophy.

His philosophy is scientific (especially according to his own idea of what is scientific) in many ways. It is very much a part of the going concerns of philosophy as a specialized discipline modelled after science. More than this, it aims at definite, piecemeal cumulative advances. It is also said to be an integral part of science. Indeed, 'epistemology in its new setting' is said to be 'a chapter of psychology.' Unlike most contemporary philosophies, Quine's is also scientific in the sense of being systematic. His system even suggests a new branch of science which specializes in discovering how science is developed and learned in the individual history of an idealized person. Of special interest to his particular approach are neurophysiology, the psychology of learning, language, and logic. In view of Quine's special emphasis on logic (as he understands it), the more restrictive and more formal adjective 'logical' seems more appropriate than 'scientific.' Hence, I have chosen to label his philosophy 'logical negativism.'

Quine's pursuit of purity takes the form of an underlying preference for the tangible. Spoken or written language is more tangible than thought, the formal is more tangible than the intuitive, behavior is more tangible than introspection, truth is more tangible than meaning, reference (extension) is more tangible than intention, individual is more tangible than society, facts (typified by those in geography and dictionaries) are more tangible than values, natural science is more tangible than other intellectual pursuits. His first major book, *Mathematical Logic*, is a model of formal (i.e., in the restricted sense of being syntactical) perfection. (As we know, formal precision of this type is precarious. This is illustrated by the fact that even after a contradiction had been discovered in the original system of *ML*, Quine failed to find the natural correction needed.)

He is an avowed behaviorist and behaviorists typically waver between strict and broadened positions. He played with sense data and nominalism in his earlier days. He would like to see philosophy becoming a science (perhaps like organic chemistry). To compensate for this preference of dependable and tangible narrow beginnings, Quine proposes and defends broad negative theses which spread over and shake up much of analytic philosophy. For those who do not agree with his beginnings, the inference drawn from his theses would yield counterfactual statements; or, for those who are convinced of the falsity of his theses, the inference would be a *reductio* of his beginnings. Such conditional conclusions would still be interesting as a sort of impossibility argument if one could be convinced that the beginning is a natural one which can be determined fairly exactly.

It is a little hard to give a fair exposition of Quine's system by singling out the several aspects of his preferences and fit them together. The preferences include behaviorism, physicalism, logic and regimentation, psychogenesis of theories (particularly of reference), empiricism, holism, extensionalism, and a (scientific) theory as a 'fabric of sentences.' Epistemology is transformed into a branch of psychology (of learning); ontology is made to center on first order logic (particularly the quantifiers); and language (particularly its acquisition and its regimentation) is the vehicle to carry out these ideas. The better-known negative theses are the rejection of the analytic-synthetic distinction, synonymy, meanings, propositions, attributes, relations, and modal logic; the indeterminacy of translation, the inscrutability of reference (and its generalization to ontological relativity), and the underdetermination of theories by experience. Many of these theses have broader implications than his system and have provoked much discussion because they appear paradoxical when taken out of the context of behaviorism.

In the critical exposition to follow I have deliberately disregarded his more definite contributions in reformulating elementary logic (in his several textbooks) and in his careful analysis of linguistic grammar (particularly in *WO*), on the ground that these results are of philosophical interest only from a very special conception of philosophy, which I certainly do not share.

Let me try to describe some of the components of Quine's system.

16.1. Empiricism

According to Quine, 'Whatever evidence there *is* for science *is* sensory evidence,' 'we recognize with Peirce that the meaning of a sentence turns purely on what would count as evidence for its truth,' and (therefore) 'all inculcation of meanings of words must rest ultimately on sensory evidence' (*OR*, p. 75 and p. 80). These are for him cardinal tenets of empiricism from Hume to Carnap's *Aufbau* of 1928 which remain unassailable. Here we have examples of general philosophical theses which must be true when properly understood and employed. Different views result from the different roles assigned to them in a comprehensive position. For example, there is a familiar tension between empiricism and holism. The word 'ultimately' in the last thesis is of course notoriously indefinite, and its absence in the first thesis seems to call for an explanation of how the thesis is adequate to all the complex relations between alternative theories and sensory experiences.

16.2. Behaviorism and the central place of language

These two preferences are mutually supporting because the concern is primarily with the public rather than the private character of scientific inquiry. Behaviorism is for Quine chiefly a behavioristic theory of linguistic meaning and linguistic learning: 'Language is a social art which we acquire on the evidence solely of other people's overt behavior under publicly recognizable circumstances' (*OR*, p. 26). One may question whether language can adequately represent our thoughts and mental activities or whether language in a richer form is a fully publicly observable behavior. Do we not lose much by leaving out of consideration the open-ended multiple interactions of behavior and our inner life? Moreover, scientific language is only a small part of the publicly observable uses of language and other forms of expression (say in art, music, architecture, etc.).

However that may be, Quine's central philosophical interest is in an 'epistemology naturalized' (*OR*, pp. 69–90), an 'enlightened' empiricism or a 'liberated epistemology' (*RR*, p. 3). It is for this new epistemology that the importance of language and language learning is argued (*NNK*, pp. 74–75):

> We see, then, a strategy for investigating the relation of evidential support, between observation and scientific theory. We can adopt

a genetic approach, studying how theoretical language is learned. For the evidential relation is virtually enacted, it would seem, in the learning. This genetic strategy is attractive because the learning of language goes on in the world and is open to scientific study. It is a strategy for the scientific study of scientific method and evidence. We have here a good reason to regard the theory of language as vital to the theory of knowledge.

Scientific method and its study mean many different things. A familiar and appealing idea is to learn to be a good scientist. In this case the purpose is concrete enough and there are visible successful examples. But it is doubtful whether there could be a 'scientific' study of how to become a good scientist. We seem to move from the particular to the particular rather than be able to ascend to a theory that would be effective in any general way. On a different level the study of a few well-chosen examples in the history of science may give one with normal adult intelligence some idea about better and worse ways of doing science. Clearly these things are not what Quine has in mind. In view of Quine's novel combination of psychology, logic, and linguistics in the envisaged subject, there would seem to be the dual question: Is it a fruitful field of scientific research? What are its credentials to the pretension of being the successor of the old epistemology (or first philosophy)?

Quine's preference for language over other data is further illustrated by his homogeneous way of transforming private experiences into public language. According to him, the way out of the subjectivity of observation 'consists in talking neither of sensation nor of environing situation, but of language,' 'I propose that we drop the talk of observation and talk instead of observation sentences,' and 'the observation *sentence* serves nicely to pick out what witnesses can agree on' (*RR*, p. 39).

16.3. Quine's physicalism

He, so to say, tries to capture the mental from two ends, the behavioral and the physicalistic, and assumes that the two ends do not clash. The subjective is thus tackled from both sides by the objective, and Quine, I believe, considers this approach the only scientific way. For example, he distinguishes sensory reception (at nerve ends) from perception. 'Reception is flagrantly physical. But perception also, for all its mentalistic overtones, is accessible to behavioral criteria. It shows itself in the conditioning of responses' (*RR*, p. 4). His physicalism (or 'hyper-Pythagoreanism,' *WPO*, p. 503) claims (*FM*, p. 166 and p. 167):

> Simply that there is no difference in matters of fact without a difference in the fulfillment of the physical-stage predicates by

space-time regions. Again this is not reductionism in any strong sense. There is no presumption that anyone be in a position to come up with the appropriate state predicates for the pertinent regions in any particular case.

Mental states and events do not reduce to behavior, nor are they explained by behavior. They are explained by neurology [neuro-physiology], when they are explained. But their behavioral adjuncts serve to specify them objectively. When we talk of mental states or events subject to behavioral criteria, we can rest assured that we are not just bandying words; there is a physical fact of the matter, a matter ultimately of elementary physical states.

A remarkable feature of Quine's physicalism is that, in his drive to get rid of unnecessary things, we are left with objects of pure set theory only (TT, p. 17, and FM). This is very different from his early views of finitism and nominalism. This shows a readiness to revise his basic positions as he develops and acquires new perspectives. At the same time I find here an illustration of a difference in preference: such drastic changes seem to me to reflect an approach to philosophy that depends too much on precarious first principles, while I would like to hold on to more stable material at the center.

This disappearance of physical objects or 'anti-physical sort of re-duction' is also the occasion to revise his emphasis on what he calls 'ontology.' He calls it an 'ontological debacle.' 'It has to do with ontology and not with ideology.' It induces us to attach 'less importance to mere ontological considerations than we used to do. We might come to look to pure mathematics as the locus of ontology as a matter of course, and consider rather that the lexicon of natural science, not the ontology, is where the metaphysical action is' (WPO, pp. 503–504). If, as I suggest elsewhere in the book, we include set theory in logic, then 'pure math-ematics' can be replaced by 'logic'; such a change, apart from other advantages, seems to me to suit Quine's framework better. It would bring 'the locus of ontology' closer to Quine's home ground and agree better with the tradition of Frege and Russell on the importance they attribute to logic and 'logicism.' (Compare section 13.3.)

Quine's physicalism retains to some extent the spirit of Carnap's conceptions of physicalism and the unity of science. The general idea is perhaps that the language of physics can in some idealized sense be made the universal language of all science, social science included. I take this to be what Quine has in mind when he stresses 'physical-state predicates' and when he says: 'The principle of physicalism must thereupon be formulated by reference not to physical objects but to physical vocabulary' (FM, p. 165). As quoted above, Quine dissociates himself from 'reductionism in any strong sense.' Here we have a rather ambiguous situtation which is illustrative of the relation between Carnap and Quine. Carnap's optimistic program had a wide and strong appeal. When the program yielded little success, Quine's criticisms came at the right time and appeared to locate the source of its weakness. (Personally I am inclined to think that the source goes deeper.) Quine then develops a modified program that is less ambitious and loses most of the strong and wide appeal. While Carnap's program was utopian in a negative sense, Quine's project suffers from, in addition to or in combination with the doubt of its feasibility, a widespread failure to see the point of it or any sharable purpose in it. This is probably the reason why Quine's system receives less attention than his negative theses from which totally different conclusions from Quine's own are drawn by others (for example, Richard Rorty in his 1979).

What is Quine's reductionism in a weak sense? Does it include a proposal to develop the language of physics into a universal language of science? If so, is he again doing a form of what he calls 'first philosophy' to which he repeatedly objects? For example, as more and more physics and chemistry are applied in the study of biology, we seem to create more and more links between biological concepts and those of physics and chemistry. But we do not presently see any practical possibility of eliminating biological concepts altogether, and in the task of creating more links the philosopher's role, particularly one who is preoccupied with language, is at best unclear.

An essential component of Quine's physicalism is his physical monism. According to him, for each mental state the correlated bodily state is specifiable simply as the state of accompanying a mind that is in that mental state. 'We can just reinterpret the mentalistic terms as denoting these correlated bodily states, and who is to know the difference?' (TT, pp. 18–19). The word 'can' certainly does not mean a practical possibility of specifying the bodily state; in practice we cannot always dispense with the mentalistic terms. As a matter of fact, in real life, the mentalistic terms enable us to make many distinctions which we cannot make in terms of bodily states. Even the theoretical possibility is not a proven conclusion but a postulate or a belief shared by a group which includes probably a majority of the people whose opinions Quine respects.

Quine takes 'it as evident that there is no inverse option here, no hope of sustaining mental monism by assigning mental states to all states of physical objects.' On this issue we have a natural tendency to interconnect different components (such as cosmology, natural history, economics, morality, and politics) and thereby complicate the issue. If we follow Quine in looking at the matter separately, then mental monism is not so evidently impossible and has indeed been favored by Leibniz (in his *Monadology*) and Gödel (in conversations). Indeed, since mentalistic terms are in an obvious sense richer than physical terms, it is easier rather than harder to extend the former to the latter (in ways less artificial than Quine's quick correlation). But in either case we seem to sacrifice much that comes naturally to us for nothing but a dubious mechanical 'economy.' The appeal of physicalism has undoubtedly much to do with the success of physics. But just because it so happened in human history that a particular way of looking at aspects of nature has turned out to be amazingly successful, it does not follow either that only those aspects are real or that all other aspects must be reducible to them.

Generally speaking we have in many situations a choice between an inclusive and an exclusive approach. In philosophy my own preference is for the inclusive approach which, in aiming to get order out of chaos, tries to retain as much as possible the shape of the different areas of human knowledge which make up the chaotic data we begin with. In particular, I certainly prefer to retain both the physical and the mental.

16.4. Quine's 'liberated epistemology'

In his *External World* (1914) and elsewhere, Russell indicated a program of accounting for the external world as a logical construct of sense data. Carnap made a famous effort to execute this program in his *Aufbau* (1928). The work can be viewed as a modernized version of parts of Hume's *Treatise* which was an empiricist revision of the Cartesian project in quest for certainty. Carnap was seeking a 'rational reconstruction' in terms of observation and logic (including set theory). The effort failed not only in getting deductions of the desired propositions but also in getting the definitions of the terms to give a translation into the primitive notation. Later in 1936 the requirement of translation was given up by Carnap (for details, see section 12.2 and *OR*, pp. 76–78). It is in this context that Quine introduces his new epistemology:

> If all we hope for is a reconstruction that links science to experience in explicit ways short of translation, then it would seem more sensible to settle for psychology. Better to discover how science is in fact developed and learned than to fabricate a fictitious structure to a similar effect.

As I understand it, the program of rational reconstruction includes much more than what is attempted by Carnap in his *Aufbau*. For instance, attempts to axiomatize physics, biology, etc., and Carnap's and Reichenbach's study of induction and probability all are efforts at reconstruction. The aim is to see more clearly and more systematically what is known rather than to discover afresh how things in fact have happened. Hence, it seems strange that Quine should consider his project a successor to the program of reconstruction. Of course, once the program is considered a failure, there are many alternative ways of modifying it. But I cannot see how Quine's 'liberated epistemology' even shares the basic spirit of the program of reconstruction; this of course does not mean that it may not be interesting for other reasons. More generally, there are alternative ways of modifying the original Cartesian quest for certainty and the Kantian project, including particularly ones which are not in the empiricist tradition. Indeed, I would like to think that by now we are ready to go beyond the contrast between empiricism and rationalism. At any rate there is a different contrast between studying how I know and what we know. Unlike Quine, I am interested in beginning with what we in fact know, much as Kant began with the fact that we do have mathematics and physics. This, I believe, is also the aspect in which reconstruction, unlike most of Quine's practice, is in the Kantian tradition.

It is certainly of interest to find out 'how science is in fact developed and learned.' But this suggests directly the history of science and biographies of (good) scientists, which are commonly thought to be different from epistemology. Indeed, Quine does not mean such studies but rather how an idealized child would learn language to the extent of being able to refer by relative clauses or, in regimented form, by quantifiers; or at least that seems to be the center of Quine's attention, viz., to search for 'the roots of reference.' According to him, the liberated epistemologist 'is out to defend science from within, against its self-doubts.' His project is to study, 'within natural science, how it is that man works up his command of that science from the limited impingements that are available to his sensory surfaces.' 'Its philosophical interest is evident. If we were to get to the bottom of it, we ought to be able to see just to what extent science is man's free creation; . . . to see whatever there is to see about the evidence relation' (RR, pp. 3–4).

These promissory notes are hard to evaluate. As the plan for a branch of science, it is not sufficient to ask important questions; it is familiar that there are many problems of great concern to us which are not ripe for a fruitful systematic study. Quine's novel approach with the help of logic and linguistics has so far not produced stable and substantive results sufficient to evoke impartial confidence in the approach. As philosophy one wonders whether there is not too much abstraction and 'semantic ascent' to obscure the more natural connections with the concrete situations. To get to a more considered assessment, let me turn to some of Quine's actual results which combine introspective (or speculative) psychology with grammatical and logical analysis. By the way, Quine also speaks of epistemology as 'the science of science' (*WP*, p. 226), as semantics (*OR*, p. 89), as containing 'the methodology of ontology' (*TT*, p. 21), etc.

Language is learned by ostension and analogic synthesis (see the index to *RR* under ostension and analogy). Quine's grammatical categories are terms, particles, and constructions. The initial stage of learning terms is by occasion sentences. A leap comes with predication which is 'the basic combination in which general and singular terms find their contrasting roles.' A further leap toward objective reference is the relative clause which is an absolute general term (adjectival in status) that has the form of a sentence with a relative pronoun taking the place of a singular term and with the word order often switched; thus, 'which I bought' corresponds to a sentence that is true of just those things x such that I bought x. The rewriting with 'x' (a relative pronoun) and 'such that' is for Quine the way to plural predication and quantification. 'All men are mortal' becomes 'objects x such that x are men are objects x such that x are mortal.' Using an artifice, Quine translates 'for all x, Fx' by 'objects x such that not Fx are objects x such that Fx.' [These ideas are developed at length in *WO* (Chapters III and V) and *RR*; a concise summary is given in *TT* (pp. 3–8).]

One purpose of these technical developments is to proceed from language learning and grammar to 'regimentation' according to the standard notation of elementary logic (the predicate calculus or the first order logic). In this way a new argument for the naturalness of elementary logic is introduced, while the grammatical analysis of language learning was initially also guided by the standard apparatus of elementary logic. At any rate we are led to an austere canonical notation which is nothing but that of the elementary logic and supplies for Quine 'a framework for theory.' The notation contains just these basic constructions: predication, the quantifiers (or quantification), and the truth functions. The ultimate components are the variables and general terms; and these combine in predication to form the basic open sentences. Quine tends to leave out identity as a primitive predicate, contrary to current practice; I shall, without distorting Quine's intentions, assume its presence. (These points are discussed by Quine at various places; see, for example, *WO*, pp. 226–232.)

16.5. Reference and elementary logic at the center
I see here a point of convergence of many of Quine's major interests such as 'word and object,' 'theories and things,' 'the roots of reference,' 'the flight from intension,' as well as the various exercises in his text-

books of elementary logic. Let me try to pull together some of the threads.

(a) The framework for theories. Elementary logic is Quine's canonical framework for the regimented formulation of (scientific) theories. Quine is of course centrally interested in science which is for him to be studied as scientific theories (i.e., fabrics of connected sentences); and as a philosopher he would like to put scientific theories under a formally exact uniform form. His preferred uniform form is just what is known in technical literature as the first order theories. For example: 'The basic structure of the language of science has been isolated and schematized in a familiar form. It is the predicate calculus' (*FM*, p. 160). It is, however, well known that there are serious difficulties in trying to axiomatize familiar science and scientific theories in this form [compare section 14 and my 1984(83)].

(b) Ontology. Speaking of (or referring to) objects and the place of things in theories is a central ingredient of all cognitive discourse, scientific or otherwise. Quine locates the heart of the matter in the use of quantifiers which play an essential part in elementary logic. If a theory is put in the first order form, then we are quite explicit about the use of quantifiers and therefore about what are said to exist. If a theory permits quantification over certain objects, it makes an 'ontic commitment' to these objects because 'to be is to be the value of a variable.' For Quine ontology is a matter of saying so, and it is primarily an aspect of theories which are all thought by him to be in principle formulable in the first order form; the concern for public explicitness is obvious in this connection.

It is clear that Quine's conception is very different from the concept of reification for G. Lukacs or M. Heidegger's concept of Being and beings with a distinction between the 'ontic' and the 'ontological.' I trust the differences in conceptions of ontology are related to the ambiguity of the concept of what is *real* or really real, which is often intimately connected with people's deep emotions. It is, therefore, not surprising that philosophies centered on the human condition would use different concepts of ontology from 'scientific' philosophies. The uneasy feeling many have of Quine's concept may be a result of the fact that scientific philosophies usually do not talk about ontology and that when they do, one fails to see the point of it.

(c) Grammar and language learning. Elementary logic serves to guide Quine's study of language learning and grammatical analysis; it sets the (preliminary) goals to be attained. In this connection it is interesting to find out whether or how Quine's work influences linguists and child psychologists.

(d) Extensionalism. Quine's concentration on reference and elementary logic (and set theory) is closely related to his extensionalism (or 'flight from intension'). The idea of extensionality is quite central to Wittgenstein's *Tractatus* in the form that all composite propositions are truth functions of their component propositions. For example, Russell discusses in this connection propositions such as 'A believes p,' 'A doubts p,' 'A desires p,' etc. (in his introduction, pp. xviii–xx). The motivation of Quine's extensionalism is quite in the same spirit. Quine singles out three requirements of extensionality which permit substitution by a (codesignative) singular term referring to the same object, by a (coextensive) general term true of the same objects, and of a component sentence by one with the same truth value. In all these cases, the truth value of the host sentence must not be disturbed (*WO*, p. 151). These requirements are satisfied by first order theories but not by the referential apparatus of our everyday language, which contains 'various anomalies and conflicts.' Quine devotes half of his *Word and Object* (Chapters IV–VI) to uncovering and remedying these irregularities, by reformulation and by renunciation. These measures include the following list in Quine's own words. With the subjective conditional 'and the propositional attitudes set aside, and modality and intensional abstraction dropped (§41, §44), and quotation reduced to spelling (§30), and the indicative conditional canalized (§46), no reason remains for' going beyond elementary logic (*WO*, p. 228). I shall make no attempt to enter into his careful considerations on these topics.

(e) Sets. A familiar principle or axiom of extensionality is the definitional condition that sets are always taken to be identical when they have the same objects as members. 'A trouble with attributes is that we are never told, or anyway not in clear enough terms, what the further conditions of their identity might be' (*RR*, p. 102). This is a typical example of what Quine calls the lack of 'individuation.' It is for this lack of individuation that Quine is unhappy with attributes (or properties) and relations, meanings, and propositions. Quine's attitude toward attributes or concepts is wavering and ambiguous (see *TT*, pp. 98–99).

In terms of set theory, the first blur may be illustrated by the move from properties or attributes to predicative set theory. What is involved is made particularly clear by Bernays 1937 which was adapted by Quine under the name 'virtual theory' (see, e.g., *SL*). The second blur may be illustrated by the move from predicative to impredicative set theory. On this point, there is a more attractive way of viewing the matter which was introduced by Bernays in his famous paper of 1935. His idea is more of a blur or, rather, analogy between the finite and the infinite cases. By this analogy, we view 'a set of integers as the result of infinitely many independent acts deciding for each number whether it should be included or excluded.' This is using the notion of set in a 'quasi-combinatorial' sense (*BP*, pp. 275–276).

16.6. Quine's negativism

Even though Hampshire speaks of Quine as 'the most distinguished living systematic philosopher' (Hampshire 1971) and Gibson (1982) gives a systematic exposition of Quine's philosophy, the best known contributions by Quine are of a negative character in several ways. There is less interest in his system as a whole which appears remote from central philosophical concerns and stable basic concepts.

Quine's negation of Carnap's program breaks into several components. Both of them moved from phenomenalism to physicalism. But Quine negated the important place assigned to the analytic-synthetic distinction as well as a strong (local) reductionism, which, though, Carnap is not partial to. For example, 'Theoretical sentences have their evidence not as single sentences but only as larger blocks of theory' (*OR*, pp. 80–81). As mentioned in section 12.2, Carnap sponsored 'holism' in *Logical Syntax*. The major disagreement is on the analytic-synthetic distinction. The large body of responses to Quine's 1951 paper was bewildering because it is hard to locate the real point or motive of the disagreement at issue over the distinction (of analytic and synthetic). Surely the focus ought to be how the distinction is employed by Carnap and not how sharp the distinction is. Another negation is of the elimination of metaphysics by reintroducing 'ontology' in what gives the appearance of exact terms.

This concern with ontology and especially with its economy and reduction I take to be another aspect of Quine's negativism. It is negative largely because putting economy as a first priority rather than a subsidiary concern arising out of particular circumstances is for me a negative attitude. In his own words, 'I cleave to my arid little S-R dialectic where I can, rather than try to make an analytical tool of the heady luxuriance of experience untamed' (*TT*, p. 185). True, fruitful idealized experiments have benefited from isolation of the factors; but they usually arise in more natural contexts. Moreover, Quine's criterion for ontology is usually inapplicable in the more interesting cases because we do not have unique or natural first order formulations of the theories under consideration.

In the area of set theory Quine negates Russell's respect for 'logic common sense' and concerns himself with formal precision (in notation and in 'ontology') plus ingenious constructions of insufficiently motivated systems. The sharable philosophical interest in a comprehensive fundamental logic is replaced by a quest for economy. It was only gradually that Quine came to see the basic advantages of standard set theory over his clever curiosities.

Developmentally Quine started with meaning construed as more or less explicit linguistic conventions such as 'a bachelor is an unmarried man.' Since we are familiar with the fact that meanings are not mere conventions but can be much more complex, Quine chose to give up meanings, synonymy, analyticity, and related concepts. He was left with truth and reference. Truth seems to give way to 'warranted belief' (*TT*, p. 39). Before long he decided that reference was also not a sharp enough concept and began to speak of its indeterminacy and inscrutability. Since reference is indispensable, he went on to introduce a relativity and to study its roots. (Even though we get back to the community of language users, he does not study this community as, e.g., J. Habermas does.) In this extended pursuit for tangible beginnings, he has introduced a few memorable negative phrases or slogans which have special technical meanings.

Let me list and explain some of his interrelated negative theses. These theses all seem to share to some extent an indefiniteness in the sense that they are true in some situations and under certain conditions (such as a suitably interpreted behaviorism). But it is not easy to see how one can derive much information or draw significant positive consequences from them.

(1) Holism. This view is often also attributed to Duhem. 'It is only the theory as a whole, and not any one of the hypotheses, that admits of evidence or counter-evidence in observation and experiment'; 'Evidence against the system is not evidence against any one sentence rather than another, but can be acted on rather by any of various adjustments' (*PL*, p. 5). If we look at particular examples in the history of science, we would find different degrees of local and global readjustments. Moreover, we generally arrive at a consensus in each case and do not consider it reasonable to adhere to a rejected statement come what may. A famous example is the negative consensus on Poincaré's suggestion that we adhere to Euclidean geometry come what may. From this thesis, we can infer that a single theoretical sentence need not have a 'meaning' of its own and that its translation into observational sentences is indeterminate.

(2) Rejection of synonymy and analyticity. If we assume that logical truths are analytic, then analytic truths are those obtainable from them by substituting synonyms for synonyms. But according to Quine, it is not sufficient to say that 'the synonymy of two linguistic forms consists simply in their interchangeability in all contexts without change of truth value,' because we have to require necessary (or analytic) interchangeability. Hence, we move in a circle between synonymy and analyticity.

This is an illustration of the sort of consideration elaborated in Quine's 'Two dogmas.' To the argument that he demands an unreasonably high 'standard of clarity' for synonymy and analyticity, he replies, 'Yet I ask no more, after all, than a rough characterization in terms of dispositions to verbal behavior' (WO, p. 207).

(3) Indeterminacy of translation. This was introduced as a thought experiment to magnify the difficulty in translating theoretical sentences into observational ones. It deals with 'radical translation' between natural languages where no preexisting aids to translation exist. Indeterminacy is the claim that 'manuals for translating one language into another can be set up in divergent ways, all compatible with the totality of speech dispositions, yet incompatible with one another' (WO, p. 27). This includes both the indeterminacy of intension (meaning) and that of extension (reference).

(4) Ontological relativity. Quine moves from radical translation of a remote language to communication in the same language. An extended discussion of imagined situations led to the inscrutability thesis and its solution by accepting as inevitable a relativity to some background language; it is meaningless to ask absolutely whether, in general, our term 'rabbits' really refers to rabbits rather than to some ingeniously permuted denotations. 'This was the inscrutability of reference, applied to ourselves; and it made nonsense of reference. Fair enough; reference *is* nonsense except relative to a coordinate system. In this principle of relativity lies the resolution of our quandary' (OR, p. 48).

(5) Underdetermination of theories. According to Quine, 'Physical theory is underdetermined even by all *possible* observations'; 'Physical theories can be at odds with each other and yet compatible with all possible data even in the broadest sense' (1970a, p. 178). Later he changed his mind: 'In its full generality, the thesis of underdetermination thus interpreted is surely untenable' (1975a, p. 323). This is followed by considerations about loose and tight formulations, finitely and infinitely (ill-sorted or not) many sentences, etc. With all Quine's avowed emphasis on actual science, the imagined examples and formulations appear so remote from existing physical theories that I am not able to link them with actual theories. For example, Quine seems to imagine these formulated as first order theories, but they are certainly very far from being so formulable.

On the whole, I am afraid I have not been able to find the proper motivation to appreciate the value of these negative theses. Hence, it is even harder to point out where they might have failed to attain the purposes for which they were introduced. I have included the summary for a measure of completeness in my exposition. It must be clear that my principal goal in considering Quine's work at such great length is to use it as a concrete example of a type of philosophy which is prevalent and, therefore, requires some attention by one who wishes to do philosophy today in a different manner.

17. Quine's logical ideas in historical perspective

Of course the word logic has many different meanings. For example, I. M. Copi and J. A. Gould have collected together various pieces in two volumes (*Readings on Logic* and *Contemporary Readings in Logical Theory*). A glance at the tables of contents would give an idea of the diversity of material which has been put under the heading logic. Hegel and Engels tend to construe logic in a broad sense. In a related sense Galvano Della Volpe develops *Logic as a Positive Science* (1969, English translation 1980). H. Scholz considers various senses of logic in his *Concise History of Logic* (1931, English translation 1961). There is the familiar contrast of deductive logic with inductive logic and perhaps also scientific method. Also, formal logic is contrasted with (dialectical, transcendental, etc.) logic. The older chair of logic at Oxford means something quite different from the recently created chair of mathematical logic. In their *Development of Logic* (1962), W. and M. Kneale include much which others would put under philosophy of logic. In some of these broader senses of logic, more if not all of Quine's work would be thought to be in logic.

In the present context, I shall confine my attention to Quine's work in logic in the more definite sense of mathematical logic. Even within this limited domain, I shall not consider his various elegant formulations of elementary logic but discuss primarily his work in constructing formal systems of set theory.

Before concentrating on Quine's treatment of set theory and its relation to Russell, I should like to list some of Quine's other contributions to logic. What has struck me for many years and seems to have drawn little attention is the syntactical perfection of *ML*. It has often been remarked that in a strictly formal system, a machine should be able to check the proofs. I have seen this goal stated and aimed at. But as far as I know, *ML* is the only extended development which satisfies this stringent requirement. Here, we have, so to speak, the last word on whatever is being covered in the book. If I remember rightly, once Ronald Jensen told me that the reading of *ML* contributed to his making the decision to switch from economics to logic. To attain a more practical rigor, I wrote programs in 1958 to prove all theorems of elementary logic in *PM* by computers (see my *Survey*, pp. 224–268).

There is also a treatment of Gödel's first incompleteness theorem in *ML* by way of the first order theory of concatenation, probably for the first time. Later, in a paper of 1946 in *JSL*, Quine shows that this theory is equivalent to first order arithmetic (with addition and multiplication as primitive functions). More detailed considerations by others on concatenation have appeared since then, for instance, by R. Smullyan in his *Theory of Formal Systems* (1961). In particular, there is an interesting analogue of Hilbert's tenth problem first proposed independently by H. B. Löb and A. A. Markov around 1955. Take an alphabet with two symbols (say a and b) and make up equations by concatenating strings of these symbols with variables to get terms; e.g., one solution of the equation $axb = yaab$ is $x = aa, y = a$. The problem is: Is there a decision procedure for solvability of any finite set of such equations? The problem remained open for many years. Only recently did G. S. Makanin give an elaborate positive solution to this problem in his 'Equations on a free semigroup' (Russian), *Proc. of 1978 Int. Congress of Mathematicians*, Helsinki, 1980, pp. 263–268. For some earlier information, consult my *Popular Lectures* (1981), p. 58.

In the 1950s contact with computer engineers led Quine to publish several papers on the quick simplification of truth functions. These results are frequently cited and his terms such as 'core' and 'prime implicant' are widely used. Quine's considerations are related to more recent studies of feasible computability. In fact, since S. A. Cook's work of 1971, the problem whether $P = NP$ has emerged as a central open problem in mathematics. And it is equivalent to the 'tautology problem,' i.e., the problem whether there is a 'feasible' method (viz., one executable in polynomial time, certainly not a reasonable concept of *practical* feasibility) to decide whether an arbitrary truth functional formula is a tautology. It is also equivalent to many other familiar problems in graph theory, algebra, number theory, etc. A whole book has recently appeared just to summarize the results on the general problem: M. R. Garey and D. S. Johnson, *Computers and Intractability*, 1979. One exposition is given in the introductory part of my paper with B. Dunham on this problem (*Annals of Mathematical Logic*, 1975).

Quine is careful in choosing his notation and terminology to reflect what he sees as the correct usage. He has introduced and made fashionable among philosophers a number of terms which often depart from common usage among mathematical logicians. Sometimes the difference reflects divergence of philosophical views, such as Quine's preference for 'truth function theory' over 'propositional calculus.' Sometimes Quine is simply more careful in cases such as his distinction between implication and conditional, equivalence and biconditional, his use of 'denial' instead of 'negation,' 'alternation' instead of 'disjunction,' etc. Quine's term 'quantification theory' leaves out identity, while the more familiar usage today is to include identity and speak of the first order logic (or just elementary logic). There is of course a minor dilemma in deciding how far one is willing to conform to common usage, especially when nothing substantive is at stake.

17.1. The historical perspective

A convenient point to begin an examination of the place of Quine's work relative to the history of logic is 1940. For one thing, the interruption of logic by war came around this time. For another thing, the bibliographical references given in the original edition of ML in this year help to determine Quine's range of familiarity in logic at this time. Moreover, I feel that since 1940, Quine has tended to limit his attention to refining and deepening his understanding of those parts of logic which had interested him before 1940. By 1940 most of the important directions which have dominated logic for the last half century had already received their solid beginnings. But Quine, even at that time, restricted his attention to elementary logic and a single aspect of set theory (namely, its alternative formulations), undoubtedly because (at least partly) these are the areas of philosophical interest according to Quine's conception of philosophy. What I find unfortunate is that on account of Quine's great influence among philosophers, most philosophers get a distorted view of what logic is about.

Up to 1900 the most consequential work in logic was done by Frege and Cantor, and to a lesser extent by Dedekind and Peano. Frege introduced (roughly speaking) the first order logic and attempted to reduce mathematics to logic. Cantor developed a powerful concept of set and introduced infinite numbers. Recently I have argued in my *Popular Lectures* that many central results in logic have been obtained by the interplay of first order logic with (infinite) ordinals, Gödel's constructible sets and much of model theory being the most conspicuous examples. From 1900 to 1930, we see the emergence of L. E. J. Brouwer's intuitionism; Zermelo's set theory and its refinements; PM and its simplifications; Hilbert's program of 'formalism' and proof theory; seminal contributions by Löwenheim and by Skolem; the first edition of Hilbert-Ackermann; and certain isolated results by others (such as Paul Bernays, J. Lukasiewicz, W. Ackermann, J. v. Neumann, E. L. Post, L. Chwistek, M. Schönfinkel, F. P. Ramsey).

In the history of science, we encounter here and there a relatively brief period when a subject makes spectacular advances. This happened to quantum theory in the 1920s, to molecular biology for a decade or more since the early 1950s. In logic the period was the 1930s. Gödel discovered the completeness theorem (of elementary logic), the incompleteness theorems (for arithmetic and set theory), an interpretation of classical arithmetic in intuitionistic arithmetic, and the constructible sets. J. Herbrand brought out some fine structures of elementary logic. Zermelo 1930 contains a persuasive description of the concept of set underlying standard set theory. Skolem constructed an elegant non-standard model of arithmetic. G. Gentzen perfected 'natural deduction' for elementary logic and gave two consistency proofs of arithmetic. Gödel tightened a suggestion by Herbrand to introduce a definitive general concept of recursive functions. A. M. Turing produced a neat model of idealized computers and gave convincing arguments to show that it captures the intuitive concept of computability. Carnap and Tarski independently made a closer study of truth and validity as they are, for example, employed only intuitively in Hilbert-Ackermann (1928).

In 1934, Gödel lectured at the Princeton Institute and interacted with Alonzo Church, S. C. Kleene, and Barkley Rosser, who have all extended Gödel's results in several different directions and continued to exert important influence by their work and their teaching. In contrast, Quine's interactions in the 1930s were with Russell, Carnap, and Tarski. In terms of books, the most remarkable one was the monumental two-volume work by Hilbert-Bernays (1934 and 1939). Also, an extensively revised second edition of Hilbert-Ackermann appeared in 1938. The first edition of Gödel's surprisingly formal monograph on the continuum hypothesis (and constructible sets) appeared in 1940. These books contain a majority of the results listed in the preceding paragraph.

Looking back to 1940 after more than forty years, one who studies logic today must envy those good old days when only so little and such attractive material needed to be digested to get to the frontier of the whole (now vast) field of logic. But of course even in those days most logicians tended to select only a few parts from the short list of directions given above. Quine's interest then and later seems to stay away from proof theory as well as what has come to be known as recursion theory, model theory, and computation theory. Within set theory he does not seem to enter deeply into the tradition represented by Cantor and Gödel. He is of course very much at home with *PM* and sympathetic toward certain earlier work from Poland. Frege's work is important to Quine, but, I conjecture, Quine probably knew in 1940 more of Peano's work than of Frege's. Since 1940 or 1950, Quine must have made a more thorough study of Frege's work. Indeed, I believe, Frege rather than Russell or Carnap is the model for Quine's own work. I recall vaguely that at one time a copy of Frege's photo was the only displayed portrait in his study at Harvard. I have certainly heard him speak of Frege with veneration.

Quine's interest is not to discover new theorems in set theory (or 'new facts about sets') or to find new axioms which conform to an evolving yet somewhat fixed concept of set. He is not even much concerned with deriving standard results of set theory. Rather, he looks for an elegant set of axioms from which 'ordinary mathematics' can be deduced. This was the goal of Frege and to a slightly lesser extent that of Russell, who was also interested in recovering Cantor's infinite numbers. But both Frege and Russell (most of the time) also looked for true or even obvious axioms (without complete success, of course). For Quine, certainly until a few years ago, the task is rather to find neat axioms which are not demonstrably inconsistent and from which ordinary mathematics can be derived comparatively smoothly. The concluding paragraph in Chapter 6 of *ML* expresses this view in a somewhat old fashioned manner (with regard to the scope of mathematics). Similar views have also been expressed by others before and after Quine.

It is a little complex to evaluate the influence of Quine's work in logic. Viewed in a narrow way, one is inclined to say that the direct influence has been rather slight. His system NF has certainly provoked much ingenious work. His influence on his students takes different forms, but I believe it fair to say that those who have broadened their viewpoint beyond Quine's have done more interesting work in logic. Quine himself is not interested in inventing special systems for special purposes, but those who do so (mostly with philosophical orientations) probably often learn their skill from Quine's books. Of course, if we come to what are called logical theory and philosophy of logic, Quine's influence is conspicuous. Moreover, I believe that Quine's books in logic are helpful to training in computer programming in that they help to cultivate the habit of (sometimes rather artificial) formal precision. Presumably a number of students are prevented from specializing in philosophy by requirements in logic for which Quine's books set the tone.

A more substantive issue is that generally as a subject develops, concerns and even styles tend to change. This phenomenon is especially striking for logic, since it has over the last few decades grown from a young discipline into a mature one. In particular, it has become more and more like older parts of mathematics in its style of work. Among other things, this means that concern for formal precision is pushed into the background. As a result, for the working logicians much of Quine's work is thought to be off the main streams.

17.2. From NF to ML to SL
Anyone who has struggled with *PM* (as I did in 1939–1940 as a freshman in Kunming) would find the basic apparatus of *ML* amazingly simple and elegant: a single style of variable ranging over all things, with only

three primitives (one for truth functions, one for quantification, and one for membership). Admittedly it was known before *ML* that set theory could be developed with such a simple notation, but nobody had carried out such a project. If we begin with *PM*, we can trace simplifications to Leon Chwistek (in 1921 and 1922) and F. P. Ramsey in 1925 (for details, see Church's review in *JSL*, vol. 2, 1937, pp. 168–170). In Gödel's celebrated paper of 1931, we can find a similar formulation of the simple theory of types, which is commonly used today. The use of a single style of variable goes back to Zermelo (1908).

In 1936, Quine completed his term as a Junior Fellow and began to teach as a Faculty Instructor. To prepare his courses he 'tried to settle on a sanest comprehensive system of logic—or, as I would now say, logic and set theory.' The first interesting attempt is his 1936. [By the way, in this paper the reference to Skolem 1930 is a mistake (surprisingly uncorrected even in the 1966 reprint); the correct reference is to Skolem 1922.] In 1936, Quine published eight articles, all but one in logic. Moreover, for the first three years of *JSL*, he probably published more material in it than anybody else.

This early system S uses membership as the only primitive predicate, defining $=$ and $\subset$ in the familiar manner. Apart from a form of the axiom of extensionality, the only axiom (scheme) is (1) $EyAx[x \in y \equiv (x \subset z \,\&\, Fx)]$. It is shown that counterparts of the basic axioms (i.e., leaving out the axioms of infinity and choice) of the simple theory of types can all be derived. Roughly speaking, we can derive the power set axiom from (1) and also prove that the empty set exists. Hence, beginning with the empty set, we can move from each type n to the next type by using as z in (1) the power set of the universal set of type n and obtain all sets of the next type.

Several comments can be made on this system. It is a proper subsystem of Zermelo's system Z (as made more explicit by Skolem 1922). First, (1) is an easy theorem in Z. Next, it is easy to verify that the familiar finite sets built up from the empty set make up a model of S. Hence, the axiom of infinity is demonstrably underivable in S. Of course, we can add some form of an axiom of infinity to S. But in that case, we just move toward Z and its further extensions. A subsidiary matter suggested by S is the possibility of playing with neat alternative (equivalent) formulations of the axioms of set theory. For example, I did some of this many years later (*Zeitschrift f. math. Logik*, vol. 13, 1967, pp. 175–188).

A more mysterious and more interesting development of the ideas in S was the introduction of NF a few months later. It was presented to the Mathematical Association of America in December 1936 and published in February 1937. In place of (1), Quine now drops the clause

$x \subset z$ and imposes some restrictions on Fx, namely, it must be *stratified*. In other words, it must be possible to put numerals for variables in it in such a way that $\in$ comes to occur only in contexts of the form $n \in n + 1$. Thus, for example, $x \in x$ and $x \in u$ & $u \in x$ are not stratified. This device of course reminds one of type theory. In fact, it sounds very much like what Russell calls typical ambiguity which he introduces more as a mere convenience than as a serious strengthening of type theory. Ernst Specker shows (1958 and 1962) that NF is indeed equivalent to type theory plus suitable axioms of typical ambiguity. This incidentally offers an intuitively better motivated formulation of NF in the sense that it brings out more clearly in what way NF enlarges type theory. Specker's construction which makes this reformulation possible is employed, for example, in Jensen's surprising result that NFU, seemingly a slight modification of NF, can be proved consistent in elementary number theory. NFU differs from NF only in a weaker axiom of extensionality which adds the condition that x is not empty to the usual form: if x and y have the same members, then $x = y$. The modification is reasonable in that it leaves room for non-sets or urelements. By coincidence, this weakened extensionality is the one Quine uses in the preceding system S just considered.

The story of NF forms a strange chapter in the history of logic. On the one hand, NF is off the main stream and results limited to it are of only isolated interest. On the other hand, some of the cleverest mathematics are brought out in attempts to meet the seductive challenge from such a deceptively simple system either to derive a contradiction or to prove it consistent (relative to standard systems).

It is Quine's habit to combine his book-writing with his course-teaching. The book *ML* of 1940 was the first fruit of this practice. The axiom of infinity had not been available in NF until 1953, when Specker disproved the axiom of choice in NF and thereby derived the axiom of infinity. Partly for this reason Quine constructed and taught an enlargement of NF. He says in the preface to *ML*, 'The material presented is substantially that covered in my course Mathematics 19 at Harvard.' Shortly after the appearance of the book, Rosser derived the Burali-Forti paradox from its axioms. Quine promptly published repairs which introduce sets 'in driblets' and are sufficient for the limited development of his book. 'I arranged with the publisher to paste a corrigendum slip into the remaining stock of the book, indicating a makeshift repair of the system. The text of this slip was inserted in the second printing (1947).' In 1947 I managed to use even weaker axioms and develop much more mathematics than *ML* (see my *Survey*, pp. 515–534). In 1949 I discovered that there is a natural alternative to the troublesome axiom (scheme) *200 and proposed the alternative system ML. I also gave with my proposal a proof that ML is consistent if NF is (Wang 1950).

The situation is of some general interest. Let S be a given system. For convenience, we assume that S uses a single style of (set) variable x, y, etc., and that S is a set theory with membership as the only primitive predicate. Thus S could be a Zermelo type set theory or NF or the system S described above or even ML. There were two familiar ways of enlarging S before 1949: the predicative and the impredicative. In both cases we add a new type on top of S, using, say, another style of (class) variable X, Y, etc., so that x ∈ Y, etc., can also be formed. We add an axiom of extensionality for the classes. The original variables of S are said to be ranging over sets.

A predicative enlargement PS of S is formed if we add the axiom scheme:

(P) If Fx contains no bound class variables, EYAx(x ∈ Y ≡ Fx). This has the advantage that we can not only reduce (P) to a finite number of special cases but also replace the familiar axiom schemes of S (e.g., the axioms of separation and replacement) each by a single axiom (e.g., Fx by x∈X). This is the sort of enlargement developed by J. v. Neumann and Bernays.

An impredicative enlargement IS of S is just a second order theory of S or roughly the adjunction of the next higher type in a truncated part T_n (for some n) of the simple theory of types. More explicitly, what we do is to add the unrestricted axiom scheme (in the enlarged notation):

(I) EYAx(x ∈ Y ≡ Fx).

But then we also strengthen the axiom schemes of S by allowing bound class variables. For example, if S is NF, then the axiom scheme EyAx(x ∈ y ≡ Fx), where Fx is stratified, becomes in IS:

*200Q. If Fx is stratified and contains no free class variables, EyAx(x ∈ y ≡ Fx).

When we straighten out notational differences, this is the troublesome axiom in the original edition of *ML*. The restriction on free variables is necessary because otherwise every class is a set: EyAx(x ∈ y ≡ x ∈ Y). This restriction is not needed in type theory because it is not cumulative. In other words, INF is Quine's system in the original edition of *ML*.

What I did in 1949 is to introduce a new type of enlargement, which may be said to be weakly impredicative. More explicitly, such an enlargement WIS of S is obtained by adding (I) as in IS but not strengthening the axiom schemes in S. Thus, if S is NF, then the old axiom scheme remains as in NF:

*200W. If Fx is stratified and contains no class variables, then $EyAx(x \in y \equiv Fx)$.

In fact, ML is just WINF. And for my proof of the relative consistency of ML to NF, the above restriction on *200 is essential.

A puzzling thing about NF is that when S is one of the standard systems in the Zermelo tradition, the enlargement to IS introduces no contradiction and indeed adds little new content to any moderately rich S. Hence, the inconsistency of INF points to some peculiar property of NF which, I believe, is not yet fully understood (but compare the next section). Moreover, the enlargement of a system S to WIS is less natural than IS because the sets (e.g., the set of natural numbers or the set of real numbers) do not benefit from the added power in WIS as they do in IS.

Before examining the various strong results on NF (and derivatively on ML), let me briefly outline the actual content of ML (1940 and 1951) and SL (1963 and 1969).

ML leaves out transfinite numbers altogether, derives the axioms of Peano arithmetic and a few elementary theorems, and gives a few definitions for ratios and real numbers. Curiously a system of set theory includes practically nothing from set theory. This is also why much weaker axioms suffice for the material developed. In 1953, Rosser published a more extensive development of NF in his Logic for Mathematicians which is not nearly as precise as ML. Moreover, much of the original elegance of the system NF is lost through the ad hoc introduction of complex formulations of the axioms of infinity and choice which are needed for the derivation of more mathematics.

Quine's primary effort from spring 1950 to spring 1959 was devoted to the composition of Word and Object. He returned to logic in the summer of 1959 and wrote SL, which was completed in January 1963. An extensively revised second edition was prepared in 1967 and published in 1969. The book divides into three parts. Part I covers more briefly and in a different way the body of ML; Part II deals with real numbers, cardinals and ordinals; Part III compares alternative axiom systems for set theory. The last part embodies the origin of the book which grew out of a short lecture course Quine gave at Oxford in 1953–1954. In writing up the lectures he got new ideas regarding the preliminary part and decided to expand it to occupy more than two-thirds of the book.

One special feature is what Quine calls the virtual theory of classes and relations, which is closely related to some work of Bernays 1937.

A second feature is a new definition of the set of natural numbers which dispenses with an appeal to the axiom of infinity. The earliest definition with such a property goes back to Zermelo 1909. A definition closer to Quine's was proposed by Michael Dummett in 1957 to answer my question of finding such a definition more akin to Frege's (see my *Survey*, p. 440 and p. 52). But Quine's is simpler.

The most pervasive feature is the emphasis on restricting to weaker axioms as far as possible (mostly existence statements) and 'neutrality' toward axiom systems 'largely incompatible with one another.' I am sure most working set theorists are not in sympathy with this attitude. Moreover, no clear intuitive picture emerges as to what axioms are sufficient for what purpose. There is no surprising new result in the sense that axioms formerly not known to be sufficient for the purpose at hand are now shown to be enough. The revised edition removes some defects in the treatment of transfinite recursion, prompted by Charles Parsons; and it brings the section on infinite cardinals closer to common usage, following a suggestion by Burton Dreben. A special case of the axiom (scheme) of replacement is singled out for attention: the image of an ordinal is a set. If we assume the axiom of constructibility (which, by the way, is mistakenly listed as the axiom of constructivity in the index on p. 353), I believe this is equivalent to the axiom of replacement.

As far as I can determine, Quine has published no technical papers in set theory since this book. In fact, I am under the impression that since 1963, Quine's work has been mostly in philosophy. The two editions of *SL* contain a survey of work done on NF and ML up to the beginning of 1963. In the 1980 foreword to *LP*, we find some brief comments on more recent contributions.

17.3. The career of NF (and ML)

Forty-eight years have elapsed since NF was first introduced. As recently as October 1981 a meeting devoted to NF was held in Louvain. The chief challenge is to determine whether NF is consistent relative to standard set theory based on the iterative concept of set. Over the years a consensus has developed that neither NF nor ML is a serious contender for being the basic system of set theory. In the 1980 foreword to *LP*, Quine remarks on the difficulty with natural numbers and mathematical induction in NF and ML, as well as their 'allowing for self-membership, which beclouds individuation.' True, Quine still emphasizes the 'real' advantages of their 'convenience and elegance.' But this is a debatable point in view of the lack of an intuitive picture comparable to the iterative concept and the necessity to add ad hoc axioms and concepts to actually develop mathematics in them.

Soon after the publication of NF, Rosser published two papers to consider definitions by induction in it and explain how the familiar paradoxes seem to be blocked in it (*JSL*, 1939). The first definite results of NF and INF (viz., the system in the original *ML*) are:

> T1. The Burali-Forti paradox is derivable in INF (Rosser 1942).
>
> T2. There is a finite axiomatization of NF (Hailperin 1944).

Since NF is a descendant of the theory of types, the theory of (finite and infinite) cardinals and ordinals is developed in the manner of *PM* rather than in the more convenient fashion that is customary in axiomatic set theory. To derive the Burali-Forti paradox, Rosser carried out some of these developments. As I noted before, since the inconsistent system is a natural enlargement INF of NF, there must be something strange about NF. Part of this unnaturalness is brought out in the following result (Rosser-Wang 1950):

> T3. NF has no standard model: no interpretation of the membership predicate (with the right identity relation) compatible with the axioms of NF could make well-orderings of both the less-than relation among ordinals and that among finite cardinals. (Compare *SL*, p. 294.)

As mentioned before, I proved in 1949:

> T4. If NF is consistent, so is ML (viz., WINF); or Con(ML) if Con(NF) (Wang 1950).

At that time I also noted a general argument by which we can prove the consistency of S in WIS (S is related to WIS as NF is to ML), provided WIS contains a reasonable amount of arithmetic. In January 1950 I communicated this argument to Rosser in a larger context. Applied to NF, the argument shows (compare *Survey*, Chapter 18):

> T5. The consistency of NF is provable in ML; or, Con(NF) is provable in ML.

If now we combine T4 and T5, we seem to arrive at the result that Con(ML) is provable in ML. Hence, by Gödel's second incompleteness theorem, ML would be inconsistent. The subtle gap in this astonishing argument is, as pointed out by Rosser in the spring of 1950, that there is an ambiguity in the arithmetic statements expressing consistency because natural numbers behave differently in NF and ML. In other words, even though we can give formally a similar definition (say, Frege's version) in NF and ML (i.e., WINF), the two definitions mean different things. (In summer 1949 I explained my argument to Gödel, and he suggested that I should look for the flaw just in such a difference. But I did not understand his suggestion then.)

The class Nn of natural numbers in ML is the intersection of all classes (not just all sets) containing zero and closed with respect to the successor operation. Hence, we get the following undesirable result (Rosser 1952; *SL*, pp. 306–307):

T6. If NF is consistent, the class Nn of ML is not a set.

This, as noted by Quine (in the 1980 foreword to *LP*), points to an unattractive feature of ML because for any substantial development of mathematics, Nn needs to be a set.

Specker told me that he had become interested in NF through a lecture of mine during my visit to Zurich in 1950–1951. Moreover, he said on several occasions that he found a note of mine ('Negative types,' *Mind*, vol. 61, 1952, pp. 366–368) suggestive. (H. M. Sheffer also liked this simple note.) It is a sort of midway station between type theory and NF. Add to the types 0, 1, 2, . . . of type theory also the negative types −1, −2, etc., and use formally the same axiom schemes of comprehension and extensionality. For each type m and each positive n, it can then be shown that the type m includes more than n sets. On the other hand, one can prove in ordinary arithmetic that the system is consistent. This system is more homogeneous than type theory because every type is like every other type to the extent that each type has infinitely many types above and below. Hence, there is a somewhat stronger 'typical ambiguity.'

A decisive advance in the study of NF was made in Specker 1953. It not only settles the outstanding question on the axiom of infinity in NF but brings out more sharply the complications with well-orderings in NF.

T7. The axiom of choice is refutable in NF.

Since the axiom of choice for finite sets is provable in NF, this implies that there must be infinite sets in NF.

T8. The axiom of infinity is derivable in NF.

Before the publication of these results, I had reflected on Hailperin's finite axiomatization of NF (T2 above). By a suitable axiom of choice, we seem able to enumerate a model required by the finitely many axioms by a formula in NF. In this way we can formulate an axiom of limitation which says that only the sets thus enumerated exist. But then, by the diagonal argument, we can also define a set distinct from the enumerated ones. We would seem to get an alternative refutation of the axiom of choice in NF, except that the new set is not defined by a stratified formula. The situation remains unclear despite T7, because a different axiom of choice is employed (*Math. Zeitschr.*, vol. 59, 1953, pp. 47–56). Since it is hard to obtain an intuitive grasp of stratification, making natural deviations in NF often turns out to violate the stipulated restrictions.

The next interesting result with ingenious constructions again came from Specker (see his 1958 and 1962; *SL*, p. 292):

> T9. NF is consistent if and only if the theory of types has a typically ambiguous model, i.e., a model such that for any sentence p without free variables and p* obtained from p by raising all indices by 1, $p \equiv p*$ is true in the model.

As I have mentioned above, Jensen produced a surprising result in 1969, using a whole battery of powerful tools. Let NFU be obtained from NF by slightly weakening the axiom of extensionality to require x nonempty (as specified before):

> T10. The consistency of NFU can be proved in ordinary arithmetic (i.e., elementary number theory) (Jensen 1969).

Further refinements of the results listed above have appeared in recent years; for a summary see, e.g., Boffa 1977; see also his 1981, which proves the consistency of some more subsystems of NF. At any rate, it is clear that everyone implicitly uses the Zermelo kind of set theory in studying properties of NF or any other novel system.

In this regard it is of interest to compare the unresolved situation of NF with the fairly quick clarification of Ackermann's system of 1956. This is usually tidied up by adding the axiom of foundation. Let the resulting system be AS. Soon afterwards, A. Levy in his 1959 shows that AS is no stronger than ZF. W. N. Reinhardt then showed in his thesis that ZF is no stronger than AS. This last result and a review of previous work is published in his 1970. Here, the question of relative consistency is not the main concern. Rather, the relationship between the two systems is brought out more explicitly by interpreting sentences and theorems of each in the other.

Ackermann's set theory leads to interesting 'principles of reflection' and stronger systems which are thought to be philosophically attractive. For an extended discussion relating to these issues, the reader is referred to my 'Large sets' (1977); in particular, there is a contribution by Gödel on p. 325 of the paper.

Chapter 5

Metaphilosophical observations

18. Philosophical presuppositions

There is a seductive idea tht once we succeed in uncovering the different presuppositions of philosophies and philosophers, we would be able to see their respective limitations and their relativity to special circumstances. In that way we would acquire a satisfactory classification and even an illuminating surview of the diverse main trends and their variant branches. It would then be possible to construct a more universal theory of relativity that is comprehensively absolute in giving all special philosophies their appropriate places. This unrealistic idea contains at least two dubious presuppositions of its own. It assumes an ability to locate the presuppositions of others from a viewpoint that is without presuppositions or at least with only more reliable or correct presuppositions. Moreover, it assumes that the presuppositions of others can be adequately made explicit in more or less clear propositions; but deep-rooted presuppositions take the form of interests and concerns which lie below the more explicit questions asked and the goals consciously pursued.

If we make a large assimilation, we might wish to say that every intellectual endeavor is to answer some question (or perhaps that every statement is made as an answer to some question) and that the ultimate causes of the questions are the (ultimate) presuppositions. (This convenient manner of speaking is, familiarly, to be taken with a large grain of salt. It is not unlike saying that every human action is done for some purpose; its universality is then protected by considering purposeless and disinterested purposes, etc.) Once a question A is asked (e.g., an open problem in mathematics), it is comparatively easy to motivate other questions believed to be capable of supplying steps which would lead to an answer of A. The question A may be said to be the relative presupposition of the other questions, and in most intellectual pursuits there are enough hard questions to keep people fully occupied. There is a temptation to say that philosophy (or at least first philosophy) is unique in attempting to uncover the ultimate presuppositions. But such a position is ambiguous and seems to demand some sort of investigation of which we have little successful experience. For example, it may be taken as a historical question of how an individual or an epoch is conditioned to ask certain basic questions. Or it may be taken as a conceptual problem of singling out the really primitive concepts together with the basic propositions (or axioms) which are true of these concepts. In either case, we do not (yet) possess noncontroversial and fruitful ways of tackling the formidable task.

18.1. Asking different questions

What is more easily observable is rather the phenomenon that philosophers of different schools are interested in different aspects of human activity and talk about different things. They set out with different goals to attain, tasks to accomplish, and problems to solve. Those who are interested in ethics, esthetics, or political theory may find Carnap and Quine disappointing because they say so little in these areas. If we limit our attention to one of the traditionally central parts of philosophy which revolves around what may be called scientific knowledge, we find Carnap and Quine put more emphasis on language and the form rather than the content of particular natural sciences (physics in most cases) and pay more attention to logic (including induction and probability in the case of Carnap) than mathematics. They are little interested in the history of philosophy.

But why do people choose diverse goals in philosophy much more than in most disciplines? For one thing, philosophy has a longer history and a larger diversity of traditions to select from. Related to this is the indefiniteness of the scope of philosophy and its relevance which leaves more room for particularizing factors to operate: the hardly separable complex of genetic and social conditioning (including the ambiguous headings of temperament, personal history, and social milieu), the historical period (with its available knowledge and dominant trends), as well as the current local and global state of the discipline matrix of philosophy. Given these interlinked factors, the number of people with wide ranges of ability who choose to pursue philosophy varies greatly with cultural units and historical periods. Ever since philosophy emerged as an academic profession, somebody who chooses philosophy for one reason or another is faced with a tough practical puzzle of squeezing out a meaningful course that would lead to some significant contribution; this is especially true of philosophy for the last hundred years or more. It is for these reasons and for wishing to be 'ultimate' in some sense that philosophy includes a larger portion of self-reflection ('metaphilosophy') than other subjects.

In a large context, leaving out varieties of pure philosophy with less definite specific purposes, I can crudely and metaphorically list six types of philosophy: philosophy as the handmaiden (or public relations agent) of religion; as the queen or partner or servant of science; as the theoretical underpinning of politics; a philosophy to live by; philosophy as guide to action; and as interpretation of classical texts (in particular, *ching hsueh* in the Chinese tradition, which may be a predecessor of the type of study of which hermeneutics is a theory). Unfortunately the objective is usually mixed and concealed. All may claim to strive for truth or wisdom but the concepts of truth and wisdom also differ. A philosophy to live by usually implies private, negative, esthetic, passive, and even escapist elements. It is an attempt to find something to rely on in order to make life less unbearable or at least to fill up a large spiritual gap (such as the need for some private mental resources or to belong to some special group). In contrast, philosophy as guide to action tends to be active and positive. If it is public, it contains a prominent political element.

The handmaiden (or queen or underpinning) philosophies can perform a variety of functions for their masters. For example, since the Renaissance, philosophy has on the whole sided in one way or another with science in its war with religion. There are also philosophers, especially in this century, who find science irrelevant to the central concerns of humanity (Sartre and Wittgenstein are possibly examples) or regard science and technology as the chief source of evil since they are the chief suppliers of the instruments for control (possibly Heidegger and M. Foucault). The attitude toward science is a chief divisive factor between continental philosophers and analytic philosophers as well as between the scientific wing and the common sense (or linguistic) wing of the latter group. The Chinese tradition combines two of the six types by interpreting classical texts to serve current politics.

'Of the three main flows of philosophical thought, it has been maintained that the Indian is otherworldly, the Greek unworldly and the Chinese worldly. No philosophy is ever plainly worldly; to say that it is so is merely an attempt to caricature it in order to bring out certain features into striking relief' (Yueh-Lin Chin 1981; it was written in 1943 in Kunming and mimeographed for limited circulation). Professor Chin singles out several features of Chinese philosophy for discussion. 'One of the features characteristic of Chinese philosophy is the underdevelopment of what might be called logico-epistemological consciousness.' This implies a lack of system and, in particular, a lack of systematic development of science. A more elusive feature is the emphasis on 'the unity of nature (*t'ien*) and person (*jen*).' (Collingwood devotes a whole book to *The Idea of Nature*, 1945, yet it contains no explanation which corresponds quite completely to the Chinese term *t'ien.*) There is in Chinese philosophy less emphasis on conquering physical nature or revolting against one's self. 'Quite without exception, Chinese philosophy is at the same time political thought.' 'Chinese philosophers were all of them different grades of Socrateses.'

Indian philosophy has had little impact on Western philosophy, Schopenhauer being clearly an exception. With Chinese philosophy we seem not to have even such exceptions; possible influences of neo-Confucianism on Leibniz are discussed in Needham 1970 (pp. 496–506). I still do not quite understand how two conflicting traditions affect somebody who is strongly immersed in both. I can see some of the surface phenomena. For instance, my professional training is nearly all in Western philosophy (much of it even logic-oriented), yet my formative years were lived in China. I have tried hard but have not been able to shake off my early conviction that philosophy is not just one subject more or less like any other, but something special. Even today such a belief, I think, persists in China.

I continue to believe that philosophy should somehow be comprehensive and aim at a unified (and preferably with a moderate degree of structure) outlook. In particular, it should find a place for each of the different types of emphases I am familiar with, for example, by understanding the sources of differences and disagreements. I find myself attached to the Chinese tradition of mixing together philosophy, literature, and history—a tradition that conditions and is conditioned by the central concerns of its philosophy; the interest in politics ties it to history, the interpretation of texts merges philosophy with its history, and the concern with the unity of nature and person overlaps with art and literature. Given the conflict of training and tradition in me, it is perhaps not surprising that for many years I have found satisfaction in neither kind of philosophy. This may largely be my own fault, but I do think that it reflects a difference between philosophy and a more homogeneous discipline. I am certain that if I specialized in physics or biology, I would not have encountered this type of frustration. In any case, I am in this book concerned primarily with recent Western philosophy.

Nietzsche sees some order in the chaos of divergent philosophies: 'How unfailingly the most diverse philosophers always fill in again a definite fundamental scheme of *possible* philosophies.' 'The wonderful family resemblance of all Indian, Greek and German philosophizing is easily enough explained. In fact, where there is an affinity of language, owing to the common philosophy of grammar—I mean owing to the unconscious domination and guidance of similar grammatical functions—it cannot but be that everything is prepared at the outset for a similar development and succession of philosophical systems; just as the way seems barred against certain other possibilities of world-interpretation' (*Beyond Good and Evil*, 1886, no. 20). I have not searched to find out what sort of history or classification of philosophy he would offer. But it is familiar how histories of philosophy vary with the philosophers who write them; some familiar examples are Hegel, Feuerbach, Windelbind, Russell, Reichenbach, and Copleston.

We have all heard of the memorable contrast between tender-minded and tough-minded philosophers by William James. If we take the concept of temperament broadly and flexibly, we may speak of Quine and Whitehead as philosophers of different temperaments. Quine was quite close to Whitehead from 1930 to 1947 and wrote two or more articles in honor of Whitehead. Moreover, both of them spent many years doing mathematical logic. The impression is, however, that Whitehead had little (positive) influence on Quine in philosophy. I am not aware of any published comments by Quine on Whitehead's philosophy. The closest approximation I can find is the following neutral statement: 'Other constructions in the 1906 paper go far outside geometry; this was the beginning of a quest for the broadest, most basic concepts and principles of nature, and in the decades since *Principia* the quest has issued in a metaphysic' (last sentence of Quine 1941a).

I do not know the extent to which Quine agrees with Dewey. They certainly began differently (one in mathematical logic and the other in Hegelian philosophy) and cover different grounds (for example, Dewey deals with education, ethics, and esthetics). But there seems to be a certain partial convergence of views which possibly has something to do with the elusive concept of an American spirit. When Quine went to Columbia as the first John Dewey Lecturer in 1968, he observed: 'I listened to Dewey on Art as Experience when I was a graduate student in the Spring of 1931. Dewey was then at Harvard as the first William James Lecturer.' He goes on to list his agreements with Dewey: both of them are naturalistic philosophers, they both oppose 'private language,' they agree that meaning 'is not a psychic existence; it is primarily a property of behavior' (*OR*, pp. 26–29).

18.2. Philosophy and specialization
Up to the early part of the nineteenth century, it was still possible for a person to grasp more or less all the available significant knowledge which is of more than provincial interest. Indeed, most of the leading philosophers until that time probably did possess such a command. Hence, roughly, they were philosophizing over the same data, using, as Nietzsche observed, the same grammar. For a long time this has become impossible owing to extensive fragmentation and intensive specialization. This introduces a new divisive factor which separates

philosophers from one another according to the different areas of specialized knowledge with which they are comfortable. Since the ratio of a philosopher's knowledge to what is available decreases greatly, he or she is forced to stay on a higher level of abstraction or with only homely illustrations in order to say something of general significance which, moreover, is also conditioned by his or her specialized equipment, which may be classics, logic, physics, biology, history, literature, or politics and economics, etc.

Approaches which make philosophy independent of more specialized knowledge, as for instance by G. E. Moore and Wittgenstein, are greatly welcomed by many. A related tendency is to learn the art of argumentation so that, once fed with the data, one can discourse sensibly on any subject. The pressure to specialize does not, however, stop with these neutral devices. Philosophy also wishes to have its own home ground, to be an autonomous discipline with its own technical apparatus. Two natural models are mathematics and literature. But it is not natural or fruitful or possible for philosophy to be precise in the same way mathematics is precise. And the great advantage of literature is that, on the whole, it shuns a technical jargon and yet is capable of a rich content.

Since there are so many different ways of making philosophy into a specialty and since, moreover, fragmentation multiplies in philosophy itself, the central part is greatly weakened by diversification. Invasions from specialists in other subjects have become commonplace: J. Piaget from child psychology, C. Levi-Strauss from anthropology, N. Chomsky from linguistics, T. S. Kuhn from the history of physics, etc. Sartre combines philosophy with literature (by his own account, he had set out to combine Hegel and Shakespeare but did not quite succeed). It almost appears to be the royal road to philosophical eminence to select at first or simultaneously an appropriate (other) specialty. An additional advantage is the unbeatable retreat, frequently employed, of defending one's position by stating that, after all, I intruded into philosophy only for the good of my own discipline. For example, I recall reading somewhere Levi-Strauss reply to a critic in something like just these words. This phenomenon of specialty-originated ideas drawing more attention is perhaps not too hard to understand. Advance or novelty in these other areas is somewhat more concrete and, therefore, leads to something more memorable or striking when transferred to philosophy. Respect for the specialists is so deep and widespread that I have recently been assured by an historian admirer of M. Polyani's philosophy that, after all, he was formerly such a good biochemist whose ideas were worked out by his students to get the Nobel Prize.

Undoubtedly, Quine's eminence in philosophy comes to a consid-

erable extent from his work in logic and especially the extensive use
he puts logic to in his philosophical work. Since, however, logic is, so
to say, a member of the family, this is not considered an invasion from
outside, except perhaps by those philosophers who dislike and detest
mathematical logic. At any rate, Quine's interests in logic and philosophy
are exceptionally well integrated: they serve one another, but perhaps
his logic is more an instrument for his philosophy than the other way
around. It may be possible to view logic as a ladder to his philosophy
which in its developed form can be expounded to a large extent independently of technical logic. Quine would probably agree that his
philosophy is in the tradition of Hume and Comte (and Duhem) but
with more emphasis on language (words in place of ideas, etc.).

Some differences get obscured at a distance. Typically, outsiders and
adversaries of a group of related but distinct doctrines would miss the
trees and see only the wood and tar them with a single brush. In this
way Quine is classified as a logical positivist (or empiricist) or an analytic
philosopher. Quine, of course, dissociates himself strongly from the
linguistic philosophers, on one side, and distinguishes himself more
mildly from the empiricists with (the two) dogmas, on the other. Since
Quine stresses explicitly his differences with, for example, Carnap, it
is desirable to examine the beliefs he shares with Carnap and his comrades. (I did just this in section 2.) For example, they and many others
consider themselves the 'tough-minded' philosophers who form the
union of the empiricist, sensationalistic, materialistic, pessimistic, ir-
religious, fatalistic, pluralistic, skeptical, etc. This classification is not
particularly helpful not only because it throws incompatible views under
one heading but more because most philosophies would seem to combine certain tough-minded elements with certain tender-minded ones,
even if we do not limit ourselves to those attempts to have it both
ways, such as the Kantian dualism and dialectic materialism which
resist such classification, however we would refine James' bifurcation.

A somewhat less crude classification is developed by L. Kolakowski
under a broad conception of positivism in his *The Alienation of Reason:
A History of Positivist Thought* (1966 and 1968). It appears likely that
Quine would be counted as a positivist according to the spirit of this
book. For example, Duhem, whom Quine finds so congenial, is dealt
with in the chapter 'conventionalism—destruction of the concept of
fact.' It is amusing to quote some of the exposition of Duhem's 'ideology'
(pp. 147–148):

> Duhem, in particular, says explicitly that his interpretation of science
> forestalls all objections to the Catholic faith and Church. For, since
> natural science makes no statements about the real world (as his

criticism of the laws of physics shows) it cannot come into conflict
with religious dogmas that are statements about real existents . . . .
In his *Physics of a Believer* Duhem discloses the conscious intention
behind his analysis of scientific method: they are an attempt to
neutralize scientific knowledge in relation to metaphysical and
religious controversies, to deprive naturalists and materialists of
the advantages they derive from equating scientific assertions and
metaphysical beliefs, and to defend Catholic dogmas.

This passage reminds me of an observation by Paul Bernays many
years ago: When one construes what is *rational* so narrowly (as by
logical positivists, etc.), a large vacuum is created in the domain of
vital human concerns which gets moved beyond the realm of rational
considerations. Duhem may be exceptional in being conscious of and
explicit about the 'ulterior' motive behind his philosophizing.

18.3. Philosophy and 'the scientific method'

This is related to the ambiguity of the central belief or presupposition
or dogma, shared by Carnap and Quine, viz., the unity and universality
of the scientific method. (I should mention that I find their conception
of 'scientific method' defective; but I am here mostly limiting myself
to what I take to be their conception.) One aspect of the ambiguity
may be clarified a bit by the complementing presupposition of what
might be called nonessentialism. It would be less awkward to speak
of phenomenalism and nominalism had their broader meaning not
been preempted by recent usage according to which Carnap and Quine
emphatically believe in neither. In a broader sense, phenomenalism
recognizes no real difference between phenomenon and essence, and
nominalism recognizes fundamentally only individual concrete objects.
It is not denied that we also construct ideal situations and mathematical
objects as auxiliaries and make existence statements about them. But
the meaning of their existence is derived only from their function in
the ordering and description of empirical reality. Hence, in particular,
as Quine stresses on many occasions, even though we are forced to
speak of the existence of sets and numbers, the constraint on a satisfactory set theory is primarily elegance and convenience. This is somewhat analogous to the philosophy of mathematics expounded by
Abraham Robinson (among others), according to which we need only
pretend that infinite sets exist. Gödel's reply is that as a matter of fact
such pretending is not as fruitful as his objectivism of numbers and
sets.

In two long letters written to me around the beginning of 1967, Gödel
gives a convincing story of how his objectivism played an essential

part in arriving at all of his most basic discoveries in logic (see *MP*, pp. 8–11). I may add that this conception helps also in securing a firmer intuitive grasp of the meaning of his theorems and their proofs. If the substance of the two preceding sentences is accepted, what can one infer that is relevant to Quine's empiricism with its 'extended nominalism' (as explained above)? I am inclined to take this example as an illustration of the fact that fruitful scientific method does rely more on 'essence' or stable 'constructs' than Quine's empiricism is willing to concede and that science contains firmer structures than Quine's holism seems to suggest.

A related presupposition is to limit cognition and cognitive value to a domain that excludes value judgments. This, I believe, departs from common usage. On the whole, the several presuppositions imply a recommendation of a 'better' use of the terms 'knowledge,' 'cognition,' 'science,' etc., and therefore a normative or regulative element. Both as a consequence and in conformity with the general spirit, there is also a strong interest in economy and reductions. We do expect that scientific method will continue to change, develop, and improve. Is scientific method the only appropriate instrument which is to bring about its own further development in the light of new observations or new experience?

A mundane concern is the fact that humanity is faced with a vast number of problems which 'scientific method' (say, in Quine's sense as explained in *WB*) cannot solve or at least solve quickly enough to guide our action or decision which often has to be taken with cruel time limits. Somewhere Joan Robinson remarks that economics generally only finds solutions to actual problems after they cease to be pressing and some makeshift measure had to be taken meanwhile. This suggests the necessity of supplementing the scientific method used in economics with some other 'method' for arriving at quicker solutions which is more rational than alternative makeshift measures. How do we apply or enlarge scientific method to become more rational in facing emergencies, the necessity of making fast or complex decisions, suffering, death, family and social clashes, ideological conflict, etc.? 'Stubborn diseases or social ills invite,' according to Quine, 'rash or superstitious measures for want of sound ones. Responsible scientists may remain properly perplexed, whereupon an eager and impatient public hearkens to the irresponsible hypotheses' (*WB*, p. 121). But to wait for sound measures is itself a choice which may or may not be the rational one in a given case.

Quine does say that professional philosophers have no 'peculiar fitness for helping to get society on an even keel.' But I believe the point at issue is, rather, the universality of the scientific method. If the advice is to apply the scientific method on every occasion, then in situations where scientific solutions cannot be found (in time) the advice is empty or worse in frustrating a relatively more rational course of action. If rationality is a proper concern of philosophy, then philosophers need not limit their concern to scientific method in Quine's sense. Moreover, since fear, death, choice, freedom, etc., are actual concerns which have been studied in philosophy, it is difficult to find convincing impartial arguments to exclude the 'unscientific' study of them in philosophy.

Both Descartes (*Method*, III) and Spinoza (*Improvement of the Understanding*, the eighth paragraph) say something like this: while I was in the process of searching for the proper norms of action, I followed the commonly accepted rules. On the whole, Quine seems to recommend caution and suspension of judgment (and action?) in situations for which we have no scientifically sound solutions. 'The psychology of motives and character traits is in its infancy, but there is no call to conspire in arresting its development' (*WB*, p. 124). In philosophy, Quine's strategy of isolation leads him to say, 'I cleave to my arid little S-R dialectic where I can, rather than try to make an analytical tool of the heady luxuriance of experience untamed' (*TT*, p. 185). This presumably is an application of the scientific method in philosophy. The application has so far yielded nothing as striking and memorable as the law of free falling bodies. More likely it is meant to be the beginning of a 'rational reconstruction' or the foundations of a new science. If it is meant to be preparations, then history will tell whether it is only idle preparations. The difficulty at present is that I do not know what type of criterion to use in order to evaluate the work, partly because I do not quite understand its purpose. This may be because I have not found strong enough motivation to study it carefully.

Natural selection is mentioned at two crucial junctures (*WB*, p. 117 and p. 137). In particular: 'This, and not training, is probably the main reason for there being widespread agreement on basic moral issues, even among very dissimilar peoples.' Intersubjective agreement plays an important role in Quine's treatment of knowledge (e.g., in the definition of observation sentences). This would, however, seem to call for a systematic analysis of communication structures within the community of investigators, as emphasized by J. Habermas in, e.g., his 1968 and other books considered in McCarthy 1982. The remark just quoted on natural selection points to the view that language and knowledge are primarily instruments of biological adaptation.

According to Engels, thought and consciousness 'are products of the human brain and that man himself is a product of nature, which has developed in and along with its environment; hence it is self-evident that the products of the human brain, being in the last analysis also products of nature, do not contradict the rest of nature's interconnections but are in correspondence with them' (*Anti-Dühring*, p. 49). Abner Shimony has for years developed similar ideas of relating epistemology to evolution. Undoubtedly the idea contains an important element of truth which is a healthy guidepost. But it is not clear how one can determine to what extent such a view can eventually be carried out. For the foreseeable future such a view will probably not yield quick specific results for improving our understanding of human knowledge and scientific method.

Carnap reports on Wittgenstein's influence on his work and their personal interactions in considerable detail (*IA*, pp. 24–29). I have earlier mentioned what I take to be Carnap's misunderstanding and misapplication of the *Tractatus*. But the personality differences and clashes between them are probably closely related to the style and result of their work. They look for totally different things from philosophy. For example, their attitudes toward Esperanto, Schopenhauer, and constructed language systems are entirely incompatible. In 1948, Wittgenstein wrote in his journal: 'Make sure you really do paint only what you see!' (*CV*). I am sure he would consider most of Carnap's work as violating this sacred principle. The type of conflict between them seems to me better formulated in some evaluations of novels.

In April 1919, Virginia Woolf said things about the works of Wells and others in her essay on 'Modern fiction,' which I can imagine Wittgenstein saying about Carnap's books (if he had read them), except that the elusive word 'materialist' must be understood in a metaphorical sense (*The Common Reader*, 1925, p. 151):

> Mr. Wells, Mr. Bennett, and Mr. Galsworthy have excited so many hopes and disappointed them so persistently that our gratitude largely takes the form of thanking them for having shown us what they might have done but have not done; what we certainly could not do, but, as certainly, perhaps, do not wish to do. No single phrase will sum up the charge or grievance which we have to bring against a mass of work so large in its volume and embodying so many qualities, both admirable and the reverse. If we tried to formulate our meaning in one word we should say that these writers are materialists. It is because they are concerned not with the spirit but with the body that they have disappointed us.

19. From how I know to what we know

Surprisingly, Quine agreed to respond to Mortimer Adler on the question: Has philosophy lost contact with people? (*TT*, pp. 190–193). His answer seems to amount to this: Yes, but this is as it should be. He wisely recommends that we assess the changing scene of philosophy by looking 'to actual endeavors and activities old and new, exoteric and esoteric, grave and frivolous, and let the word "philosophy" fall where it may.' (This reminds one of the familiar idea that philosophy is what philosophers do, voiced once by Isiah Berlin.) But to achieve an instructive account of such a complex diversity of things seems to call for a survey of various traditions and the doctrines of the numerous mixtures of them, as well as the role they play in different societies of the world today.

Instead, Quine limits himself to a single strand of 'scientific philosophy,' centering on his own type of work. We detect a familiar interplay of valuation with cognition in his normative description of the history and the contemporary state of philosophy. Eight of the big names in Western philosophy, thus leaving out, e.g., Gautama (the Buddha or Sakyamuni) and Confucius, are selected for their concomitant work in natural science. The list ends with Kant and the eighteenth century but leaves out Socrates, Augustine, Aquinas, Francis Bacon, and Spinoza. We are reminded that Plato was a mathematician and cosmologist, Aristotle a pioneer physicist and biologist, Descartes and Leibniz were mathematicians and in part physicists, and 'Locke, Berkeley, Hume, and Kant were in large part psychologists.' Physics, mathematics, and biology all have made spectacular advances since these philosophers occupied themselves with these subjects. It has long been realized that Galileo and Newton not only made more permanent contributions to physics than Descartes and Leibniz but also had a much firmer grasp and more helpful things to say on the methodology of physics. This would suggest that even in the seventeenth century and on this highest level, physics was more effectively pursued as a primary concern rather than as a part of philosophy.

19.1. Philosophy and psychology: now and before 1800
The matter of psychology and its relation to philosophy presents a good deal more of unresolved puzzle. I believe that many people must have felt at one time or another that psychology provides the key for philosophy. Yet it remains to this day controversial and unclear whether or how psychology as it is professionally studied can help the pursuit of philosophy in a basic way. If much of Kant's work is viewed as falling under psychology, then there are no obvious successors to his work that have further advanced psychological studies. In fact, founders of different schools of 'scientific' philosophy, notably Frege and Husserl, took pains to dissociate themselves from psychology. Applied psychology in advertising and management is successful enough to create

demands for experts in that field; the success is undoubtedly related to the limited scope and relatively clear goals. Psychoanalysis has attracted a few highly speculative philosophers. Cognitive psychology and particularly the psychology of language have received a fair amount of attention; yet, owing to my own bias, I have so far failed to notice any definite connection with philosophy that would generate in philosophy as much enthusiasm and ramification as, for instance, Frege's attempt to reduce arithmetic to logic.

Piaget published extensive discussions of ('genetic') epistemology centered on his study of child psychology. His experimental work is suggestive but not definite enough to exclude greatly diverse interpretations. To reflect on or do philosophical analysis of his results is more likely to lead to additional questions for clarification which suggest new experiments than to find a stable foothold as in the case of mathematics, physics, or biology. Piaget criticizes some of Sartre's and Merleau-Ponty's work under the heading of philosophical psychology: 'Where the anti-intellectualism of Sartre sees "magic" everywhere, that of Merleau-Ponty discovers ambiguities, which is already much more rational' (*Insights and Illusions of Philosophy*, trans. Wolfe Mays, 1971). I believe, on the other hand, that Sartre and Merleau-Ponty would regard Piaget as a shallow and weak philosopher.

Piaget and his colleagues tested 'experimentally the famous problem of synthetic and analytic relations' and produced a book, *Les liaisons analytiques et synthètiques dans les compartements du sujet*. The report was sent to 'the well-known Harvard logician Quine' who 'wrote us a very encouraging letter, recognizing the scope of the collected facts, while making reservations as to the mode of definition adopted, and accepting retrospectively membership on the Board of the Center' (ibid., pp. 31–33). S. Papert, a disciple of Piaget, has extended his ideas to conduct experiments with nonroutine applications of computers in teaching children 'how to think' and published a stimulating summary and discussion in his *Mindstorms* (1980). There is also a considerable literature on 'artificial intelligence,' as well as its relation to philosophy and to psychology: for example, H. Dreyfus, *What Computers Can't Do*, 1972 and 1981; M. Boden, *Artificial Intelligence and Natural Man*, 1977; D. Dennett, *Brainstorms*, 1978; and my 'Computer theorem proving and artificial intelligence' (1984).

This mindless tabulation of diverse attempts to relate the study of psychology to philosophy is meant to convey the impression that while there are many research projects which can get supported, I do not see how a good psychologist today can hope to attain an eminence in the (future) history of philosophy or of culture comparable to what Locke, Berkeley, Hume, and Kant have done. To regard Kant or Locke with his political philosophy or even Hume with his work in history as primarily a psychologist seems to me to be stretching usage and at least pointing to something rather different from what we take psychologists to be today.

According to Quine, the eight chosen great philosophers and others 'were scientists in search of an organized conception of reality.' If we wish to learn from historical experience and to try to glean some lessons from these examples, it is hard to know how to construe Quine's statement. Is the emphasis on scientific knowledge or on scientific method or on important discoveries in science? A more familiar statement is easier to accept and probably more crucial: 'Until the 19th century, all available scientific knowledge of any consequence could be encompassed by a single first-class mind.' (I would be inclined to delete even the word 'scientific' from the statement.) That encompassing is what is no longer possible today (indeed, has not been so for nearly two centuries). Hence, one might argue, a 'psychologist' can no longer hope to achieve a comparably appealing organized conception of reality as Kant did in his day.

Quine, it seems to me, chooses to single out one type of scientific philosophy which he considers most fruitful. He points out that what we now consider distinctly philosophical in the eight philosophers were their struggle with broader and more basic concepts and their quest for a system on a grander scale, but stresses that these efforts 'were integral still to the overall scientific enterprise.' This leads to his thesis of continuity: 'What is pursued under the name of philosophy today, moreover, has much these same concerns when it is at what I deem its technical best.' I feel I discern an implicit transition in the phrase 'integral to.' For example, according to this formulation, Kant's philosophy on 'the starry heavens above me and the moral law within me' is integral to the scientific enterprise, but Quine's conception of scientific philosophy largely gives up the second half as a lost cause. Being integral to, I feel, gives way to Quine's exclusive concern with the enterprise of natural science to be studied by the same method of natural science, of which, by the way, Quine has, I believe, only a one-sided understanding conditioned by his clinging to the 'tangible.' Moreover, for the eight philosophers their more general and speculative reaches are integral not only to their scientific pursuit but also to their encompassing of all available knowledge of their times. How do we know that by continuing with 'much these same concerns' more in isolation we can still claim to be their true successors?

19.2. Philosophy and organic chemistry
For Quine, it is important for its progress that philosophy become a

technical, specialized discipline (with subdisciplines) and give up contact with people much as 'physics, microbiology, and mathematics.' 'Now philosophy, where it was continuous with science, progressed too.' But philosophy so specialized is for Quine in a worse situation than physics and more akin to organic chemistry, in that popular expositions of physics are of interest to the layman while those of philosophy and organic chemistry are not. To complete the gloomy side of the story, Quine concedes that 'the separation of philosophers into sages and cranks seems to be more sensitive to frames of reference.' He attributes this to the 'unregimented' and speculative character of the subject. Quine warns the aspiring candidate that professional philosophy has no 'peculiar fitness for helping to get society on an even keel' or for 'inspirational and edifying writing,' which is admirable, but its place 'is the novel, the poem, the sermon, or the literary essay.'

On the brighter side, Quine claims that good professional philosophy in his sense satisfies intellectual curiosity. For Quine, the rewarding recent advances in philosophy are largely connected with the use of the powerful new logic and the increasing concern with the nature of language. As I reported before, Quine's three original interests (even before college) were philosophy, language, and a certain type of mathematics (which in his case quite naturally was soon concretized in a part of mathematical logic). Hence, we find in Quine's development an unusually fortunate coincidence of his primary interests with the chief requirements of one central trend in philosophy. It is rare indeed to be so fortunate as to meet with such circumstances and be able enough to achieve such harmony of interest, talent, and the demands of the subject at the particular historical juncture. With the mention of the importance of language for philosophy, Quine is obliged to dissociate himself from the linguistic wing of analytic philosophy. Here we have another instance where the normative factor guides the descriptive account of the 'actual endeavors and activities.'

Given the highly confusing state of philosophy at the time when Quine began his study, it is certainly a great achievement on his part to be able to select a course of work which, according to a majority of his professionally influential colleagues, has yielded fundamental advances in the central part of current philosophy. The objective question of how solid these advances are, or whether they have served or will serve as steps toward more advances of 'scientific' philosophy, is more debatable. If we accept Rorty's account of philosophy today (as reported in section 11.4), the answer would appear to be more in the negative than in the positive. But this is undoubtedly another question which is 'sensitive to frames of reference.'

I find Quine's account of philosophy and 'scientific' philosophy less than impartial. Let me just mention some alternative conceptions of scientific philosophy. As I have mentioned before, Quine and Reichenbach share a negative attitude toward history, history of philosophy, and nineteenth century philosophy. Yet Reichenbach pays less attention to language and gives inductive logic and probability theory a more central place than deductive logic. Wittgenstein would undoubtedly refuse the title of scientific philosopher, yet his later treatment of language and its relation to social practice is for many people more stably fundamental than Quine's treatment of scientific languages. Kant's conception of scientific philosophy is broader than Quine's. Husserl's and Gödel's 'philosophy as rigorous science' is quite different from Quine's. Quine would probably find them violating empiricism, while Gödel would consider Quine's notion of experience too narrow in not giving enough weight to the experience of introspection. As remarked elsewhere in this book, it is possible to question whether Quine's or Duhem's philosophy is indeed empiricism. A widely influential and broader conception of scientific philosophy is that of the tradition of Marx, which may be briefly characterized by the suggestive second thesis on Feuerbach: 'The question whether objective truth can be attributed to human thinking is not a question of theory but is a *practical* question. In practice man must prove the truth, that is, the reality and power, the this-sidedness of his thinking. The dispute over the reality or non-reality of thinking which is isolated from practice is a purely *scholastic* question.'

Quine's comparison of philosophy with organic chemistry seems to me unsatisfactory on three levels. I consider it an open question whether philosophy can best be pursued only as a specialized discipline like a branch of natural science, especially since it certainly aims at a larger view of things ('an organized conception of reality'). We have a pretty good idea of the place of organic chemistry in our intuitive and institutionalized tree of knowledge, but to determine the place of philosophy is itself a major concern in the pursuit of philosophy. Even if philosophy has to be studied as a specialized discipline, its place must be in some sense more neutral (or basic) and more comprehensive than organic chemistry.

19.3. Intuition and new disciplines
Rorty voices, as I noted before, the disappointments thirty years later in the original optimistic expectations from making scientific philosophy into an autonomous discipline matrix in American philosophy departments. Independently of the traditionally special character of philosophy, there is a general question about the necessary conditions for the successful emergence of a new discipline. I believe that a primary

condition is a stable basis which treats of some rich natural concepts and problems and links the new area to solid beliefs and vital human concerns. In such cases the pursuit promises some form of accumulation of experience acquired through investigating the area.

Mathematical logic, a much poorer and more esoteric subject than philosophy as it is commonly understood, has, with some resistance from mathematics, gradually been accepted as another branch of mathematics, admittedly one that is somewhat off the main stream. In this case, set, formal proof, computability, and a special sense of model have acquired rich and stable explications which correspond sufficiently closely to our natural intuitive concepts so that, with some training, practitioners not only reach easy agreement but can also work with the concepts rather effortlessly. Moreover, familiar tools in mathematics can quickly be adapted to the pursuit. In contrast, the new philosophy undertakes to isolate itself from its messy past and its messy large problems, such as freedom, the meaning of history, the wish to believe in the possibility of a better society, and even the more intuitive aspects of scientific practice. More precise artificial concepts are introduced to substitute for vaguer intuitive concepts so that before long one forgets what started the whole thing off. This type of thing happens often in mathematics too, but, unlike philosophy, it has firmer roots for its precision which supply a more efficient mechanism of natural selection.

The unhappy state of American philosophy is undoubtedly also related to a general decline of academic life in the last two decades or so. In terms of job opportunities I understand that professional philosophers (especially the younger ones) are among the hardest hit during this period. Moreover, if, as Rorty suggests, the graduate departments compete with the law schools for candidates of the same kind of quality and qualification, one would expect that the majority of the abler candidates would choose law over philosophy. On top of all these troubles, Rorty also deplores the ill feeling between the analytic and the continental philosophers. This phenomenon is certainly not unique to philosophy departments. I have often watched the conflict between pure and applied mathematicians, as well as both groups combining forces to exclude the statisticians. Some time ago I read about the Harvard sociology department in the *New York Times* (October 18, 1981). 'As a discipline, sociology is extremely divided. At Harvard, there are two warring factions. One is the quantitative school of sociology, people who rely on statistics, surveys and mathematical models. The other is the qualitative school whose members work in the more theoretical or historical tradition of the classical German sociologist Max Weber.' This cleavage into warring factions is a familiar one. It seems to resemble the one between the analytic and the continental, and the one between the tough-minded and the tender-minded.

A generalization of the contrast between quantitative and qualitative is often misleadingly described as objectivism against subjectivism. It has been suggested that the work of Marx and Wittgenstein points to the way of developing a social theory which avoids the one-sided pitfalls of subjectivism and objectivism (D. Rubinstein 1981). I would have thought that any systematic study of the human situation would have to find a proper mixture of the subjective and the objective. In fact, I would prefer to speak of the general and the particular and their interplay. In this regard, I believe that dialectics is the much abused 'method' (or rather, style) or guidance toward a judicious organization of the complex interrelations (say, between the general and the particular, between subject and object, subject and subject, etc.). But what is needed of dialectics is a knowing how rather than a knowing that, a skill to use it rather than a doctrine to expound it. That is probably why Marx never wrote any extended treatment of dialectics. Wassily Leontief praises Marx highly for his impressive contributions to economics but attributes his accomplishment more to an extraordinary intuitive grasp of a vast body of empirical data rather than to the use of any special dialectical 'method' (see D. Horowitz 1967, p. 98). In my opinion, philosophy also needs such an intuitive grasp, whether it is called dialectics or not.

19.4. Using what we know

Quine's emphasis on empirical psychology is related to his idea of a 'liberated epistemology,' which proposes to make the study of the psychology of language learning a successor subject to epistemology. But I take his proposal to be in the tradition of asking 'how I know,' rather than 'what we know.'

A familiar experience in mathematics is that one is often convinced of the truth of a proposition or something close to it but cannot quite prove it or gets only a defective proof. A good and experienced mathematician seldom errs far in such situations because intuition seems to be a less exact but more dependable guide than a formally exact proof, just as the human brain can tolerate more error and indefiniteness than a computer. More generally, we often have perfectly reasonable beliefs but cannot give good reasons for the beliefs. Russell and his followers often teach us to distrust such beliefs. Russell, for example, criticizes Descartes and Kant for pretending 'that deep-seated prejudices were heaven-sent intuitions.' More strongly, Russell says, 'Morally, a philosopher who uses his professional competence for anything except a disinterested search for truth is guilty of a kind of treachery' (*History*,

p. 863). I agree that we should try hard to see whether our deeply held beliefs can be disproved, especially when we make crucial decisions on the basis of such beliefs. But for me a more fruitful approach to philosophy than systematic doubt would seem to be to search for reasons to support our basic beliefs, which may be somewhat indefinite and are relative to the historical period, etc.

L. W. Beck gives an exposition of Kant's philosophy in which he views Kant's philosophical development as a continued attempt to give a structure to his Weltanschauung, which remained pretty much invariant throughout Kant's changes in his doctrines:

> By *Weltanschauung* I mean here: a set of philosophical ideas and opinions held together in a personal attitude, but without benefit of the technical discipline of analysis and argumentation which, it is to be hoped, raises philosophy above the merely subjective, individual, and existential and gives it some claim to more than biographical and historical interest. . . . We find a high degree of likeness between conclusions reached in works written over five decades during which profound changes occurred in his premises and modes of argumentation.

Beck then offers a list of eleven principal beliefs and attitudes of Kant which need not be discussed here (see his 1969, pp. 426–430).

I believe that constructing a comparable list today relative to the existing knowledge of nature and experience of human history would help to clarify what are the principal goals of the philosophical enterprise. For example, in place of Kant's question 'What can I know?' I would put the question, 'What do we know?' In place of Kant's belief in the immortality of the soul, I would put a basic belief which I think is widely shared today and expressed by Einstein in a talk to a group of children (first published in 1934) in the following manner (1954, p. 56):

> Bear in mind that the wonderful things you learn in your schools are the work of many generations, produced by enthusiastic effort and infinite labor in every country of the world. All this is put into your hands as your inheritance in order that you may receive it, honor it, add to it, and one day faithfully hand it on to your children. Thus do we mortals achieve immortality in the permanent things we create in common. If you always keep that in mind you will find a meaning in life and work and acquire the right attitude toward other nations and ages.

The importance of selecting a good problem or topic or project is familiar in all research. But the task appears particularly difficult and important for philosophy. It is comparable to solving an intricate set of simultaneous equations which may have no solution at all or only relative solutions in the sense that we have often to choose between giving more weight to satisfying (more adequately) one equation or another. To illustrate what I mean and to give a crude preliminary formulation of what I look for in philosophy, let me give a set of conditions which a right (or good) topic for doing philosophy ought to satisfy. Related to this matter of good topics is the larger task of trying to arrive at a philosophy which can be viewed as a topic itself or, more likely, a combination of a number of topics. An intermediate task is to attain a 'fundamental' philosophy which is less comprehensive than a 'whole' philosophy but in some sense includes its fundamental parts. What makes up fundamental philosophy seems to change with time: for example, metaphysics was taken as the first philosophy for many centuries; epistemology seems to have largely supplanted it since the seventeenth century; in recent years I have heard it said that the theory of meaning is the new occupant of the position. I am inclined to think that the talk of a fundamental philosophy generally begs the question.

Allow me to offer a provisionary list of conditions for a right topic for doing philosophy by a person:

(1) the person can get motivated (and not by fashion or promotion or profit only) in studying it;
(2) it deals with relatively stable issues, at least potentially, of more than limited interest (to a few specialists);
(3) its study involves some of our larger intuitions;
(4) a connected study of it is possible (it contains interlinked parts);
(5) its study has wide implications yet can be isolated from too many minute details;
(6) it is 'philosophical' in not being a part of some specialized science only;
(7) it is universal or at least has a high degree of universality and, in the latter case, the limitations of its universality can be made explicit in a fairly natural way;
(8) it can be fitted into some good comprehensive philosophy.

In terms of these conditions, the extended work on 'justice as fairness' by John Rawls seems to fare very well. It has its impact not only on political theory, but also on law and economics. It belongs to political philosophy, an area not in the center of current academic philosophy, and it is explicitly nonuniversal in that it is almost exclusively concerned with an idealized form of only a particular kind of society, a particular 'form of life.' This example of substantive work seems to support the revolt against the entrenched persistence in looking for a privileged access to truth by selecting one special area of human activity as the philosophically fundamental.

A challenging, large philosophical problem has been suggested in Goldmann 1973. Let me just quote his formulation. 'Will Western industrial society as it develops guarantee the values of *content* in intellectual life, or will the socialist form of society be able to develop into the guardian of the values of the Enlightenment: equality, freedom, toleration and individual conscience of every one of its members?' This would seem to command even more interest than justice as fairness and to require a different sort of treatment. But it is not easy to see where to look for a fruitful approach to it.

According to a view congenial to me, the central aim of philosophy is to see in a comprehensive way how things hang together; to attain and express in a coherent way a comprehensive, relatively stable, and reasonable view of the world. What can be achieved of course depends heavily on the historical circumstances of the particular period and on the contingent facts about each aspiring philosopher. A first condition on the enterprise seems to me to be a humility toward the collective human experience which requires that one be as faithful as possible to the best available knowledge and understanding in each major region of human thought and feeling. Hence, potentially, such a comprehensive view promises wide acceptance, not so much in its details but more in its general intent, by those who reflect on it. Given the widespread confused state of the thinking minds, even a moderate degree of coherence in any such comprehensive outlook will not 'leave everything as it is.'

Since the scope is so large, a division of labor (vertically and horizontally) seems necessary. Crudely speaking, one has to select and charter out a few regions which are to be studied by different agents or at different stages by the same agent; there are the tasks of making the pieces and putting them together. But these tasks are closely interrelated in such a way that the structure and its various pieces all more or less condition one another. Hence, they are not to be done in linear succession but dialectically in the sense that less definite ideas of the whole and its components lead to more definite ones at each stage. It is in this connection that we can appeal to the fact that bodies of knowledge and understanding do exist in the world. This fact, if used carefully and with a measure of reverence, seems to offer a pretty dependable guide to the choice of preferred regions and to the making of the corresponding pieces. Looked at in this way, there are different particular choices as to what regions are taken as the more important. Moreover, the danger of eclecticism is generally quite real and usually even accompanied by the complementary tendency to distort the local regions to suit the global structure. Hence, putting together the pieces must be a highly demanding creative process. Indeed, concentrating on one or two well-chosen regions may be a more realistic course. This is one aspect of the metaphilosophical task of finding the right topics for doing philosophy, which seems to me to present a particularly acute problem today.

If we take from the history of philosophy Plato, Aristotle, and Kant as very different successful examples of carrying out such a project, we would have to say there are no comparable achievements in this century. Undoubtedly the added social and intellectual experiences over the last two hundred years have much to do with this. Kant paid little explicit attention to the historical dimension or the dimension of individual development (certainly in his three *Critiques*), even though E. Cassirer speaks of his papers on history as his fourth critique. To take into consideration these additional dimensions would undoubtedly promise a more adequate perspective yet at the same time make the task more complex. Moreover, we are increasingly aware of the importance of the differences within the general category of the human species: different nations, different cultural traditions, different races, different economic classes, men and women, different age groups, etc.

As human knowledge and understanding increase, one would expect to see things clearer and therefore to be capable of creating more adequate philosophies. Yet, seeing things clearer has brought to light a good deal of complexity that was concealed before, and global developments in every direction have generated more particularities; we begin to realize how different and complex people are and how ignorant we are on important questions such as education, the prevention of war, the reconciliation of incompatible perspectives, alienation, the meaning of progress, and so on. We are more aware of important different forms of the unconscious masking of our beliefs, such as those pointed out by Marx, Nietzsche, and Freud. Moreover, there is an absolute increase of the relative ignorance of every individual person measured against what is known today by the various different communities. What is more serious than the sheer quantity of material is the divergence of beliefs of the different interest groups (including, in particular, even the different specialized disciplines). It is this divergence that seems to preclude not only unification but also cooperative efforts to attempt a coherent position which gives each group its due. An 'outsider' may be better situated to achieve impartiality but would probably fail to appreciate the central concerns of any group. Moreover, when social reality is under consideration, nobody can claim to be a genuine outsider.

Everyone may be said to be 'thrown into' the world and to have grown and acquired beliefs in a haphazard manner, with more or less conscious effort to scrutinize and modify the beliefs from time to time, more, or less, successfully. The striving for universality is always tinted by particularity in this second level sense. Moreover, even when one aims at more general conclusions, it often seems better to begin with particular cases. In fact, at least in philosophy, generalizations often seem to be incompletely justified by the particular cases and therefore lose some of the purity and richness of the latter. Related to this is the practical necessity of 'conditional beginnings.' For example, Descartes reduced the self to a thinking substance or an elusive abstract consciousness, which is independent of everyday life, gender, age, class, nation, the degree of abnormality, and the historical context. Kant and Husserl broadened the conception of consciousness and deepened the reflections on it, but continued with a homogeneous image of the self ('the intersection'), irrespective of familiar basic differences (within 'the union').

As can been seen from Goldmann's problem, the full meaning of the values of Enlightenment remains insufficiently understood today. For Kant, according to Beck (op. cit., p. 427), 'The interests of humanity are the ideals of the Enlightenment.' In his response to the question 'Was ist Aufklärung?' (Berlinische Monatschrift, November 1984), Kant formulates the slogan 'dare to know' and characterizes the spirit of Enlightenment as releasing us from the status of 'immaturity.' Two centuries have passed, and we are still far from attaining mature adulthood. Indeed, the growth of autonomy has not kept pace with the growth of capacities.

The slogan 'reverence for what we know' sounds bland and negative. How do we reach what we know? It is, first of all, necessary to single out what is 'essential' from the vast domain of what the human species knows today. And then, how do we use the data in an appropriate way? One source of comfort might be a belief, right or wrong, that existing philosophy has developed useful tools for handling data and its defect is rather its not using a wide enough range of data. In a letter of September 1912 to Lady Ottoline, Russell wrote in connection with his attempt to write a novel (Forstice): 'I feel so hampered by want of art and lack of knowledge. I long to know all human life and all history and everything. Arnold Bennett gets his effects through his immense knowledge of industrial life' (Clark, p. 181). Wanting to know all is certainly not by itself a royal road to philosophy. Even after overcoming the 'lack of knowledge' for writing a novel or for doing philosophy, there remains the serious obstacle of 'want of art,' which is presumably remediable only by actually plunging in. That is probably why, even though many philosophers cannot resist the temptation to metaphilosophize, they fortunately do become sick of it after too heavy a dose.

References

I shall begin with a table of abbreviations used in the body of the book and in the list of references to follow. The list itself will be in alphabetic order according to author and in chronological order according to dates of publication (and occasionally according to dates of composition). When important changes are made in different editions, the different dates will be given and page references are, unless otherwise indicated, to the most recent edition. In cases where the dates of composition are known, they will be attached in parentheses. Sometimes the references are given in the text and not listed here.

Abbreviations

AMM:	*American Mathematical Monthly.*
AMS:	American Mathematical Society.
Aufbau:	Carnap 1928.
BP:	Benacerraf-Putnam 1964/1983.
CV:	Wittgenstein 1980.
External World:	Russell 1914.
FG:	Heijenoort 1967 (*From Frege to Gödel*).
FM:	Quine 1979.
History:	Russell 1946.
Human Knowledge:	Russell 1948.
IA:	Carnap's *Intellectual Autobiography* in Schilpp 1963.
IMP:	Russell 1919.
JP:	*The Journal of Philosophy.*
JSL:	*Journal of Symbolic Logic.*
Lackey:	Lackey 1973.
Logical Syntax:	Carnap 1934/37.
LP:	Quine 1953.
MD:	Russell's 'My mental development' in Schilpp 1944.
ML:	Quine 1940/51.
ML:	Wang's corrected system of *ML*, presented in Wang 1950 and adopted in the 1951 edition of *ML*.
MP:	Wang 1974.

NF:	Quine's system presented in Quine 1937, reprinted with addition in *LP*.
NNK:	Quine 1975.
OC:	Wittgenstein 1969.
OD:	Russell 1905.
OR:	Quine 1969.
PD:	Russell 1959.
PI:	Wittgenstein 1953.
PL:	Quine 1970.
PM:	Whitehead-Russell.
PNAS:	*Proceedings of the National Academy of Sciences of U.S.A.*
PP:	Russell 1912.
Principles:	Russell 1903.
RMM:	*Revue de métaphysique et de morale.*
Σ_ω:	The simplest of a scheme of systems proposed in Wang 1954.
SL:	Quine 1963/69.
Survey:	Wang 1962.
Tractatus:	Wittgenstein 1921/22.
TT:	Quine 1981.
WB:	Quine (and Ullian) 1970/78.
WO:	Quine 1960.
WP:	Quine 1966/76.
WPO:	Quine 1976.

List of books and articles mentioned elsewhere in this book

W. Ackermann
   1956.   *Math. Annalen*, vol. 131, pp. 336–345.

Henry S. Ashmore (editor)
   1968.   *Britanica Perspectives*, 3 volumes.

A. J. Ayer
   1936/46.   *Language, Truth and Logic.*
   1959.   (Editor). *Logical Positivism.*
   1977.   *Parts of My Life.*

Francis Bacon
   1620.   *The New Organon and Related Writings*, edited with an introduction by F. H. Anderson, 1960 (compare also Anderson's *Philosophy of Francis Bacon*, 1948).

W. W. Bartley
   1974.   *Wittgenstein.*

L. W. Beck

1965.   *Studies in the Philosophy of Kant.*
1969.   *Early German Philosophy.*

P. Benacerraf and H. Putnam
1964/83.   BP: *Philosophy of Mathematics: Selected Readings* (the second edition is an extensive revision; all page references are to the 1964 edition).

I. Berlin and others
1973.   *Essays on J. L. Austin.*

Paul Bernays (1888–1977)
1935.   Sur le platonisme dans les mathématiques, reprinted in English translation in BP, pp. 274–286.
1937.   A system of axiomatic set theory, *JSL*, vol. 2, pp. 65–77.

Kenneth Blackwell
1981.   Early Wittgenstein and middle Russell, *Perspectives on the Philosophy of Wittgenstein*, ed. I. Block.

M. Boden
1977.   *Artificial Intelligence and Natural Man.*

M. Boffa
1977.   *JSL*, vol. 42, pp. 215–220.
1981.   *Bull. Soc. Math. Belg.*, vol. 33, pp. 21–31.

B. Bolzano
1837.   *Wissenschaftslehre.*

Georg Cantor (1845–1918)
1932.   *Gesammelte Abhandlungen*, ed. E. Zermelo.

Rudolph Carnap (1891–1970)
1922.   *Der Raum*, separate issue of doctoral dissertation of 1921.
1926.   *Physikalische Begriffsbildung.*
1928.   *Aufbau: Der logische Aufbau der Welt.* English translation of this and 1928a by Rolf A. George appeared in 1967.
1928a.   *Scheinprobleme in der Philosophie.*
1929.   *Abrisse der Logistik.*
1932.   Die physikalische Sprache als Universalsprache der Wissenschaft, *Erkenntnis*, vol. 2, pp. 432–465.
1934/37.   *Logical Syntax: The Logical Syntax of Language.* The German text appeared in 1934 and the expanded English version appeared in 1937.
1936.   Testability and meaning, *Philosophy of Science*, 92 pp.
1939.   *Foundations of Logic and Mathematics.*
1942.   *Introduction to Semantics.*
1943.   *Formalization of Logic.*
1947.   *Meaning and Necessity.*

218   References

1950.   *Logical Foundations of Probability.*

C. Chihara
1973.   *Ontology and the Vicious-Circle Principle.*

Yueh-lin Chin
1981 (1943).   Chinese philosophy, *Social Science in China,* no. 1, pp. 83–93.

R. Clark
1975.   *The Life of Bertrand Russell.* (The text used in this book is the 1976 edition by Alfred A. Knopf of New York.)

R. G. Collingwood
1945.   *The Idea of Nature.*

S. A. Cook
1971.   *Proc. 3rd ACM Conf. on Theory of Computing,* May 1971, pp. 151–158.

R. Crawshay-Williams
1970.   *Russell Remembered.*

D. Davidson and J. Hintikka (editors)
1969/75.   *Words and Objections.*

D. Dennett
1978.   *Brainstorms.*

John Dewey
1929.   *The Quest for Certainty.*

C. Diamond (editor)
1976.   *Wittgenstein's Lectures on the Foundations of Mathematics.*

H. Dreyfus
1972/81.   *What Computers Can't Do.*

Pierre Duhem
1906.   *La théorie physique: son objet et sa structure.*

M. Dummett
1975(70).   Wang's paradox, *Synthèse,* vol. 30, pp. 301–324 (reprinted in his 1978).
1978.   *Truth and Other Enigmas.*

Albert Einstein
1954.   *Ideas and Opinions.*

Encyclopaedia Britannica, the fifteenth edition, 1975

P. Engelmann
1967.   *Letters from Ludwig Wittgenstein with a Memoir.*

F. Engels
1878/85/94.   *Anti-Dühring*, 1969. English edition, Progress Publishers, Moscow.

H. Feigl and W. Sellars (editors)
1949.   *Readings in Philosophical Analysis.*

A. Fraenkel and Y. Bar-Hillel
1958.   *Foundations of Set Theory.*

G. Frege (1848–1925)
1879.   *Begriffshrift*, reprinted in *FG*, pp. 1–82.
1884.   *Foundations of Arithmetic*, 1950 translation by J. L. Austin.
1893.   *Grundgesetze*, I.
1903.   *Grundgesetze*, II.

R. F. Gibson, Jr.
1982.   *The Philosophy of W. V. Quine—an Expository Essay.*

Kurt Gödel (1906–1978)
1931.   Famous paper on incompleteness results, reprinted in *FG*, pp. 596–616.
1939.   The elegant version of his constructible sets and relative consistency proof of the continuum hypothesis, *PNAS*, vol. 25, pp. 220–224.
1940/51/63.   *The Consistency of the Continuum Hypothesis.*
1944.   Russell's mathematical logic, in Schilpp 1944 and reprinted in BP.
1947/64.   What is Cantor's continuum problem? *AMM*, vol. 54, pp. 515–525; revised version reprinted in BP.

Lucien Goldmann
1973.   *The Philosophy of Enlightenment.*

Nelson Goodman
1951.   *The Structure of Appearance.*

I. Grattan-Guinness
1977.   *Dear Russell-Dear Jourdain.*
1979.   *Historia Mathematica*, vol. 6, pp. 294–304.

J. Habermas
1968.   *Knowledge and Human Interests.*

T. Hailperin
1944.   *JSL*, vol. 9, pp. 1–19.

S. Hampshire
1971.   Conversations, *Modern British Philosophy*, ed. Bryan Magee.

C. G. Hempel

1963.   Schilpp, pp. 685–709.

J. Herbrand
1930.   His dissertation, partly reprinted in *FG*, pp. 525–581.

D. Hilbert and W. Ackermann
1928/38.   *Grundzüge der theoretischen Logik.*

D. Hilbert and P. Bernays
1934–1939.   *Grundlagen der Mathematik*, in 2 volumes.

J. Hintikka (editor)
1975.   *Rudolf Carnap, Logical Empiricist.*

D. Horowitz (editor)
1967.   *Marx and Economics.*

P. Hylton
1980.   Russell's substitutional theory, *Synthèse*, vol. 45, pp. 1–31.

R. Jager
1972.   *The Development of Bertrand Russell's Philosophy.*

R. B. Jensen
1969.   Davidson and Hintikka, pp. 278–291.

I. Kant (1724–1804)
1781/87.   *Critique of Pure Reason.*
1785.   *Metaphysical Foundations of Natural Science.*
1800.   *Logic.* English translation by R. S. Hartman and W. Schwarz,
1974.

A. Kenny
1973.   *Wittgenstein.*
1976.   From the Big Typescript to the *Philosophical Grammar, Essays on Wittgenstein*, ed. J. Hintikka.

J. M. Keynes
1949.   *Two Memoirs.*

L. Kolakowski
1966/68.   *The Alienation of Reason: A History of Positivist Thought.*

D. Lackey (editor)
1973.   *Essays in Analysis* (of Russell).

A. Levy
1959.   *JSL*, vol. 24, pp. 154–166.

C. I. Lewis (1883–1964)
1918.   *Survey of Symbolic Logic.*
1929.   *Mind and the World-Order.*

1946.   *Analysis of Knowledge and Valuation.*

C. G. Luckhardt (editor)
1979.   *Wittgenstein: Sources and Perspectives.*

G. Lukacs (1885–1971)
1923/68.   *History and Class Consciousness,* with 1967 preface.

N. Malcolm
1958/84.   *Ludwig Wittgenstein: A Memoir.*

T. McCarthy
1982.   *The Critical Theory of Jürgen Habermas.*

G. E. Moore (1873–1958)
1899.   The nature of judgment, *Mind,* vol. 8, pp. 176–193.
1903.   *Principia Ethica.*
1903a.   The refutation of idealism, *Mind,* vol. 12, pp. 433–453.
1955.   Wittgenstein's lectures in 1930–3, III, *Mind,* vol. 64, pp. 1–27.

Joseph Needham
1970.   *Science and Civilization in China,* II.

Otto Neurath (with assistance of Hans Hahn and R. Carnap)
1929.   *Wissenschaftliche Weltanschauung: der Wiener Kreis.*

F. Nietzsche
1886.   *Beyond Good and Evil.*

A. Orenstein
1977.   *Willard Van Orman Quine.*

A. Pap
1946.   *The a priori in Physical Theory* (compare also his *Semantics and Necessity,* 1958).

S. Papert
1980.   *Mindstorms.*

C. Parsons
1983.   *Mathematics in Philosophy.*

Fania Pascal
1979.   Wittgenstein: a personal memoir, Luckhardt, pp. 23–60.

G. Peano
1895–1903.   *Formulaire de mathématiques,* 4 volumes.

David Pears
1967.   *Bertrand Russell and the British Tradition in Philosophy.*
1971.   *Wittgenstein.*
1977.   The relation between Wittgenstein's picture theory of

propositions and Russell's theory of judgment, *Philosophical Review*, vol. 86, pp. 177–196.
1981.   The logical independence of elementary propositions, in the volume cited under Blackwell, pp. 74–84.

C. S. Peirce (1839–1914)
1878.   How to make our ideas clear, *Popular Science Monthly*; the term 'pragmatism' was first introduced.

J. Piaget
1971.   *Insights and Illusions of Philosophy*, trans. Wolfe Mays.

W. V. Quine
1930.   Review of Nicol's *Foundations of Geometry and Induction*, AMM, vol. 37, pp. 305–307.
1933.   A theorem in the calculus of classes, *Jour. London Math. Soc.*, vol. 8, pp. 89–95.
1934.   *A System of Logistic*, xii + 204 pp.
1934a.   Ontological remarks on the propositional calculus, *Mind*, vol. 43, pp. 472–476. Reprinted in 1966/76.
1936.   Set theoretical foundations for logic, *JSL*, vol. 1, pp. 45–57. Reprinted in 1966.
1936a (1935).   Truth by convention, *Philosophical Essays for A. N. Whitehead* (ed. O. H. Lee), pp. 90–124. Reprinted in 1966/76.
1937 (1936).   New foundations for mathematical logic (NF), *AMM*, vol. 44, pp. 70–80. Reprinted with additions in 1953/61/80.
1939.   A logistical approach to the ontological problem, *J. Unified Science*, vol. 9, pp. 84–89 (preprints only). Reprinted in 1966/76.
1940/47/51.   *ML: Mathematical Logic*, xii + 344 pp.
1941/66.   *Elementary Logic*, vi + 170 pp.
1941.   Element and number, *JSL*, vol. 6, pp. 135–149. Reprinted in 1966. This was a response to the discovery of a contradiction in the system of *ML*.
1941a.   Whitehead and the rise of modern logic, Schilpp 1941, pp. 125–163. Reprinted in 1966.
1946.   Concatenation as a basis for arithmetic, *JSL*, vol. 11, pp. 105–114. Reprinted in 1966.
1947.   Steps toward a constructive nominalism (with Nelson Goodman), *JSL*, vol. 12, pp. 97–122.
1948.   On what there is, *Review of Metaphysics*, vol. 2, pp. 21–38. Reprinted in 1953/61/80.
1950/59/72.   *Methods of Logic*, xxii + 272 pp.
1951.   Two dogmas of empiricism, *Philosophical Review*, vol. 60, pp. 20–43. Reprinted in 1953/61/80.
1952.   The problem of simplifying truth functions, *AMM*, vol. 59, pp. 521–531 (continued in the same journal, vol. 62, pp. 627–631, and vol. 66, pp. 755–760; the last piece is reprinted in 1966).
1953/61/80.   *LP: From a Logical Point of View*, vii + 184 pp.

1957.   The scope and language of science, *Brit. Jour. Phil. of Sci.*, vol. 8, pp. 1–17. Reprinted in 1966/76.

1960.   *WO: Word and Object*, xvi + 294 pp.

1960a (1954).   Carnap and logic truth, *Synthèse*, pp. 350–374. Reprinted in 1966/76 and Schilpp 1963 (pp. 385–406).

1963/69.   *SL: Set Theory and Its Logic*, xvi + 359 pp.

1966/76.   *WP: The Ways of Paradox and Other Essays*, x + 257 pp. and xii + 335 pp.

1966.   *Selected Logic Papers*, x + 250 pp.

1966a.   Russell's ontological development, *JP*, vol. 63, pp. 657–667, reprinted in *TT*.

1969.   *OR: Ontological Relativity and Other Essays*, x + 165 pp.

1970.   *PL: Philosophy of Logic*, xv + 109 pp.

1970a.   On the reasons for indeterminacy of translation, *JP*, vol. 67, pp. 178–183.

1970/78.   *WB: The Web of Belief* (with J. S. Ullian), 95 pp. and vii + 148 pp.

1974.   *RR: The Roots of Reference*, xii + 151 pp.

1975.   *NNK: the nature of natural knowledge*, *Mind and Language*, ed. S. Guttenplan, pp. 67–81.

1975a.   On empirically equivalent systems of the world, *Erkenntnis*, vol. 9, pp. 313–328.

1976.   *WPO: Whither physical objects? Boston Studies in Philos. of Sci.*, vol. 39, pp. 497–504.

1979.   *FM: Facts of the matter.* Shahan and Swoyer, pp. 155–169.

1981.   *TT: Theories and Things*, xii + 219 pp.

1983.   'Ontology and ideology revisited,' *JP*, pp. 499–502.

F. P. Ramsey
1931.   *The Foundations of Mathematics.*

Hans Reichenbach
1951.   *The Rise of Modern Philosophy.*

W. Reinhardt
1970.   *Annals of Mathematical Logic*, vol. 2, pp. 189–249.

J. Richard
1905.   Note on his paradox and its solution (by the 'vicious-circle principle'); reprinted in *FG*, pp. 142–144.

Paul Ricoeur, rapporteur
1979.   *Main Trends in Philosophy.*

Richard Rorty
1979.   *Philosophy and the Mirror of Nature.*
1982.   *Consequences of Pragmatism.*

J. B. Rosser

1942.   *JSL*, vol. 7, pp. 1–17.
1952.   *JSL*, vol. 17, pp. 238–242.
1953.   *Logic for Mathematicians.*

J. B. Rosser and Hao Wang
1950.   *JSL*, vol. 15, pp. 113–129.

D. Rubinstein
1981.   *Marx and Wittgenstein.*

Bertrand Russell (1872–1970)
1896.   *Germany and Social Democracy.*
1897.   *An Essay on the Foundations of Geometry.*
1900.   *A Critical Exposition of the Philosophy of Leibniz.*
1903/37.   *Principles: Principles of Mathematics.*
1905.   On denoting, *Mind*, reprinted in Lackey.
1906 (1905).   Transfinite numbers, reprinted in Lackey.
1973 (1906).   On the substitutional theory of classes and relations, first published in Lackey.
    [According to Lackey, Russell wrote in September 1906 a paper on 'the paradox of the liar' in which he observed, 'Whatever can be an apparent variable must have some kind of being.' This is taken as an anticipation of Quine's slogan about 'to be.' See Lackey, p. 134 and p. 332.]
    In 1906, Poincaré began an exchange with Russell in *RMM*, vol. 14, by attacking Russell's paper 'transfinite numbers' (pp. 17–34 and pp. 294–317). Russell replied (pp. 627–650; the English version was published in Lackey as Essay 9) and Poincaré added some more remarks (pp. 866–868). After Russell published his type theory paper (1908 below), Poincaré criticized it in *RMM* (vol. 17, 1909, pp. 451–482); Russell responded again (*RMM*, vol. 18, pp. 263–301; also included in Lackey as Essay 10). A shortened version of Poincaré's articles appeared in English translation in *Science and Method* (1914).
1908 (1907).   Mathematical logic as based on the theory of types, *Am. J. Math.*, vol. 30, pp. 222–262; reprinted in *FG*.
1910/25.   (with A. N. Whitehead) *PM: Principia Mathematica*, 3 volumes, 1910, 1912, 1913; second edition, 1925 and 1927. The first volume was largely Russell's work.
1912.   *PP: Problems of Philosophy.*
1984(1913).   *Theory of Knowledge*, typescript of 1913 which was discontinued as a result of criticisms by Wittgenstein. First published in 1984 as vol. 7 of *Russell's Collected Works.*
1914.   *External World: Our Knowledge of the External World as a Field for Scientific Method in Philosophy.*
1918.   The philosophy of logical atomism. *Monist* (in four issues from October 1918 to July 1919); reprinted in his *Logic and Knowledge* (1956).
1919.   *IMP: Introduction to Mathematical Philosophy.*
1921.   *The Analysis of Mind.*
1927.   *The Analysis of Matter.*

1940.   *An Inquiry into Meaning and Truth.*
1944 (1943).   *MD*: My mental development, in Schilpp 1944.
1946.   *History: History of Western Philosophy and Its Connection with Political and Social Circumstances from the Earliest Time to the Present Day.*
1948.   *Human Knowledge: Human Knowledge, Its Scope and Limits.*
1949.   Logical positivism, *Actas del primer congreso nacional de filosofia*, II, pp. 1218–1219.
1956.   *Portraits from Memory.*
1959.   *PD: My Philosophical Development.*
1967–9.   *Autobiography: The Autobiography of Bertrand Russell*, in 3 volumes, 1967, 1968, 1969.

G. Santayana
1953.   *Persons and Places* (third volume of *My Host the World*).

K. G. Sauer (editor)
1981.   *Bertrand Russell: A Bibliography of His Writings, 1895–1976.*

P. A. Schilpp (editor)
1941.   *Philosophy of Alfred North Whitehead.*
1944.   *Philosophy of Bertrand Russell.*
1949.   *Albert Einstein: Philosopher-Scientist.*
1963.   *Philosophy of Rudolf Carnap.*

M. Schlick
1918/25.   *Allgemeine Erkenntnislehre.*

R. W. Shahan and C. Swoyer (editors)
1979.   *Essays on the Philosophy of W. V. Quine.*

Th. Skolem
1922.   Remarks on axiomatized set theory, reprinted in *FG*.

J. Sneed
1971.   *The Logical Structure of Mathematical Physics.*

E. Specker
1953.   *PNAS*, vol. 39, pp. 972–975.
1958.   *Dialectica*, vol. 12, pp. 451–465.
1962.   *Logic, Methodology, and Philosophy of Science*, edited by E. Nagel and others, pp. 116–124.

C. Spector
1955.   Recursive well-orderings, *JSL*, vol. 20, pp. 151–163.

P. F. Strawson
1950.   On referring, *Mind*.

A. Tarski
1956.   *Logic, Semantics, Metamathematics*. (This includes an English translation of his 1936 paper on the concept of truth which consists of a

German translation of his 1933 paper in Polish, on pp. 152–268, plus an interesting postscript, on pp. 268–278. I am not able to find a mention of the date when the postscript was written; but it was probably in 1934 or 1935, in any case long after Gödel's letter of 1931, now published in Grattan-Guinness 1979.)

L. H. Tharp
1971.   *JP*, vol. 68, pp. 151–164.
1974.   *JSL*, vol. 39, pp. 700–716.
1975.   *Synthèse*, vol. 31, pp. 1–21.

Miguel de Unamuno
1921.   *The Tragic Sense of Life.*

Galvano Della Volpe
1980.   *Logic as a Positive Science*, Italian editions in 1950, 1956, 1969.

F. Waismann
1979.   *Wittgenstein and the Vienna Circle.*

Hao Wang
1944.   The metaphysical system of the New Li-Hsueh (in Chinese), *Philosophical Review* of the Chinese Philosophical Society, vol. 9, no. 2, pp. 39–62.
1945.   Language and metaphysics (in Chinese), ibid., vol. 10, no. 1, pp. 35–48.
1947.   A note on Quine's principles of quantification, *JSL*, vol. 12, pp. 130–132.
1948.   A new theory of element and number, *JSL*, vol. 13, pp. 129–137.
1949.   *PNAS*, vol. 36, pp. 448–453.
1950(49).   *JSL*, vol. 15, pp. 25–32.
1951(50).   *Methodos*, vol. 3, pp. 217–232; *Transactions AMS*, vol. 71, pp. 283–293.
1952.   *Transactions AMS*, vol. 73, pp. 243–275 (reprinted in *Survey* as Chapter 18).
1953.   *Philosophical Review*, vol. 62, pp. 413–420 (compare *MP*, pp. 416–424).
1954(53).   *JSL*, vol. 19, pp. 241–266 (reprinted as Chapter 23 in *Survey*; compare also last section of Chapter 3 in *MP*).
1955.   *Theoria*, vol. 21, pp. 158–178.
1957.   *JSL*, vol. 22, pp. 145–158 (also *Survey*, Chapter 4).
1958.   *Dialectica*, vol. 12, pp. 466–497 (*Survey*, Chapter 2).
1960(58).   *IBM Journal*, vol. 4, pp. 2–22 (*Survey*, Chapter 9).
1961.   *Essays on the Foundations of Mathematics*, pp. 328–351 (compare *MP*, Chapter 7).
1962(59).   *Survey: A Survey of Mathematical Logic*, Science Press, Peking, 652 pp. + x; also distributed by North-Holland Publishing

Company, Amsterdam, 1963. Reprinted by Chelsea, New York, 1970, under the title *Logic, Computers and Sets*.

1965.   Russell and his logic, *Ratio*, vol. 7. pp. 1–34 (compare *MP*, Chapter 3 and section 4 of Chapter 11).

1966.   Russell and philosophy, *JP*, vol. 63, pp. 670–673.

1971(66).   Logic, computation and philosophy, *L'âge de la science*, vol. 3, pp. 101–105.

1970(68).   A survey of Skolem's work in logic, *Selected Logical Works of Th. Skolem*, ed. E. Fenstad, pp. 17–52.

1974 (1972).   *MP: From Mathematics to Philosophy*, Routledge & Kegan Paul, 431 pp. + xiv. (Italian translation, Boringhieri, 1984; Chapter 6 is reprinted in the 1983 edition of BP as the concluding essay.)

1975(72).   Metalogic, *Encyclopaedia Britannica*, vol. 11, pp. 1078–1086 (all except the part on model theory makes up Chapter 5 of *MP*).

[After the completion of *MP* in June 1972, a period of diversified explorations followed. A number of examples are listed here to fulfill a promise made toward the end of section 3.2 in the Introduction.]

1973(72).   *Reflections on a Visit to China* (in Chinese), 37 pp. (widely reprinted also in newspapers and journals).

1974(73).   Concerning the materialist dialectic, *Philosophy East and West*, vol. 24, pp. 303–319.

1976(74).   (with B. Dunham). Toward feasible solutions of the tautology problem, *Annals of Mathematical Logic*, vol. 10, pp. 117–154.

1977(75).   Large sets, *Logic, Foundations of Mathematics, and Computability Theory*, ed. R. E. Butts and J. Hintikka, pp. 309–333.

1981(76).   Some facts about Kurt Gödel, *JSL*, vol. 46, pp. 653–659.

1977(76).   Dialectics and natural science, *The Overseas Chinese Life Scientists Association Newsletter*, vol. 1, no. 2, pp. 48–55.

1977.   To learn from Lu Xun's searchings (in Chinese), *Dousou Bimonthly*, vol. 19, pp. 1–16.

1981(78).   *Popular Lectures on Mathematical Logic*, 273 pp. + v, Chinese and English versions by Science Press, Beijing, and Van Nostrand Reinhold, New York.

1979(78).   Mechanical treatment of Chinese characters and the means of information transmission (in Chinese), *The State of the Art Report of Computer Technology*, Beijing, June issue, pp. 1–5.

1979.   Sixty years after the May Fourth Demonstration (in Chinese), *Wide Angle*, vol. 86, November issue, pp. 32–49.

1981(80).   Gödel and Wittgenstein (Chinese translation by Y. Z. Li from manuscript), *Philosophical Research Monthly*, no. 3, pp. 25–37.

1983(82).   Philosophy: Chinese and Western, *Commentary* (Singapore), vol. 6, no. 1, pp. 1–9.

1984(82).   Computer theorem proving and artificial intelligence, *Automated Theorem Proving: After 25 Years*, ed. W. W. Bledsoe and D. W. Loveland, vol. 29 of AMS series on contemporary mathematics, pp. 49–80.

1984(82).   Wittgenstein's and other mathematical philosophies, *The Monist*, vol. 67, pp. 18–28.
1984(83).   The formal and the intuitive in the biological sciences, *Perspectives in Biology and Medicine*, vol. 27, pp. 525–542.

A. N. Whitehead and B. Russell
1910/25.   *Principia Mathematica* (*PM*), three volumes published in 1910, 1912, 1913, respectively; second edition with revisions by Russell in the first volume published in 1925; the other volumes (unchanged) were reprinted in 1927. A planned fourth volume on geometry, largely to be written by Whitehead, never appeared.

D. C. Williams
1965.   Clarence Irving Lewis 1883–1964, *Philosophy and Phenomenological Research*, vol. 26, pp. 159–172.

W. Windelbind
1901.   *A History of Philosophy*, English translation by James H. Tufts.

L. Wittgenstein (1899–1951)
1961/79.   *Notebooks, 1914–16.*
1921/22.   The *Tractatus: Tractatus Logico-philosophicus*, with introduction by Russell.
1956/78.   *Remarks on the Foundations of Mathematics.*
1953.   *Philosophical Investigations.*
1969 (1949–51).   *On Certainty.*
1980.   *Culture and Value.*

Alan Wood
1957.   *Bertrand Russell: The Passionate Sceptic.*

Harry Woolf (editor)
1980.   *Some Strangeness in the Proportion.*

Virginia Woolf
1925.   *The Common Reader.*

G. H. v. Wright
1955.   Biographical sketch of Wittgenstein, reprinted in Malcolm.
1969.   The Wittgenstein papers, *Philosophical Review*, vol. 78, pp. 483–503.
1974.   *Wittgenstein's Letters to Russell, Keynes, and Moore.*

E. Zermelo
1904.   Paper introducing the axiom of choice, reprinted in *FG*, pp. 139–141.
1908.   Paper introducing his system of set theory, reprinted in *FG*, pp. 199–215.

1909.   Sur les ensembles finis et le principe de l'induction complete, *Acta mathematica*, vol. 32, pp. 183–193. First definition of natural numbers not needing infinite sets.

1930.   Über Grenzzahlen und Mengenbereiche, *Fund. math.*, vol. 16, pp. 29–47. A preliminary account of the iterative concept of set.

Chronological table

For the purpose of a quick surview, I have compiled a table listing some of the major items in the life and work of Russell, Wittgenstein, Carnap, and Quine. Since I am considering the matter from my perspective, I have included also items directly and indirectly related to my contact with their work. Incomplete citations of their publications depend on the preceding list of references (and the table of abbreviations).

There are many volumes on Russell's life, including his three volumes of autobiography, his *Portraits from Memory* (1956), his *PD* (1959), and a big volume by Ronald W. Clark (1975) which draws from various sources. When detailed sources are not given below, they can usually be found by consulting Russell's autobiography or his *PD* or Clark's book. Malcolm's memoir (including Wright's biography) and *CV* are major sources of quotations from and about Wittgenstein. (Brian McGuinness has checked this part of the table and given a few corrections.) Data about Carnap are mostly derived from his *IA* in Schilpp 1963. Orenstein 1977 contains some information from an unpublished brief autobiography of Quine's. I have also received a few corrections and additions from Quine on an earlier version of the part about him. Quine has completed a book-length autobiography which is to appear before this book, by the same publisher.

There are different ways of dividing Russell's life into stages. A standard way is into three stages: (1) 1872 to 1910 or 1914; (2) 1910 or 1914 to 1938 or 1944 or 1948; (3) 1938 or 1944 or 1948 to 1970. 'He had been beautifully educated by private tutors at Pembroke Lodge.' From his entrance into Trinity College in 1890 to the summer of 1900, his education was completed in a remarkable manner. This was followed by a decade of intensive and fruitful work, from the *Principles* to *PM*. He was happily married from the end of 1894 to the end of 1901, and unhappily married from 1902 to the beginning of 1911.

From 1910 to 1921, Russell tried to start a big new philosophical project, became very famous, worked as a pacifist, was in prison (1918), visited Russia and China, and had three extended and serious affairs. This was a period of transition and he was two-minded about his philosophical interest. From 1921 to 1938, he became a father and went from his second to his third marriage; philosophy occupied only a subordinate place over this period until toward its end when he decided to return to philosophy. From 1938 to 1948 he was engaged in doing philosophy in one form or another; he left England September 1938 and stayed in America till May 1944.

Wittgenstein was educated at home until he was fourteen and continued for three years thereafter at a school at Linz, finishing in 1906. He then did some engineering work for several years but apparently began to study Russell's *Principles* some time previous to April 1909. For nearly ten years he did work which led to the completion of his *Tractatus* in 1918. This was followed by a decade of other activities, including teaching in elementary schools for six years (1920–1926). In January 1929 he returned to philosophy and to Cambridge to begin the development of a different philosophy from the *Tractatus*. Professor von Wright stresses the continuity over this period, with three distinguishable phases: from 1929 to 1933, ending with the Big Typescript; from the Brown Book (1935) to the completion of *PI*, I (1945); and from 1946 to 1951. The two main centers of activity were Vienna and Cambridge (England). He did a good deal of lecturing to small groups from 1930 to 1947 and was professor from 1939 to the end of 1947. From February 2, 1929, to a few days before his death in April 1951, he wrote a huge amount and got a substantial portion typed.

Carnap lived in Europe from his birth in 1891 to the end of 1935, and in America from 1936 to his death in 1970. From 1910 to 1914 he attended three courses by Frege. He studied *PM* in 1919 and *External World* in 1921, which were the decisive influences on his first major book, the *Aufbau* (1928), essentially completed by 1926. From 1926 to 1931 he was an instructor in Vienna; this was followed by a professorship in Prague till the end of 1935, when he emigrated to America. He spent 1936 to 1952, with several years on leave, at the University of Chicago; in 1954 he succeeded Reichenbach at the University of California (Los Angeles). Carnap's most influential work was probably his *Logical Syntax*, written chiefly during his Prague period. From 1935 to 1945 he worked on semantics; from 1946 on he devoted his energy to studying the logic of induction and probability.

Quine went to Harvard as a graduate student in 1930 and has stayed there, except for leaves and visits, ever since. He began to read Russell's work in college (probably around 1928), and got excited about Carnap's work when they met around the beginning of 1933. From that time on, he 'was Carnap's disciple for six years.' From 1936 to 1950 he wrote three famous articles largely, in one way or another, as responses to the work of Russell and Carnap: NF (1936), 'On what there is' (1948), and 'Two dogmas' (1950). Since these papers concentrated on central themes of the time, his own general outlook in philosophy (including philosophy of logic) was only sketched or implied in them. From 1950 on, Quine started a more systematic development of his own philosophical ideas; he began with the largest project in his career, the fruit of which was his *WO*, completed nine years later. Further improvements, revisions, and extensions of his system have continued since 1960 in articles and books, including *OR* (1969), *RR* (1974), and *TT* (1981). He is at present engaged in preparing replies to his critics who have contributed to the volume to honor him in the 'Library of living philosophers' series.

1872.   Bertrand Arthur William Russell was born on May 18 at 5:45 P.M., big and fat, the second son and third child.

His father, Viscount Amberley, was the eldest son of the first Earl Russell who was twice Prime Minister, from 1846 to 1852 and from 1865 to 1866.

His mother was the daughter of the second Lord Stanley of Alderley.

Their lives and characters were depicted in *The Amberley Papers* (1937) which Russell edited with Patricia Spence, his third wife.

1873.   John Stuart Mill, Russell's lay godfather, died.

1874.   Russell's mother and sister died of diphtheria.

1876.   His father died on January 9 of bronchitis and grief; he and his elder brother went in February to live with their grandparents at Pembroke Lodge, where he was to live fourteen years. His grandfather lived only three years longer, but his grandmother lived until 1898; she once gave Russell a Bible with the inscription: 'Thou shalt not follow a multitude to evil.'

His childhood was solitary but not unhappy. He was educated by governesses and tutors. In adolescence, he began to suffer from loneliness. 'I was a solitary, shy, priggish youth. I had no experience of the social pleasures of boyhood and did not miss them' (*Portraits*, p. 9).

1883.   His brother Frank began to give him lessons in Euclid on August 9. He objected to taking the axioms on trust.

'Bertie showed me his schoolroom at Pembroke Lodge, and his old notebooks on the various subjects that he had studied. It was perfectly princely education, but a little like cultivating tropical flowers under electric light in a steaming greenhouse. The instruction was well selected, competently given, and absorbed with intense thirst; but it was too good for the outdoor climate' (Santayana 1953).

'It turned out that while not without aptitude for pure mathematics, I was completely destitute of the concrete kinds of skill which are necessary in science' (for source, see Clark, p. 31).

1888.   First heard of *Das Kapital* and non-Euclidean geometries from his tutor, Mr. Ewen, a stout defender of reason and an acquaintance of one of Marx's daughters.

In the spring he was sent to 'an Army crammer at Old Southgate' to prepare for college.

1889.   Went to Cambridge in December for entrance scholarship examination; Whitehead was the examiner.

Ludwig Joseph Johann Wittgenstein, born on April 26 in Vienna, the youngest of five brothers and three sisters.

1890.   Russell entered Trinity College in October with a minor scholarship, specializing in mathematics.

'I like mathematics because it is *not* human and has nothing particular to do with this planet or with the whole accidental universe.'

Met Alys Pearsall Smith (on vacation from Bryn Mawr) for the first time in the summer.

1891.   Began to take part in the University Moral Science Club in February.

On June 4, Russell proposed, to the Magpie and Stump Debating Society, the motion: 'That this house consider it both just and expedient that women should be admitted to equal political rights as men.'

Carnap was born on May 18, exactly nineteen years younger than Russell, in Ronsdorf near Barmen, in northwest Germany, of very religious parents. When a child, his mother worked on a large book about her late father, and Carnap 'was fascinated by the magical activity of putting thought on paper.'

1892.   G. E. Moore (1873–1958) entered Trinity with a classical scholarship and soon took part in the Moral Science Club.

Russell was elected to 'the Society' (known as the Apostles).

1893.   Russell became friends with Moore and persuaded him to turn his attention from classics to philosophy. Russell said of Moore that 'for some years he fulfilled my ideal of genius.'

Russell was bracketed Seventh Wrangler in the Mathematical Tripos. After the examination he 'swore that I would never look at mathematics again and sold all my mathematical books.' (A few years later, when Einstein graduated from college, he had a similarly negative reaction to the final examinations, after which 'I found the consideration of any scientific problems distasteful to me for an entire year'—Schilpp 1949.) The (temporary) disillusion turned him to philosophy ('Moral Science' at Cambridge); he soon discovered 'all the delight of a new landscape on emerging from a valley.'

Russell came of age in May and acquired legal and financial independence, with a fortune of twenty thousand pounds inherited from his father. From this moment his relations with Alys (Pearsall Smith) 'began to be something more than distant admiration.' In September he proposed to Alys and 'was neither accepted nor rejected.'

1894.   Took a First with distinction in the second part of the Moral Science Tripos. About this time Alys consented to become definitely engaged to him; also he 'went over completely to a semi-Kantian, semi-Hegelian metaphysic.'

Spent three months in Paris as an honorary attaché, beginning in August. Married Alys on December 13.

1895.   Spent the first three months in Berlin, chiefly studying economics but also continuing to work at his Fellowship dissertation. He 'resolved not to adopt a profession, but to devote myself to writing.' His 'intellectual ambitions were taking shape.'

One day 'I walked by myself in the Tiergarten, and made projects of future work. I thought that I would write one series of books on the philosophy of the sciences from pure mathematics to physiology, and another series of books on social questions. I hoped that the two series might ultimately meet in a synthesis at once scientific and practical. My scheme was largely inspired by Hegelian ideas. Nevertheless, I have to some extent followed it in later years,' except that he never, according to himself, attained the desired 'synthesis.'

It might be of interest to compare this early project with the 'great instauration' discussed in section 4.3. The more concrete objective of book-writing (and in two series) seems to put form before substance and gives the impression of waiting for the synthesis to emerge by itself as the pieces (in the form of books) get made. As it was, Russell did not appear to have assigned the final goal of synthesis an appropriate commanding role in writing his numerous books. Rather, he either looked for 'fundamental' or 'scientific' philosophy, or dealt with concrete particular ethical and social issues in a direct and somewhat isolated (from a striving for synthesis) manner. He was, in Santayana's words, 'caught and irresistibly excited by current discussions.'

To be able to write so many widely and directly influential books (and mostly not journalistic) is in itself an extraordinary achievement. His form of life was very different from that of Kant and Hegel, who were among the early professors of philosophy living at a time and in a society respectful toward and receptive of complex philosophical treatises. According to G. H. Hardy's *A Mathematician's Apology*, however, Russell was more interested in the relative 'immortality' of his work: he dreamed of a librarian in the next century hesitating over whether to dispose of *PM*.

He and Alys then travelled in Italy before settling down to finish his Fellowship dissertation by August. This he did and was elected Fellow, with six free years; his 1897 was based on the dissertation. He then returned in autumn to Berlin to study German Social Democracy, which resulted in his 1896.

1896.   Russell lectured on the Social Democrats at the London School of Economics and studied Cantor's work on set theory; 'finished my book on the foundations of geometry in 1896, and proceeded to what I intended as a similar treatment of the foundations of physics, being under the impression that problems concerning geometry had been disposed of' (*PD*, p. 41).

In autumn he and Alys went to America for three months.

1897.   Russell settled down to mathematics; also studied the principles of dynamics and Maxwell's work.

1898.   He and Alys 'began a practice, which we continued till 1902, of spending part of each year at Cambridge.' He was, assisted by Moore, 'beginning to emerge from the bath of German idealism.' 'On re-reading what I wrote about the philosophy of physics in the years 1896 to 1898, it seems to me complete nonsense' (*PD*, p. 43).

He began work on his 'big book' which eventually became his *Principles*.

Toward the end of the year, Russell and Moore rebelled against both Kant and Hegel (*PD*, p. 54).

Carnap's father died and he moved to Barmen with the family.

1899.   Russell lectured on Leibniz, as a stand-in for McTaggart; the lectures led to his 1900.

1900.   The Russells and the Whiteheads attended the philosophy congress in Paris from late July to early August. It 'was a turning point in my intellectual life, because I there met Peano.'

Russell's further work with his *Principles*, his discovery of and struggle with the paradoxes, his theory of descriptions of 1905, his debates with Poincaré, and the *PM* project: all these are reviewed in section 6 and will not be repeated here.

'Every day throughout October, November and December, I wrote my ten pages, and finished the MS [of a draft of the *Principles*] on the last day of the century.'

1901.   'Oddly enough, the end of the century marked the end of this sense of triumph, and from that moment onwards I began to be assailed simultaneously by intellectual and emotional problems which plunged me into the darkest despair that I have ever known.'

The intellectual problem of that time was undoubtedly the discovery of Russell's paradox in May or June. The emotional problem had a lot to do with his disenchantment with his first marriage. It has been conjectured that between February 1901 and February 1902 he fell out of love with Alys and fell in love with someone else, presumed (in Clark's book) to be Evelyn Whitehead.

Russell's fellowship at Trinity ran out in the summer and he was invited in the autumn to lecture on mathematical logic for two terms.

1902.   'I went out bicycling one afternoon, and suddenly,' he recalls, 'I realized I no longer loved Alys.' This took place during the first weeks of the year.

The marriage continued somehow. On May 29, 1911, Alys finally agreed to a complete parting. The divorce eventually became official on September 21, 1921. He married Dora Winifred Black on the 27th, left her in 1932, and was divorced by her in 1935. He then married Patricia Helen Spence in 1936 and was divorced by her in 1952 after she had left him in 1949. On December 15, 1952, he married Edith Finch, and the marriage was a success.

1903.   Completed and published his famous paper 'The free man's worship.' Was interested in free trade; began giving political lectures.

Wittgenstein was educated at home until he was fourteen; beginning of three years at a school at Linz in Upper Austria; 'read Schopenhauer's *Die Welt als Wille und Vorstellung* in his youth' that gave him 'his first philosophy' (Wright 1955).

1904.   Even though Russell has often emphasized the unhappy marriage and the hard work on *PM* from 1901 to 1910, he also observed: 'It must not be supposed that all my time was consumed in despair and intellectual effort.' In particular, he had a good deal of political and social activity. 'Throughout this period my winters were largely occupied with political questions.' 'In 1907 I even stood for Parliament at a by-election, on behalf of votes for women.'

Once this year, when Russell was living in an isolated village, J. M. Keynes asked for and was promised a restful weekend. But by Monday morning the Russells 'had had twenty-six unexpected guests, and Keynes, I fear, went away more tired than he came.'

1905.   The Russells decided to live near Oxford. Shortly after they had moved in he discovered his theory of descriptions.

1906.   Began an exchange with Poincaré in *RMM* (see Russell 1906 under 'References').

Wittenstein finished school and entered the Technische Hochschule in Berlin-Charlottenburg to study engineering.

1907.   Russell developed his theory of types.

1908.   Elected a fellow of the Royal Society of London.

Wittgenstein (W for brevity) left Berlin to go to England; registered at the University of Manchester in the autumn to study aeronautics; elected to a research studentship in 1910 and again in 1911. Over this period W did successively experiments with kites, construction of the jet engine, and design of the propeller.

As the last project lent itself to a completely mathematical treatment, W's interest shifted to mathematics and the philosophy of mathematics. Read Russell's *Principles of Mathematics* (1903), which led him to a study of Frege's work. 'It was Frege's conceptual realism which made him abandon his earlier idealistic views' (Wright 1955).

On April 20, 1909, Jourdain noted that Russell had 'said that the views I gave in reply to Wittgenstein (who had "solved" Russell's contradiction) agree with his own' (Grattan-Guinness 1977).

Willard Van Orman Quine was born on June 25.

He grew up in Akron, Ohio and attended the local high school, where he exhibited an aptitude for mathematics and pursued the scientific, rather than the classical, technical, or commercial courses. During several summers he drew and sold maps of nearby places. Poe was his favorite author. In his last year in high school, he developed a serious interest in language, particularly in grammar and etymology.

1909.   Carnap moved to Jena with the family.

1910.   Russell was made a lecturer, for five years, at Trinity College.

In the autumn Carnap attended Frege's course Begriffschrift.

1911.   Russell became intimate with Lady Ottoline Morrell. They continued extensive correspondence until her death in April 1938. Russell wrote her 1,775 letters, all preserved in his Archives.

Met Wittgenstein for the first time on October 18; they were thirty-nine and twenty-two.

R. B. Perry wrote in the spring to invite Russell to Harvard for one year; he declined. Early in 1912, Santayana, visiting England, renewed the invitation. Not until November did he agree to a three-month visit to begin in March 1914. When Josiah Royce (1855–1916) asked if he would 'go to Harvard permanently as their chief professor,' he firmly refused (February 6, 1913). It seems very likely that Harvard was eager to secure Russell, probably as successor to William James (1842–1910). When Russell went to Harvard in 1914, he wrote on March 19: 'Nobody here broods or is absent-minded, or has time to hear whispers from another world—except poor old Royce, whom I like, though he is a garrulous old bore. Everybody is kind, many are intelligent along the narrow lines of their work, and most are virtuous—but *none* have any quality.'

In January 1916, Harvard invited him for another visit; before the end of the month he had accepted. When he applied for a passport in May, he was refused and the British ambassador in Washington wrote on June 8 to Harvard's president to apologize for the refusal. From 1919 on, 'I used to send periodical cables to President Lowell' to testify on behalf of H. M. Sheffer (*Autobiography*, II, p. 151, after a letter by Harold J. Laski). In 1923, Whitehead (1861–1947), over sixty, joined Harvard's philosophy department and went on to write several major books. Russell lectured at Harvard in 1929 and 1931, with Whitehead in the chair. In 1930, Harvard also asked him to make a long visit, but he declined.

Toward the end of 1936, Russell had a very strong desire to get back to philosophy and began to look for an academic position. Among other inquiries he wrote to ask Whitehead whether the offer six years ago could be renewed. To Warder Norton, he wrote on February 16, 1937, 'I should *very much* like to succeed Whitehead at Harvard.' Nothing came of this, except that later he was invited to be the William James Lecturer for the autumn of 1940, when Carnap and Quine were both there.

Wittgenstein visited Frege at Jena and was advised by him to study under Russell at Cambridge; met Russell on October 18, followed by close interaction. Asked Russell for advice on choosing between aviation and philosophy on November 27. (For this entry and much about W under 1912 and 1913, see Blackwell 1981.)

1912.   Russell published 'The essence of religion,' which Wittgenstein detested.

At this time Russell became much interested in studying physics for developing his philosophy of knowledge. On November 17 he wrote: 'When I have read enough [popular books on physics] to know my way about, I will start on things that are not popular. A new big piece of work like this provides the sort of tightening-up and sudden alertness that you see in a dog who startles a hare. It is a fine big canvas that may easily take me ten years to fill. The mere thought of it makes my blood tingle.'

Wittgenstein proposed to Russell 'a definition of logical *form*' on January 26. In March, Russell wrote (to Lady Ottoline Morrell): 'Yes, Wittgenstein has been a great event in my life—Whatever may come of him.'

W told David Pinsent that he had suffered from a terrible loneliness for some nine years, with thoughts of suicide constantly in his mind.

In October, Russell wrote about Wittgenstein's detesting his newly published article 'The essence of religion': 'He felt I had been a traitor to the gospel of exactness, and wantonly used words vaguely; also that such things are too intimate for print.'

1913.   Russell started on a big book on theory of knowledge but did not complete it. He had written 350 pages which would be less than one-third of the projected book. [This is 1984(1913).]

Wittgenstein wrote a 'Review of Peter Coffey's *The Science of Logic,*' *Cambridge Review*, March 6 (reprinted in E. Homberger et al., eds., *The Cambridge Mind*, 1970).

Friends of W at Cambridge included, apart from Russell, G. E. Moore, A. N. Whitehead, J. M. Keynes, G. H. Hardy, W. E. Johnson, and David Pinsent.

W criticized Russell's unfinished book manuscript (350 pages written from May 7 to June 6).

W moved to Norway at the beginning of the autumn, after six terms at Cambridge, and lived in isolation until the outbreak of the War in 1914. 'Notes on logic' written in September and early October (reprinted in *Notebooks 1914–16*). Parts of a version of this were apparently read to Russell in a brief visit to England and caused Russell to write on October 4, 'It is as good as anything that has been done in logic.' Later Russell finally dragged this version out of him, 'with pincers,' wanting to use it 'for lecturing on logic at Harvard.'

In the summer, Carnap attended Frege's Begriffsschrift II.

1914.   Russell taught at Harvard and gave his Lowell Lectures in Boston, which resulted in his 1914.

Wittgenstein's 'Notes dictated to G. E. Moore in Norway,' April 1914 (published in *Notebooks 1914–16*).

W enlisted (as a volunteer) on August 7 in a garrison artillery regiment; served first on a vessel in the Vistula and later in an artillery workshop at Cracow.

'Notebook from August 9 to October 30' and 'Notebook from October 30 to June 22, 1915,' published in *Notebooks 1914–16*.

Carnap attended Frege's Logik der Mathematik course in the summer.

During the first years of the war, Carnap was at the front most of the time; he was transferred to Berlin in summer 1917. 'Military service was contrary to my whole attitude, but I accepted it now as a duty, believed it to be necessary in order to save the fatherland.'

1915.   Russell's pacifist views and activities generated much tension between him and a number of his friends.

His lectureship at Trinity was renewed for five years, with permission to be on leave for the first two terms of 1915–1916; for a leaflet of his, he was dismissed from the lectureship on July 11, 1916. After the war, the Council decided on December 12, 1919, to offer Russell 'a lectureship in Logic and the Principles of Mathematics tenable for five years from 1 July, 1920.' After some delay, he accepted the lectureship; before the end of 1920, when he was in Peking, he had resigned.

Helped T. S. Eliot who had been his student at Harvard.

Wittgenstein read and was overwhelmed by Tolstoy's version of the Gospels; also his Folk Tales.

W was stationed near Lwow from end of July.

1916.   Russell toured South Wales in the summer, giving political speeches.

Wittgenstein went to the front by March; decorated in June and October. Probably in October, went to Olmuetz (now Olomouc, Czechoslovakia) to attend the artillery training school there as a 'one-year conscript.'
Made friends with Paul Engelmann in Olmuetz.
Notebooks 1914–16, 1961, revised edition 1979.

1917.   In September, Russell said: 'My interest in philosophy is reviving, and I expect before long I shall come back to it altogether.'
Wittgenstein returned to the Eastern Front by January 26; at least once on leave at Olmuetz, probably before July.

1918.   For an article he wrote, Russell was put in Brixton Prison early in May and released on September 18. A draft of his *IMP* was written while in prison.
Wittgenstein was transferred to the Italian Front in March. On leave in the Salzburg area and in Vienna, July and August.
W wrote an immediate predecessor of *Tractatus*, published 1971 under the title *Protractatus*.
Tractatus, completed in August. Immediately approached a publisher and received a negative answer; resumed the pursuit of publication a year later and continued till July 8, 1920, when he wrote to Russell: 'For the present I won't take any further steps to have it published. But if you feel like getting it printed, it is entirely at your disposition.'
Only with Russell's 'Introduction' and intervention was it published in the final issue of W. Ostwald's *Annalen der Naturphilosophie* in 1921.
The book, with an English translation, was published in 1922.
W was taken prisoner on November 3 by the Italians, upon the collapse of the Austro-Hungarian army.

1919.   Russell completed his *Analysis of Mind*.
Met Wittgenstein at The Hague for seven days to discuss the *Tractatus* (in December).
Wittgenstein was released from prison in August; reached home on August 25.
Talked of suicide incessantly. (For the next few years, see Bartley 1974 and Engelmann 1967.)
Enrolled by September 16 in a Teachers Training College.
Moved from the family mansion to become a lodger on September 25.
October has been described 'as his cruelest month.'
Moved to a friend's home in November and stayed till April 20, 1920.
Visit to The Hague and meeting with Russell in December.
Carnap studied *PM* around 1919.

1920.   Russell met Romain Rolland in Paris and signed his appeal for European peace.
Russell visited Russia from May 19 to June 25. He saw Gorky, Trotsky, Kamenev and was granted an hour's interview with Lenin. Shortly after the visit he published *The Practice and Theory of Bolshevism*.

He and Dora Black visited China from October 22 to July 10, 1921. After brief visits in Shanghai, Hangchow, Hankow, and Changsha, they arrived at Peking on October 31 and he began lecturing soon after. In Changsha he met John Dewey for the first time. He gave five sets of 'official' lectures on: mathematical logic, the analysis of matter, the analysis of mind, the problems of philosophy, and the structure of society. Their interpreter and companion was the linguist Y. R. Chao.

Wittgenstein wrote to Engelmann on May 30: 'I have had a most miserable time lately. Of course only as a result of my own baseness and rottenness. I have continually thought of taking my own life, and the idea still haunts me sometimes.' More of this sort of talk is contained in the letter of June 21.

Completion of training course for teachers in July; assistant gardener at the Klosterneuberg Monastery during late July to August 23.

Went to Trattenbach as a primary-school teacher in September; 'I am happy in my work at school,' for the first month or two; teacher at three schools till April 1926.

Asked for a copy of Frege's *Grundgesetze* in letter of October 31.

1921.   Russell became seriously ill on March 14 and recovered full consciousness only on April 28.

He married Dora Black on September 27; their first child, John Conrad, was born on November 16.

In letter of January 2, Wittgenstein said, 'I have been morally dead for more than a year!'

Spent August in Norway.

Left Vienna for Trattenbach on September 13; teacher there through the academic year.

Read some work of Tagore in October; became afterwards more interested in Tagore's work. 'I am as stupid and rotten as ever.'

Publication of the *Tractatus* in Ostwald's journal.

In the winter of 1921, Carnap read Russell's *External World*, which made a specially vivid impression on him.

Carnap's dissertation *Der Raum* at Jena was completed; the degree, Dr. Phil., was granted on December 9.

1922.   When John Conrad was born, Russell 'felt an immense release of pent-up emotion, and during the next ten years my main purposes were parental.' 'Parenthood had made it imperative to earn money.'

Russell had given away most of his inherited money by 1916. Meanwhile, with his *Principles of Social Reconstruction* (1916), he had discovered that he could earn money by writing, to which he added also lecturing from 1924 on. From 1923 to 1930 he published, apart from numerous articles, over a dozen books, mostly popular and including at least three bestsellers. He made lecture tours in America in 1924, 1927, 1929, and 1931.

He stood for Parliament in Chelsea in 1922 and 1923.

Meeting of Wittgenstein with Russell at Innsbruck in the summer.

W was attached briefly to a secondary school at Hassbach in the autumn.

W was elementary schoolteacher at Puchberg-am-Schneeberg for the academic years 1922–1923 and 1923–1924.

In letter of September 14, W said: 'The idea of a possible flight to Russia which we talked about keeps on haunting me. The main reason for this is that . . . they [teachers, parish priests, etc. at Hassbach where I am going to teach] are not human *at all* but loathsome worms.'

From 1922 to 1925, Carnap's major occupation was considerations out of which grew his *Aufbau* (1928).

1923.   A daughter, Katharine Jane, was born to Russell and Dora.

Ramsey visited Wittgenstein at Puchberg in September.

A small conference at Erlangen in March was regarded by Carnap as the 'initial step in the movement of a scientific philosophy in Germany.' Among the participants were Heinrich Behmann, Carnap, Paul Hertz, Kurt Lewin, and Reichenbach. After the conference, Carnap and Reichenbach met frequently and interacted in a way fruitful for both.

1924.   Russell completed in September his additions to the 1925 edition of *PM*; Ramsey assisted in the work.

Ramsey was in Vienna from March to October and visited Wittgenstein a number of times.

W was a teacher at Otterthal for the academic year 1924–1925 and from September 1925 to April 1926.

During the two years at Puchberg, a fairly prosperous resort town, he seems to have been less unhappy than during the years at Trattenbach and Otterthal.

Schlick wrote to him on December 25 to praise the importance and correctness of the *Tractatus.*

Through Reichenbach, Carnap became acquainted with Schlick (in the summer).

1925.   Wittgenstein visited England (including Manchester and Cambridge) in the summer; stayed with Keynes in Sussex.

Carnap 'went for a short time to Vienna and gave some lectures in Schlick's philosophical Circle.'

1926.   *On Education: Especially in Early Childhood* was published, and re-viewed by John Dewey. Russell wrote to Dewey on June 15: 'It is an amateurish and in some ways ignorant book, and I am relieved that it should not be despised by a man of your eminence as an educationalist. . . . I seriously think of emigrating, however, as I expect disaster in England before my children are grown up.'

In April one Piribauer and his neighbors at Otterthal instituted legal pro-ceedings against Wittgenstein on the ground of physical brutality to some students.

W abruptly left the tiny village, never to teach elementary school again.

Schlick and a few pupils went to Otterthal in April and found W had left.

His mother died on June 3.

Worked as a gardener at Huetteldorf in the spring and summer; entertained seriously the idea of becoming a monk.

Wörterbuch für Volksschulen, a spelling book for elementary schools, containing between six and seven thousand words.

In autumn W began with Engelmann the project of building the house on the Kundmanngasse for his sister. His contribution was, according to one account, primarily the introduction of certain engineering features and the meticulous supervision of the workmen. The house was completed two years later.

From the fall of 1926 to the summer of 1931, Carnap was an instructor in philosophy at the University of Vienna.

Quine entered Oberlin College majoring in mathematics.

1927.   Russell and Dora could not find a satisfactory (to them) school to which to send their children and began to consider experimenting with a school of their own to provide really modern education. Their Beacon Hill school opened at Telegraph House on September 22. Dora was primarily concerned with education for socialism, but Russell put the idea of the individual before the idea of the state. They jointly ran the school for a few years. Russell left Dora and the school in 1932, after which Dora took single-handed control and continued the school until the early 1940s.

Russell published his Tarner Lectures, *The Analysis of Matter.*

Wittgenstein met Schlick for several conversations; afterwards Waismann was included and, at times, also Carnap, H. Feigl, and Maria Kasper. One of the topics of discussion from 1927 to 1928 was Ramsey's article 'The foundations of mathematics' (1925). (For this and related information, see Waismann 1979.)

There was some correspondence between W and Ramsey in June to July.

Schlick visited England in October.

1928.   Brouwer gave one or two lectures in March in Vienna. According to Feigl, 'Waismann and Feigl at first had difficulty in persuading W to attend,' but after the lecture all three spent a few hours at a cafe and W 'became extremely voluble and began sketching ideas that were the beginnings of his later writings' (George Pitcher, *The Philosophy of Wittgenstein,* 1964, p. 8).

Quine started honors reading in mathematical philosophy. For this he studied Peano's *Formulaire,* Couturat's *Algebra of Logic,* PM, Russell 1903, and Russell 1919. He read more on his own, including Russell 1914, *Marriage and Morals* (1929), and *The ABC of Relativity* (1925).

1929.   Wittgenstein returned to Cambridge in January. Years later, W 'said that he returned to philosophy because he felt that he could again do creative work.'

Received his Ph.D. in June, with the *Tractatus* as the dissertation; the oral examination was given on June 6 by Moore and Russell.

'Some remarks on logical form,' *Proc. Aristotelian Soc.,* suppl. vol. 9, pp. 162–171. In place of this paper a talk on the notion of the infinite in mathematics was given at the actual meeting in July at Nottingham.

At least six meetings with Schlick and Waismann took place in Schlick's house from December 18 to January 5. More such meetings were on March 22, June 19, and September 25 of 1930, on September 21 and December 9 of 1931, and July 1 of 1932; there were six meetings from December 17, 1930, to January 4, 1931. Notes by Waismann recording these conversations are published in *Wittgenstein and the Vienna Circle* (1979).

Ramsey, who was Lecturer in Mathematics and had officially been W's supervisor, wrote on June 14 of his work at that time: 'He began with certain questions in the analysis of propositions which now led him to problems about infinity which lie at the root of current controversies on the foundations of mathematics. At first I was afraid that lack of mathematical knowledge and facility would prove a serious handicap to his working in this field. But the progress he has made has already convinced me that this is not so, and that here too he will probably do work of the first importance.'

W then received a grant from Trinity to enable him to continue his researches.

Later, Carnap reported on his experience with the Vienna Circle, particularly from 1926 to 1931, in nostalgic terms. 'Characteristic for the Circle was the open and undogmatic attitude taken in the discussions.' 'The common spirit was one of cooperation rather than competition.' 'The congenial atmosphere in the Circle meetings was due above all to Schlick's personality, his unfailing kindness, tolerance, and modesty.'

1930.   Ramsey died on January 19, not quite 27 years old.

In January 1945, W wrote, after mentioning the *Tractatus*: 'For since beginning to occupy myself with philosophy again, sixteen years ago, I have been forced to recognize grave mistakes in what I wrote in that first book. I was helped to realize these mistakes—to a degree I myself am hardly able to estimate—by the criticism which my ideas encountered from Frank Ramsey, with whom I discussed them in innumerable conversations during the last two years of his life. Even more than this—always certain and forcible—criticism I am indebted to that which a teacher of this university, Mr. P. Sraffa, for many years increasingly practised on my thoughts' (the 'two years' should be one year).

About the discussions with Ramsey in 1929, W once told Moore that Ramsey had said to W, 'I don't like your method of arguing' (Moore 1955).

W resumed philosophical writings on February 2, 1929, which had essentially stopped after August 1918 (for details, see Wright 1969). His Nachlass consists of (handwritten) manuscripts, typescripts, dictations to colleagues or pupils, notes of conversations and lectures, and correspondence. There was a steady flow of MSS from 1929 to 1951 (items 105 to 178 in Wright's list); these include rough drafts and more finished versions, from which he dictated, with alterations, to typists. Typed texts were often cut up into fragments ('Zettel') and rearranged; in a number of cases a new typescript was produced on the basis of a collection of cuttings. After W's death in 1951, books and articles from the Nachlass have been published. These include:

(1) *Philosophical Remarks*, from 1930.
(2) G. E. Moore, 'Wittgenstein's lectures in 1930–33.'
(3) *Philosophical Grammar*, based on but different from the 'Big typescript. Probably 1933. viii + 768 pp' (see Kenny 1976).
(4) *The Blue Book*, dictated to the class of 1933–1934.
(5) *The Brown Book*, dictated to two pupils in 1935.

(6) C. Diamond, ed., *Lectures on the Foundations of Mathematics*, from W's lectures in the Lent and Easter terms of 1939. (I saw a typescript of some incomplete version of this in the summer of 1950.)

(7) *Remarks on the Foundations of Mathematics*, from writings in the years 1937–1944. (I saw some of the typescripts in the spring of 1955.)

(8) *Remarks on the Philosophy of Psychology*, these preparations for Part II of (9) were published in 1980 in two volumes (previously W's cuttings of 369 fragments from these had been published as *Zettel*); the work was done from May 10, 1946, to October 11, 1947, and from November 19, 1947, to August 25, 1948.

(9) *Philosophical Investigations*, in two parts; Part I was completed by 1945; Part II was written between 1947 and 1949. This is the book which was probably regarded as closest to completion by W and had been preceded by various preliminary versions. The writing began in Norway, 1936–1937.

(10) *On Certainty*, written in 1949 to 1951.

There are also a number of publications from his observations on more general cultural matter. Anyway, the list is far from complete.

Elected in December a Research Fellow of Trinity College tenable for five years. The typescript of (1) was probably read by Russell and Littlewood in connection with their recommendations.

'Lecture on ethics,' lecture given to the Heretics Club in Cambridge on November 17, 1930; the published version was from a typescript of 1929.

W began to lecture in January; the lecturing continued, with interruptions including 1936–1937 and 1942–1944, till the Easter term of 1947.

In September, Waismann went to Königsberg to give a lecture entitled 'The nature of mathematics: Wittgenstein's standpoint'; Gödel mentioned an early form of his first incompleteness theorem at the same meeting.

From the time Waismann met W in 1927, there have been plans and work by him to give expositions of W's ideas. Some time before Easter 1934, they decided upon joint work; but the project did not materialize.

W's lectures initially (for several years) consisted of a one-hour lecture and a two-hour discussion (on another day) every week of full term.

Carnap suggested 'that the formal theory of language was of great importance for the clarification of our philosophical problems. But Schlick and others were rather sceptical at this point.' He often discussed with Gödel 'the problem of speaking about language.'

As his honors thesis Quine generalized a formula from Couturat and proved the generalization in the formalism of *PM*; an improved version was later published as his 1933. He also wrote his first scholarly publication (1930) in the spring.

Quine entered Harvard's philosophy department as a scholarship graduate student in the autumn, where he studied with A. N. Whitehead, C. I. Lewis, H. M. Sheffer, and D. W. Prall.

1931.   'I was profoundly unhappy during the next few years,' said Russell, using the year 1930 as the point of reference.

Russell succeeded to the Earldom on the death of his brother, Frank, in Marseilles.

On January 1, W said: 'Russia. The passion is promising. Our waffle, on the other hand, is impotent.'

At the Moral Science Club, 'He would talk for long periods without interruption, using similes and allegories, stalking about the room and gesticulating' (Pascal 1979).

W: 'A thinker is very much like a draughtsman whose aim it is to represent all the interrelations between things' (*Culture and Value*: quotations of W below are mostly from this collection of W's observations).

W: 'Ramsey was a bourgeois thinker. I.e. he thought with the aim of clearing up the affairs of some particular community. He did not reflect on the essence of the state—or at least he did not like doing so—but on how *this* state might reasonably be organized.' (I take the words 'state' and 'community' as referring to the beliefs and modes of thought shared by some intellectual community to which Ramsey belonged. A more specialized example might be mathematics or physics or economics as he saw it.)

From 1931 to the end of 1935, Carnap had a chair in natural philosophy in the division of the natural sciences of the German university in Prague. During much of this period, he worked on his *Logical Syntax*.

Quine completed his M.A. in the spring. Russell came to Harvard to lecture; the sight of Whitehead and Russell on the podium together was Quine's 'most dazzling exposure to greatness.'

1932.   Russell wrote *Education and the Social Order* in the summer. 'After this, having no longer the financial burden of the school, I gave up writing potboilers. And having failed as a parent, I found that my ambition to write books that might be important revived.'

'In the case of logic, there were two most important matters with regard to which he [W] said that the views he had held when he wrote the *Tractatus* were definitely wrong.' (See Moore 1955.) These refer to the matter of elementary propositions ('final analysis') and the confusion of finite sum with infinite limit. (The points are discussed in Chapter 2 and elsewhere in this book.) It appears that these mistakes became clear to W between 1928 and 1932; I find Moore's report most helpful. The shift since 1928 or 1929 of the center of his interest from the philosophy of logic to the philosophy of mathematics is manifest. A more general issue is a change from the view that the philosophy of logic is self-contained and indeed the whole of fundamental philosophy. But in these two respects the philosophy of mathematics cannot take the whole place of the philosophy of logic (in a broad sense inherited largely from Frege and Russell). Rather, in W's mind the new view relates it closely to the philosophy of psychology (or of mind) ('Theory of knowledge is the philosophy of psychology,' the *Tractatus*, 4.1121), the study of such things as understanding, intention, and expectation.

Quine completed his dissertation, *The Logic of Sequences: A Generalization of PM*, and received his Ph.D. A revised version of the dissertation was published later as his 1934.

He was elected a Sheldon Travelling Fellow for 1932–1933, and visited Vienna, Prague, and Warsaw.

Toward the end of the year (or was it early in 1933?), he met Carnap for the first time in Prague. On October 23, 1970, he talked about this visit and his other contacts with Carnap (Hintikka 1975). 'Carnap was my greatest teacher. I got to him in Prague 38 years ago, just a few months after I had finished my Ph.D.' (There he also read the German typescript of *Logical Syntax*.)

'I was then an unknown young foreigner of 23 [24?], with thirteen inconsequential pages in print and sixteen at press. It was extraordinary of anyone, and characteristic of Carnap, to have been so generous of his time and energy. It was a handsome gift. It was my first experience of sustained intellectual engagement with anyone of an older generation, let alone a great man. It was my first really considerable experience of being intellectually fired by a living teacher rather than by a dead book. I had not been aware of the lack.'

1933.   The *Philosophical Grammar* (or rather, the related 'big typescript') is by far W's longest work, which links his earlier to his later philosophy. For example, slogans from his different periods coexist in this work: a proposition has meaning in virtue of being a picture; the meaning of a proposition is the mode of its verification; the meaning of an expression is its use.

Quine was elected one of the first group of Junior Fellows of the Society of Fellows at Harvard. This freed him from teaching duties for the next three years.

B. F. Skinner was another of the group, but Quine's behaviorism has its origin in his reading John B. Watson's famous book *Behaviorism* during his college days.

After his visit to Prague, Quine continued interacting with Carnap. 'Our correspondence was voluminous. He would write in English, practicing up for a visit to America, and I in German; and we would enclose copies for correction.'

1934.   W took lessons in Russian from Fania Pascal for all three terms, together with his friend Francis Skinner. He was a fairly docile as well as outstanding pupil, and later returned (in summer 1935) for Russian conversation, in preparation for his trip to Russia. W continued to have contact with his teacher Fania Pascal afterwards.

According to Fania Pascal, W's cavalier attitude toward Freud can be understood, 'once we realize that he himself had no need of Freud. . . . There was in him no perceptible split between the ego and the super-ego. For that matter, no split of any kind.' (Compare: 'Where the id was shall the ego be.')

Carnap spent several weeks in England in the autumn.

'Above all I enjoyed meeting Bertrand Russell for the first time. I visited him in his residence some distance south of London. We talked on various problems of philosophy and also on the world situation. Among other topics he asked me whether anybody had made use of his logic and arithmetic of relations. I told him that his concept of relation number (relational structure) played an important role in our philosophy. I mentioned also my axiom system of space-time-topology using only relational logic but not real numbers. He expressed the conviction that it should be possible to go much further in representing the essential content of Einstein's general theory of relativity in the same framework without using differential equations or coordinate systems. I was deeply impressed by his personality, the wide horizon of his ideas from technicalities of logic to the destiny of mankind, his undogmatic attitude in both theoretical and practical questions, and the high perspective from which he looked at the world and at the actions of men' (*IA*, p. 33).

At Harvard, Quine gave a series of lectures on Carnap's work. Some of the material was later included in his 1936a (which was completed in 1935).

1935.   At the beginning of the year, Russell was, his doctor considered, in a state of nervous exhaustion, necessitating complete rest. He spent two months in the Canary Islands and, for two more months he was 'though sane, quite devoid of creative impulse, and at a loss to know what work to do.' He remarried in mid-January 1936.

W's research fellowship was to end in December, but sometime in the year it was extended to the end of the academic year 1935–1936. The approaching termination of the fellowship probably played a part in W's contemplating a change.

In a letter dated June 30, to J. M. Keynes, W wrote: 'I have now more or less decided to go to Russia as a tourist in September and see whether it is possible for me to get a suitable job there. If I find (which, I'm afraid is quite likely) that I can't find such a job, or get permission to work in Russia, then I should want to return to England and if possible study medicine. Now when you told me that you would finance me during my medical training you did not know that I wanted to go to Russia and that I would try to get permission to practise medicine in Russia' (Wright 1974, p. 132).

W went to Russia in September. There was a postcard to Moore dated September 18 from Moscow, indicating his intention to return in a fortnight to Cambridge, where he would remain for the academic year. There are complex and conflicting versions of an offer of a chair from the University of Moscow or the University of Kazan (where Tolstoy had studied). In a letter to Engelmann, dated June 21, 1937, W wrote: 'I am now in England for a short stay; perhaps I shall go to Russia. God knows what will become of me.'

W wrote a long letter to Schlick on Gödel's theorem (dated July 31).

Carnap left Prague in December for America. Quine reported in 1970: 'By Christmas 1935 he was with us in our Cambridge flat. Four of us drove with him to the Philosophical Association meeting in Baltimore. The others were David Prall, Mason Gross, and Nelson Goodman. We moved with Carnap as henchmen through the metaphysicians' camp. We beamed with partisan pride when he countered a diatribe of Arthur Lovejoy's in his characteristically reasonable way, explaining that if Lovejoy means A then p, and if he means B then q. I had yet to learn how unsatisfying this way of Carnap's could sometimes be' (Hintikka 1975).

On June 6, Russell wrote to Quine to comment belatedly on Quine 1934 which had been sent to him earlier. 'In reading you I was struck by the fact that, in my work, I was always being influenced by extraneous philosophical considerations.' 'I am worried—though as yet I cannot put my worry into words—as to whether you really have avoided the troubles for which the axiom of reducibility was introduced as completely as you think. . . . And do you maintain that an infinite class can be defined otherwise than by a defining condition?' (Actually, Quine was using the simple theory of types rather than the ramified theory; in other words, it followed Ramsey's approach rather than the 1925 *PM*, but it is probable that Quine did not interpret the system in Ramsey's way.) 'What you have done . . . has reformed many matters as to which I had always been uncomfortable.'

1936.   Toward the end of 1932, Russell proposed to write a recent history 'to bring out the part played by beliefs in causing political events, the part which, I think, Marxists unduly minimize.' He spent 1933 writing *Freedom and Organization, 1814–1914* (1934). While working on the book, he said, 'I enjoy writing history so much that I feel prepared to continue doing it for the rest of my natural life.' Next, in collaboration with Patricia Spence, he wrote a record of the brief life of his radical parents, *The Amberley Papers* (1937), in two volumes.

In 1936, Russell published three philosophical articles: 'Determinism and physics'; 'On order in time'; and 'The limits of empiricism.' He desired to return to purely philosophical work and began to look for an academic position. On November 30, he wrote to Warder Norton: 'I gather that there is a university somewhere in America which has given Einstein and many others purely research jobs. Do you know which it is? If I had any chance of such a job I should apply for it. I should like to live in America if it were financially feasible.' The pursuit for an academic job was to become more intensive in 1937 (see below).

W went to his hut in Norway probably in the summer (certainly before September 4) and stayed there for nearly one year. It was during this period that the composition of *Philosophical Investigations* began.

Schlick was assassinated in June, a loss deeply felt by W and by Gödel.

Carnap was a visiting professor for the Winter Quarter and then offered a permanent position at the University of Chicago, which he held from 1936 to 1952.

Quine was appointed a faculty instructor at Harvard, which he served from 1936 to 1941. He wrote the twin papers 1936 and 1937 (NF).

1937.   On March 16, Desmond MacCarthy wrote to Russell: 'It is of the utmost importance that you should have leisure to write your book clearing up the relation of grammar and philosophy and many things besides.' In September, Russell was lecturing at Oxford on 'Words and facts.' Russell wrote on September 25: 'I have gone back to philosophy and I want people to talk to about it. I am lecturing [at Oxford] and shall get to know all the people in my line, of whom, among the younger dons, there are now quite a number. In Cambridge I am an ossified orthodoxy; in Oxford, still a revolutionary novelty.' He delivered his presidential address 'On verification' to the Aristotelian Society on November 8. The Russells bought a house at Kidlington, near Oxford, and lived there for about a year.

Russell gave, at the London School of Economics in the autumn, lectures on 'The science of power.' He wrote about the work on power in July: I am very keen on it myself, I think of it as founding a new science, like Adam Smith's 'Wealth of Nations.' The result was his *Power: A New Social Analysis* (1938). Years later, Russell still thought well of the book. 'I argued that power, rather than wealth, should be the basic concept in social theory, and that social justice should consist in equalization of power to the greatest practicable degree. It followed that State ownership of land and capital was no advance unless the State was democratic, and even then only if methods were devised for curbing the power of officials' (*Autobiography*, II, p. 277).

Financial difficulties and the desire to return to philosophy combined to strengthen Russell's efforts to obtain an academic job. He tried Cambridge, the Princeton Institute and Harvard, without success. On September 2 he received some money (indirectly) from Santayana, and late in the year he received an invitation to lecture at the University of Chicago. The story with the Institute (as told in Clark, pp. 455–456) is rather remarkable. Einstein, O. Veblen, and H. Weyl all were in favor of Russell joining the Institute but were over-ruled by A. Flexner, the director. It so happened that the director's sister-in-law, Helen Thomas, was a cousin of Alys (Russell's first wife).

Wittgenstein made a brief visit to Cambridge around the New Year.

Returned to Cambridge in the summer.

W: 'I *squander* an unspeakable amount of effort making an arrangement of my thoughts which may have no value at all.'

W: 'Again and again a use of the word emerges that seems not to be compatible with the concept that other uses have led us to form.'

W: 'Language—I want to say—is a refinement, "in the beginning was the deed." '

In 1937–1938, Carnap was interested in semantics and gave a research seminar; with money from the Rockefeller Foundation he got C. G. Hempel and O. Helmer to join him as research associates.

1938.   In September, Russell, with his wife and young son, left England for Chicago, where he had a one-year appointment. His duties were: to give an undergraduate course on 'the problems of philosophy'; to run a graduate seminar on semantics ('words and facts'); and to deliver a series of lectures based on *Power*.

After the *Anschluss* in March, W became a British subject (having had to give up his Austrian passport).

In 1937–1938 I ran across a copy of Yueh-lin Chin's *Logic* (1936, probably the most advanced book in Chinese at the time), in which about 80 pages were devoted to a condensed version of the body (i.e., leaving out the intricate introductions and the more advanced parts) of the first volume of *PM*. I found the material attractive and easy. Before that I had tried, following my father's suggestion, to read, with little success, *Anti-Dühring* and *Ludwig Feuerbach and the End of Classical German Philosophy* (in Chinese translations). I thought, therefore, that I should first try to learn the easier mathematical logic so that afterwards I might be better prepared for studying dialectics.

1939.   Russell received the offer of a three-year engagement with the University of California at Los Angeles, to begin in September. They rented a house in Santa Barbara for the summer. Later, Russell recalled his year at UCLA: 'The people were not so able, and the President [Robert Sproul] was a man for whom I conceived, I think justly, a profound aversion. If a lecturer said anything that was too liberal, it was discovered that the lecturer in question did his work badly, and he was dismissed.'

Russell replied to Quine on October 16 about not being able to find a job for A. Tarski: 'They feel that they are saturated both with foreigners and with logicians.'

Wittgenstein lectured on the foundations of mathematics in the Lent and Easter terms; thirty-one lectures of two hours each (twice a week) (see Diamond 1976).

W succeeded Moore to the chair in philosophy; the war had broken out before W assumed his chair.

Malcolm visited Cambridge from autumn 1938 to February 1940 and has since written extensively on his interactions with W during and since that period.

W continued to lecture on the foundations of mathematics in the Michaelmas term.

W: 'In a way, having oneself psychoanalysed is like eating from the tree of knowledge. The knowledge acquired sets us (new) ethical problems; but contributes nothing to their solution.'

Quine was to become an assistant professor of philosophy at Harvard, but the Committee of Eight eliminated that rank and extended the rank of faculty instructor from three years to five.

In 1939–1940 I audited Professor Sian-jun Wang's course on symbolic logic, studied the first volume of *PM*, and read Hilbert-Ackermann (1938) to learn scientific German. In the latter part of 1940, I read also the first volume of Hilbert-Bernays (1934).

1940.   Early in February, Russell received and accepted the (not fully official) offer of a professorship at the City College of New York, resigning prematurely from UCLA his two remaining years of employment. This was followed by a strange chain of events which 'struck at the security and intellectual independence of every faculty member in every public college and university in the United States' (*New York Times*, April 20). Russell's appointment was revoked. Dewey said, 'As Americans we can only blush with shame for this scar on our repute for fair play.' (Detailed accounts are contained in *The Bertrand Russell Case*, ed. John Dewey and H. M. Kallen, 1941, as well as in the appendix to Russell's *Why I Am Not a Christian*, 1957).

Before the trouble in New York an engagement had been made for Russell to give the William James lectures at Harvard in the autumn. 'Perhaps Harvard regretted having made it, but, if so, the regret was politely concealed from me.' The Russells spent the summer near Lake Tahoe, where Russell finished his *Inquiry into Meaning and Truth*, the text of his lectures at Harvard.

Wittgenstein continued lectures at Cambridge until sometime in 1942, when he went to London to work as an orderly at Guy's Hospital. Afterwards he worked in the Clinical Research Laboratory at an infirmary in Newcastle-upon-Tyne till the early months of 1944.

W: 'If we look at things from an ethnological point of view, does that mean we are saying that philosophy is ethnology? No, it only means that we are taking up a position right outside so as to see things *more* objectively.'

W: 'I often write my remarks like women of old retail shops, treasuring up strings, ribbons, rags, pins because they may frequently be needed. But whenever they are actually needed, they are not on hand.' [I once saw this in the fragment of the typescript for II-47 in the 1956 edition of his *Remarks* (immediately preceding 'But in the way every proof,').]

Lu Xun (1881–1936), the greatest and most influential Chinese author of the century, wrote about his own forceful short essays (on December 30, 1935) that 'I only set up at the street corner late in the night a shop on the ground, offering nothing but a few small nails, a few clay plates; but I also hope and believe that some people can find among them things appropriate to their needs.' Elsewhere Lu Xun wrote (on October 16, 1934): 'Usually, what are described in my essays are a nose, a mouth, a hair; but when put together, there is already nearly a whole of some form which could pass before adding anything. But drawing a tail to stick on makes it even more complete.' Unlike W, Lu Xun published promptly and almost daily nearly all that he wrote. Like W, he also used the particular to express the universal, and offered a system not by 'saying' but only by 'showing.'

Carnap spent 1940–1941 at Harvard.

In the autumn, Russell, Carnap, Tarski, and Quine were all at Harvard. They met at Carnap's apartment to discuss Carnap's manuscript *Introduction to Semantics*. Midway in the reading of the first page, Tarski and Quine 'took issue with Carnap on analyticity. The controversy continued through subsequent sessions, without resolution and without progress in the reading of Carnap's manuscript.' Ten years later, some of the criticisms were crystallized in Quine's most famous paper 'Two dogmas.'

Quine published his first major book, *ML*, and taught Gödel's first incompleteness theorem at Harvard in the spring (Mathematics 19b), within the special framework of 'protosyntax' (as in the last chapter of *ML*).

1941.   In January, Russell began his duties at the Barnes Foundation (near Philadelphia), according to a five-year contract worked out during the previous summer. He lectured on the history of Western philosophy. 'On December 28th, 1942, I got a letter from him [Dr. Albert Barnes] informing me that my appointment was terminated as from January 1st.' Russell sued Barnes and eventually (after he had gone back to England) got most of the expected salary for the unexpired three years of the contract.

W: 'You must say something new and yet it must all be old.'

W: 'Philosophers use a language that is deformed as though by shoes that are too tight.'

Quine became an associate professor of philosophy at Harvard. A contradiction in the system of *ML* was found by J. B. Rosser (and independently by Roger

Lyndon). Quine wrote a paper (1941) to repair the system; the repair was printed as a label and supposedly pasted into the unsold copies in 1941. In the 1947 reprint, the repair was printed on page 154.

1942.   From 1942 to 1944, Carnap had a research grant from the Rockefeller Foundation. 'During this time, which I spent near Santa Fe, New Mexico, I was first occupied with the logic of modalities and the new semantical method of extension and intension. Later I turned to the problems of probability and induction.'

Quine began his service in the Navy, to last over three years.

I read *Logical Syntax*, took a course with Professor Yuting Shen on the *Tractatus*, and began to write a long essay on Hume's problem of induction.

1943.   Russell worked on his *History*, wrote his *MD* and his reply to criticisms (finished in July) for Schilpp 1944, and lectured at Bryn Mawr.

1944.   The Russells sailed in May to return to England. 'The last part of our time in America was spent at Princeton, where we had a little house on the shores of the lake. While in Princeton, I came to know Einstein fairly well. I used to go to his house once a week to discuss with him and Gödel and Pauli. . . . I found that they all had a German bias towards metaphysics, and in spite of our utmost endeavors we never arrived at common premises from which to argue.'

Russell was elected to a five-year lectureship and a fellowship at Trinity, where he had use of Newton's rooms. 'I dine in hall and enjoy seeing dons I used to know 30 years ago' (letter of September 20). He prepared an annual course on 'non-demonstrative inference,' which led to his *Human Knowledge* (1948). On December 3, 1946, Wittgenstein wrote to Moore to praise H. H. Price over J. L. Austin as speakers at the Moral Sciences Club, adding: 'Russell was there and most disagreeable. Glib and superficial, though, as always, *astonishingly* quick.'

W went to Swansea in the spring; returned to Cambridge afterwards.

Carnap returned to Chicago.

I wrote a critical note on Russell 1940, which was published in 1945 in *Philosophical Review* of the Chinese Philosophical Society.

1945.   Wittgenstein wrote to Malcolm in August (Malcolm 1958, also the source of much of the material on W in the remainder of this table): 'I've been working a good deal this last academic year, I mean for myself, and if everything goes well I might publish by Christmas. Not that what I've produced is good, but it is now about as good as I can make it. I think when it'll be finished I ought to come into the open with it.'

Quine returned to Harvard.

1946.   In the summer, Russell lectured for the British Council in Switzerland on 'Ethics and power.' (This was one of many lecture trips abroad.)

In the spring, Wittgenstein wrote: 'I haven't done any decent work for ages apart from my classes. They went all right last term.'

W lectured on topics belonging to the philosophy of psychology for all the three terms of the academic year 1946–1947.

W: 'And what do you experience (other than vanity)? Simply that you have a certain *talent*. And my conceit of being an extraordinary person has been with me *much* longer than my awareness of my particular talent.'

W: 'If you want to go down deep you do not need to travel far; indeed, you don't have to leave your most immediate and familiar surroundings.'

W: 'Bacon, in my view, was not a *precise thinker*. He had large-scale and, as it were, wide-ranging visions. But if this is all someone has, he is bound to be generous with his promises and inadequate when it comes to keeping them.'

Quine taught a course on the philosophy of Hume in the summer, the only course in the history of philosophy that he has ever taught. He went on leave for the autumn semester.

I arrived at Harvard as a graduate student in October, saw Quine for the first time in November, and began to study *ML*. I was soon after able to use weaker axioms to develop more mathematics than is done in *ML* and in 1947 wrote it up as my dissertation, with the quaint title (suggested by Quine): *An Economic Ontology for Classical Analysis*.

1947.   Wittgenstein gave his last lectures in the Easter term.

Away on leave in the autumn; resigned his chair and ceased to be a professor at the end of the year.

In November, W wrote to Malcolm from Cambridge, 'As soon as I returned from Austria, I tendered my resignation to the Vice Chancellor and I shall cease to be a professor on December 31st at 12 p.m. . . . . I intend to leave here for Ireland in about 3 weeks. . . . I'm very busy these days; chiefly, dictating stuff I wrote during the last 2–3 years.'

From scattered information in the literature (especially Wright 1969), I get the following picture of W's work from 1936 to 1949, centering on the two books (9) (*Investigations*, in two parts, I and II) and (7) (*Mathematics*), as listed above under the year 1930. They were initially envisaged as one book. By 1938 a first draft of them was done (MS 220 and MS 221). Shortly afterwards, some more work was devoted to polishing 221 to yield 222 and 223 which form the only relatively finished portion of (7). From then on, while continuing preparations for both parts, W began to concentrate, with regard to the composition of a finished work, on the first book. These efforts, after some interruption caused by the war, led to a finished version of Part I of (9) in the autumn of 1944. A few months before that, work on (7) had essentially stopped. After the completion of I, W concentrated on preparing II of (9).

According to the Preface to (8) (published in 1980), the nine volumes of MSS (130–138) written from May 1946 to May 1949 may be described as preparatory studies for II of (9). In late autumn 1947 and early autumn 1948 selections from the first two-thirds of these MSS were dictated to a typist to produce TS 229 and TS 232. Probably in the middle of 1949, W put together a selection (MS 144), mainly from what he had written since October 1948, but partly also from earlier MSS and TSS. This was published in 1953 as II of (9). The book (8) consists of TS 229 (based on writings from May 10, 1946, to

October 11, 1947) and TS 232 (based on writings from November 19, 1947, to August 25, 1948). The book (7) (*Mathematics*) is based on writings from 1937 to early 1944. At the end of (9) there was a suggestion that the philosophy of mathematics could be treated in the same spirit.

W moved to Ireland in December.

W: 'Science: enrichment and impoverishment. *One* particular method elbows all the others aside. They all seem paltry by comparison, preliminary stages at best.'

W: 'The most I might expect by way of effect is that I should first stimulate the writing of a *whole lot* of garbage and that then this *perhaps* might provoke somebody to write something good.'

W: 'My thoughts probably move in a far narrower circle than I suspect.'

Quine, in collaboration with N. Goodman, published their result of playing with 'nominalism' (1947).

I was assistant to Quine's courses in 1947–1948, including advanced logic and the philosophy of language.

1948.   Russell gave the first of the Reith Lectures, on 'authority and the individual.'

Wittgenstein lived mostly in Ireland; visited Austria and Cambridge in the autumn.

Wrote from autumn to spring 1949 the material published posthumously as Part II of *Investigations*.

Moved from remote Galway to (a hotel in) Dublin in the autumn.

W: 'Make sure you really do paint only what you see!'

W: 'But the bad thing about it was that he [Bacon, and W himself too?] launched polemical attacks on the real builders and did not recognize his *own* limitations, or else did not want to.'

At Harvard, Quine became full professor and senior fellow of the Society of Fellows. He published his famous paper, 'On what there is.'

1949.   The king of England conferred the Order of Merit on Russell and remarked, 'You have sometimes behaved in a way which would not do if generally adopted.'

Russell wrote on February 4 to thank Quine for his paper, 'On what there is.'

Wittgenstein stayed in Dublin till July except for a trip to Vienna from the middle of April to May.

Went to Ithaca, New York, to visit the Malcolms around the end of July; returned to England in October.

Early in December, W wrote to Malcolm: 'The doctors have now made their diagnosis. I have cancer of the prostate.'

Went to Vienna in December and remained there until the end of March 1950.

W: 'One reason why authors become dated, even though they once *amounted* to something, is that their writings, when reinforced by their contemporary setting, speak strongly to men, whereas without this reinforcement their works die, as if bereft of the illumination that gave them their colour.'

Quine went on leave for the spring semester; I taught the advanced logic course in his absence, thereby introducing Gödel's incompleteness results at Harvard in a fairly complete manner.

I discovered and corrected an error in *ML*; the corrected system ML was later adopted in the revised edition of *ML* (1951).

1950.   Russell was awarded the Nobel Prize for Literature and heard the news while visiting Princeton briefly. On December 11, he gave his Nobel lecture: 'What desires are politically important?'

'In April 1950 he [Wittgenstein] was back in England. He had received an invitation to give [the first series of] the John Locke lectures in Oxford. . . . He declined this invitation and the reason he gave to me [Malcolm] was "I don't think I can give formal lectures to a large audience that would be any good." ' (In spring 1954 I was invited to give the second series of these lectures in 1954–1955. I was told at Oxford that, after W had declined, they did succeed in getting Oets Bouwsma to lecture on W's views.)

During part of 1950, W lived in Oxford in Anscombe's home. W used to visit the Bouwsmas who were in Oxford that year.

Went to Norway for five weeks in the autumn.

W: 'Philosophy hasn't made any progress?—If somebody scratches the spot where he has an itch, do we have to see some progress? Isn't it genuine scratching otherwise, or genuine itching? And can't this reaction to an irritation continue in the same way for a long time before a cure for the itching is discovered?'

Quine published his most polished textbook on elementary logic and began to work on his largest philosophy book (1960); the work was to continue for nine years.

1951.   In January or February, Wittgenstein went to Cambridge to stay in the home of his physician, Dr. Bevan.

On April 16, W wrote he had been able to work again for the last five weeks: 'It's the first time after more than two years that the curtain in my brain has gone up.'

W died in his physician's home on April 29. (I happened to go to Oxford on April 29. The next morning I went to see Gilbert Ryle. The first thing he said to me was, 'Wittgenstein died last night!' Recently I saw Peter Strawson who reminded me that I had gone to see him afterwards and repeated the sentence immediately on seeing him.)

In his will, dated January 29, W gave to Mr. R. Rhees, Miss G. E. M. Anscombe, and Professor G. H. von Wright the copyright in all his unpublished writings with the intention that they should publish from the papers as many of them as they considered fit.

Carnap and Quine held a symposium on ontology in Chicago.

1952.   Carnap left Chicago and visited the Princeton Institute from 1952 to 1954.

1953.   Quine published his first collection of essays and served as George Eastman Visiting Professor at Oxford for 1953–1954.

I introduced extensions of the ramified theory of the 1925 *PM*, which are more adequate to the development of ordinary mathematics.

1954.   Carnap succeeded Reichenbach at U.C.L.A.

Quine wrote a paper (1960a) on Carnap's work and succeeded C. I. Lewis as Edgar Peirce Professor of Philosophy at Harvard.

1955.   The Russell-Einstein Manifesto (on the nuclear peril overriding the ideological split) was issued at the end of May.

I was at Oxford giving the John Locke Lectures and had an opportunity to read parts of Wittgenstein's manuscripts on the philosophy of mathematics.

1956.   Quine was a member, for 1956–1957, at the Institute for Advanced Study (Princeton).

In the autumn I led a seminar at Oxford, discussing Wittgenstein's *Remarks on the Foundations of Mathematics*, which was attended by most of the leading philosophy dons of Oxford.

1957.   Crawshay-Williams (see his 1970, p. 125) happened to mention in 1956 to Russell Strawson 1950, 'in the course of a discussion of the reasons why his later work had not been taken sufficiently seriously.' Russell wrote a rejoinder, 'Mr. Strawson on referring' (*Mind*, 1957, reprinted in *PD*). 'Russell was somewhat resentful about Strawson's never answering his rejoinder.'

Quine gave his presidential address, 'Speaking of objects' (reprinted in *OR*), to the eastern division of the American Philosophical Association.

Hiram McLendon, who knew Russell from Cambridge around 1945, offered to arrange for me to visit Russell; I saw him at his London flat on February 16. I had tea with him and tried unsuccessfully to explain to him the extensions of his ramified type theory.

1958.   Quine was, for 1958–1959, a fellow at the Center for Advanced Study in the Behavioral Sciences (Stanford).

I designed effective programs to prove on a computer (IBM 704) all the theorems of first order logic included in *PM*, in a few minutes.

1959.   Quine completed his *Word and Object* in June and soon after began to work on his *SL*, which was finished in January 1963.

Russell wrote an introduction to E. Gellner's *Words and Things: A Critical Account of Linguistic Philosophy and a Study in Ideology* (1959). (I understand that Quine had previously intended to entitle his book *WO* 'words and things' also.) Russell published his *PD*.

1960.   By now, Russell had come through pneumonia, removal of the prostate, and trouble with the muscular reflexes of his throat which forced him to live on liquids; he remained quite energetic and had been settled in North Wales for five years, with a flat in London. (A particularly illuminating account of Russell's life from 1945 to 1970 is given in Crawshay-Williams 1970.) Ralph Benedek Schoenman became his 'left-hand man' (for the next six years, with increasing misgivings on Russell's part).

1962.   In connection with the Cuban crisis, Russell sent telegrams to Kennedy, Khrushchev, U Thant, Macmillan, and Gaitskell on October 23.

On May 12, Carnap wrote to Russell 'a message of best wishes and of deep gratitude for all I owe to you,' on the occasion of Russell's ninetieth birthday (May 18). The letter mentioned that Carnap's birthday falls on the same day and that he was going to retire from teaching in a few weeks. 'Throughout my life I have followed with the greatest interest not only your philosophical work but also, especially during the last years, your political activities, and I admire your courage and your intensity of energy and devotion.' 'I am in complete agreement with the aims for which you are fighting at present: serious negotiations instead of the Cold War, no bomb-testing, no fall-out shelters. But, not having your wonderful power of words, I limit myself to participating in public appeals and petitions initiated by others and to some private letters to President Kennedy on these matters.' Carnap emphasized especially 'the inspiring effect on me of your appeal for a new method in philosophy, on the last pages of your book [External World].'

In reply (June 21), Russell thanked Carnap 'immensely' and said: 'I believe that your efforts to bring clarity and precision to philosophy will have an everlasting effect on the thinking of men, and I am very happy to see that you will continue your work after your retirement.'

1963.   The volume Schilpp 1963 to honor Carnap was published. It includes Carnap's IA (82 pages) and his replies (155 pages) to the contributions by C. Morris, R. S. Cohen, P. Frank, P. Henle, K. R. Popper, H. Feigl, A. J. Ayer, R. Feys, J. Myhill, D. Davidson, R. M. Martin, W. V. Quine, H. G. Bohnert, W. Sellars, E. W. Beth, P. F. Strawson, Y. Bar-Hillel, N. Goodman, A. Pap, A. Grünbaum, C. G. Hempel, J. G. Kemeny, A. W. Burks, H. Putnam, E. Nagel, and A. Kaplan.

1964.   In 1962 or 1963 the editor of Bertrand Russell, Philosopher of the Century (1967) invited me to write a contribution to it. I wrote 'Russell and his logic.' The editor first accepted it; later he complained that my idolization of Russell was incomplete, but failed to single out any specific deficiencies in this regard. I was soon thoroughly disgusted with the editor's obnoxious ignorance, inconsistency, and pomposity. As a consequence, I withdrew the essay and published it in Ratio (vol. 7, 1965, pp. 1–34; a revised version of the paper was included in MP as Chapter 3 and section 4 of Chapter 11).

1965.   Quine spent five months at Wesleyan University as fellow of the Center for Advanced Studies; the last of these months was devoted to putting together two collections of essays, published in 1966.

1966.   In December a special session of the American Philosophical Association meeting at Philadelphia was devoted to Russell's philosophy. Quine gave his paper 'Russell's ontological development'; C. G. Hempel and I were the commentators.

1967.   On May 9, Arnold Toynbee wrote to Russell on the occasion of his ninety-fifth birthday. 'I am grateful to you, most of all, for the encouragement and the hope that you have been giving for so long, and are still giving as vigorously and as fearlessly as ever, to your younger contemporaries in at least three successive generations.'

1968.   Quine was the first John Dewey Lecturer at Columbia University (the lectures were published in *OR*). He was invited to address the 14th International Congress of Philosophy; the address, 'Epistemology naturalized,' is also included in *OR*.

1969.   A collection (*Words and Objections*) of essays on the work of Quine appeared (revised edition in 1975), including also 60 pages of replies by Quine. Contributors are: J. J. C. Smart, G. Harman, E. Stenius, N. Chomsky, J. Hintikka, B. Stroud, P. F. Strawson, H. P. Grice, P. T. Geach, D. Davidson, D. Føllesdal, W. Sellars, D. Kaplan, G. Berry, and R. B. Jensen.

1970.   Russell died on February 2 at his home in North Wales.
Carnap died on September 14 in Los Angeles.
A memorial meeting for Carnap was held on October 23; homage was paid to Carnap by H. Feigl, C. G. Hempel, R. Jeffrey, W. V. Quine, and A. Shimony.

1971.   Quine gave his Paul Carus Lectures in December. Centering on these lectures, the book *Roots of Reference* was written between early 1970 and December 1972. It appeared in print in 1974.
Over the years Quine has interacted widely with many philosophers by oral discussions, written exchanges (published or otherwise), reviews and comments on other philosophers, replies to criticisms and expositions, forewords to books close to his work, etc. For instance, Nelson Goodman introduced him at the Carus Lectures, and acknowledgments for assistance to the resulting book include G. Harman, D. Davidson, O. Chateaubriand, D. Kaplan, R. Thomason, E. A. Martin, S. Stich; D. Føllesdal, R. Herrnstein, and especially B. Dreben.

1975.   *Rudolf Carnap, Logical Empiricist: Materials and Perspectives* (Hintikka 1975) appeared.

1978.   Quine retired from teaching (at Harvard) but continues to go to his office in Emerson Hall regularly.

1981.   Quine published another collection of essays (*TT*).

1982.   Quine completed a draft of a book-length autobiography. [The book was apparently finished in 1984 and is scheduled to appear spring 1985.]

1983.   Quine published 'Ontology and ideology revisited' half a century after he had first written on the subject (1934a).

1984.   Quine is, among other things, engaged in preparing his reply to criticism for the forthcoming volume to honor him in the Library of Living Philosophers.
To date, the following books and collections of essays dealing with Quine's

work have appeared: Davidson-Hintikka 1969; Orenstein 1977; Shahan-Swoyer 1979; Gibson 1982; M. Garrido (editor), *Aspectos de la filosofía de W. V. Quine* (1976); C. E. Caorsi (editor), *Volumen especial dedicado a la filosofía de W. V. Quine* (1982); M. Boffa et al., *La théorie des ensembles de Quine* (1982); T. E. Forster, *Quine's New Foundations* (1983); P. Gochet, *Quine en perspective* (1983); G. D. Romanos, *Quine and Analytic Philosophy* (1983); H. Lauener, *Willard V. Quine* (1983, in the 'Grosse Denker' series); and Ilham Dilman, *Quine on Ontology, Necessity, and Experience: A Philosophical Critique* (1984).

Index

⊐⊏ Bradford Books